CONTENTS
Unit 6

For information about the Unit Resources, assessing fluency, and teaching with BQ Tunes, see the opening pages of your Unit 1 Resources.

"Play Hard; Play Together; Play Smart" *from* **The Carolina Way** by Dean Smith with John Kilgo

from **the Odyssey, Part 1** by Homer

from **the Odyssey, Part 2** by Homer

Poetry by Edna St. Vincent Millay, Margaret Atwood, Derek Walcott, and Constantine Cavafy

"Three Skeleton Key" by George Toudouze

Prentice Hall *LITERATURE*

PENGUIN EDITION

Unit Six
Resources

Grade Nine

PEARSON

Upper Saddle River, New Jersey
Boston, Massachusetts
Chandler, Arizona
Glenview, Illinois

BQ Tunes Credits
Keith London, Defined Mind, Inc., Executive Producer
Mike Pandolfo, Wonderful, Producer
All songs mixed and mastered by Mike Pandolfo, Wonderful
Vlad Gutkovich, Wonderful, Assistant Engineer
Recorded November 2007 – February 2008 in SoHo, New York City, at
Wonderful, 594 Broadway

ISBN–13: 978-0-13-366455-3
ISBN–10:   0-13-366455-4
7 8 9 10 11 12 V092 17 16 15 14 13
CC

 **BQ Tunes**

Role Model, performed by The Dave Pittenger Band

We've read the papers and watched the news
A role model, the cameras are focused on you
The **standards** that we're used to are being abused

Your **character** – all the flaws and strengths
Is reflected in your decisions, all the **choices** that you make
If you're never brought to **justice** when you're **involved** in something wrong
How are we to learn?

Oooo, everyone wants to **identify** with you
The **hero,** the **hero** we look up to
The **hero** that we love

You know you're held responsible
An **obligation** lies with you
Responsibility never carried so much weight
As when we **imitate** you

Oooo, everyone wants to **identify** with you
The **hero,** the **hero** we look up to
The **hero** that we love

All we are asking is for truth and **honesty**
Consider the consequences to which a lack of **wisdom** leads

You **serve** the people by the example you set
The **morality** of your actions are judged by how much good you do
Your goals and **intentions** may be noble
But we can't read your mind

Continued

Role Model, *continued*

Oooo, everyone wants to **identify** with you

The **hero,** the **hero** we look up to

The **hero** that we love

Ahhh . . .

Song Title: **Role Model**

Artist / Performed by The Dave Pittenger Band

Vocals & Guitar: Dave Pittenger

Bass Guitar: Jon Price

Drums: Josh Dion

Lyrics by Dave Pittenger

Music composed by Dave Pittenger

Produced by Mike Pandolfo, Wonderful

Executive Producer: Keith London, Defined Mind

Name _____ Date _____

Unit 6: Themes in Literature
Big Question Vocabulary—1

The Big Question: Do heroes have responsibilities?

Small children who watch a superhero on television will often pattern their behavior after the superhero's behavior.

honesty: truthfulness, sincerity

justice: fairness

morality: conformity to the rules of proper conduct

responsibility: reliability or dependability

wisdom: good sense and judgment, especially based on life experience

DIRECTIONS: *Create a superhero that little children could respect and admire. For each of the vocabulary words, give an example of how your superhero would demonstrate this quality. Use each vocabulary word in each description.*

HONESTY: _____

_____

_____

JUSTICE: _____

_____

_____

MORALITY: _____

_____

_____

RESPONSIBILITY: _____

_____

_____

WISDOM: _____

_____

_____

1

Unit 6: Themes in Literature
Big Question Vocabulary—2

The Big Question: Do heroes have responsibilities?

Often an athlete, a movie star, or a politician will be regarded as a hero. With that hero status comes a responsibility to act in a way that is consistent with good values.

character: a combination of valued qualities, such as honesty and integrity

hero: a person of great courage who is admired for his actions

imitate: to copy the way someone else behaves and/or speaks

intention: purpose or plan

serve: to be useful or helpful

DIRECTIONS: *Think of a public figure whom you consider a hero. Answer the following questions using the vocabulary words that are in parentheses.*

1. Who is the public figure you selected? (*hero*)

   _____

2. What qualities does this person have that make him or her admirable? (*character*)

   _____

   _____

3. How is this person useful or helpful to the world or to a particular community? (*serve*)

   _____

   _____

4. What do you suppose this person's purpose is with regard to the world or his or her community? (*intention*)

   _____

   _____

5. In what ways have you and others learned from this person? (*imitate*)

   _____

   _____

Name _____ Date _____

Unit 6: Themes in Literature
Big Question Vocabulary—3

The Big Question: Do heroes have responsibilities?

If we look around our communities, we will often discover that there are "unsung heroes," or people who do not get recognition for their exceptional actions.

choices: decisions

identify: to recognize and name something

involvement: taking part in an activity or event

obligation: moral or legal duty

standard: level of quality, skill, or ability that is acceptable in a particular situation

DIRECTIONS: *Recognize someone in your community who is an "unsung hero" by creating a plaque to award him or her. In the plaque, describe your hero's achievements using all the vocabulary words. Your hero can be real or imagined.*

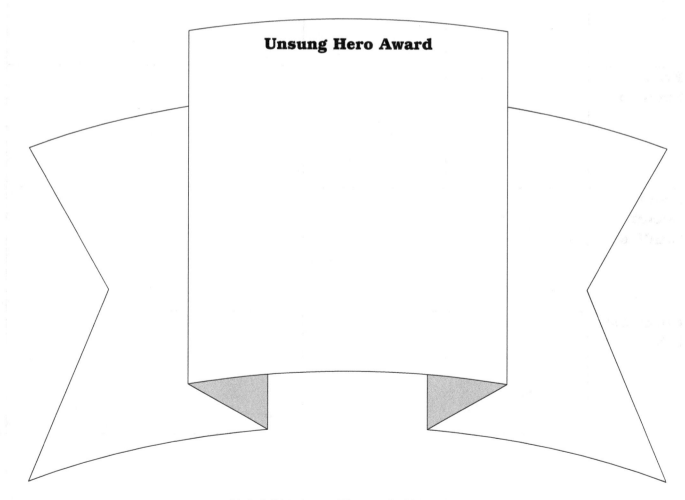

Unsung Hero Award

Unit 6: Themes in Literature
Applying the Big Question

The Big Question: Do heroes have responsibilities?

DIRECTIONS: *Complete the chart below to apply what you have learned about heroes and their responsibilities. One row has been completed for you.*

Example	The heroic act	Motivation for the act	The hero's responsibilities	What I learned
From Literature	In "Odysseus' Revenge" in the *Odyssey*, Odysseus kills his wife's suitors.	His sense of outrage and vengeance	To protect his wife, son, and the people of Ithaca	Heroes may have divided responsibilities and may give in to their emotions.
From Literature				
From Science				
From Social Studies				
From Real Life				

4

Unit 6: Themes in Literature: Heroism Skills Concept Map—1

Do heroes have responsibilities?

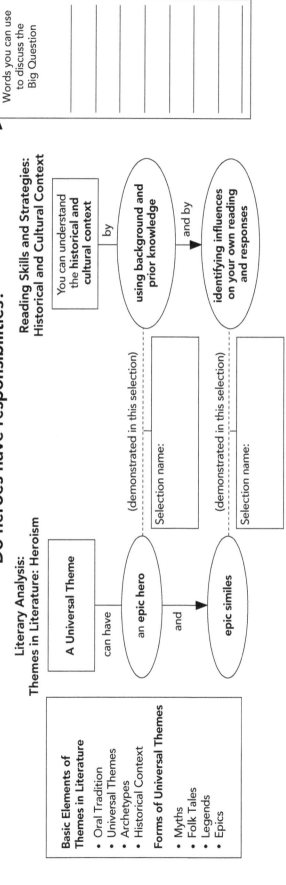

Literary Analysis:
Themes in Literature: Heroism

A Universal Theme → can have → an epic hero → and → epic similes

(demonstrated in this selection)
Selection name:

(demonstrated in this selection)
Selection name:

Basic Elements of Themes in Literature
• Oral Tradition
• Universal Themes
• Archetypes
• Historical Context

Forms of Universal Themes
• Myths
• Folk Tales
• Legends
• Epics

Comparing Literary Works:
Contemporary Interpretations

focus on → an allusion

focus on → an ancient work

(demonstrated in these selections)
Selection names:
1.
2.

Reading Skills and Strategies:
Historical and Cultural Context

You can understand the historical and cultural context → by → **using background and prior knowledge** → and by → **identifying influences on your own reading and responses**

(demonstrated in this selection)
Selection name:

Words you can use to discuss the Big Question

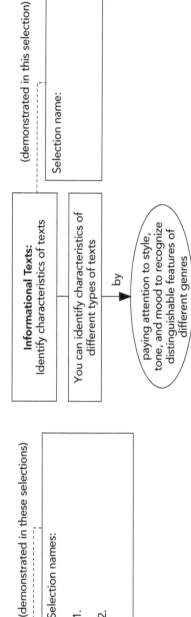

Informational Texts:
Identify characteristics of texts

You can identify characteristics of different types of texts → by → paying attention to style, tone, and mood to recognize distinguishable features of different genres

Student Log

Complete this chart to track your assignments.

	Extend Your Learning	Writing Workshop	Other Assignments
Writing			

Vocabulary Warm-up Word Lists

Study these words from the selections. Then, complete the activities.

Word List A

championship [CHAM pee uhn ship] *adj.* winning; excelling
   His <u>championship</u> spirit motivates him to always try his best.

competitive [kuhm PET i tiv] *adj.* trying to win
   They are a <u>competitive</u> team and always play hard to win.

enjoyable [en JOY uh buhl] *adj.* giving pleasure
   We had an <u>enjoyable</u> vacation at the beach filled with sun and fun.

execution [ek si KYOO shuhn] *n.* way or style of doing something
   Her <u>execution</u> of the oral report was detailed and interesting.

previous [PREE vee uhs] *adj.* earlier
   We covered this same information in a <u>previous</u> class.

professional [pruh FESH uh nuhl] *adj.* paid and specially trained
   Our new dog is so hard to handle, we need a <u>professional</u> trainer.

strategic [struh TEE jik] *adj.* done with a strategy in mind; deliberate
   Li made the <u>strategic</u> decision to take the job with more benefits.

stray [STRAY] *v.* to move away from
   She attends a local college and does not <u>stray</u> far from home.

Word List B

determination [dee ter mi NAY shuhn] *n.* trying hard; sticking with something
   It takes strong <u>determination</u> to accomplish your goals.

duplicate [DOO pli kayt] *v.* make an exact copy of
   I would not <u>duplicate</u> that mistake by doing the same thing twice.

fundamentals [fuhn duh MEN tuhlz] *n.* most basic parts
   One of the <u>fundamentals</u> of baseball is hitting a ball with a bat.

importance [im PAWR tins] *n.* significance, effect, or influence
   The <u>importance</u> of good health is clearest when someone is sick.

maximum [MAK suh muhm] *adj.* largest that is possible; most
   To get ready for the test, make a <u>maximum</u> effort to study daily.

philosophy [fi LAS uh fee] *n.* set of beliefs about something important
   My father's <u>philosophy</u> is that hard work is good for everyone.

refresh [ree FRESH] *v.* to make less tired or to make better
   A cool swim will <u>refresh</u> me after working in the hot sun.

ultimate [UHL tuh mit] *adj.* greatest and often most important
   The <u>ultimate</u> disappointment is losing when you know you could win.

"Play Hard; Play Together; Play Smart" *from* **The Carolina Way**
by Dean Smith with John Kilgo
Vocabulary Warm-up Exercises

Exercise A *Fill in each blank in the paragraph with an appropriate word from Word List A.*
Use each word only once.

Baseball is a sport that requires excellent teamwork in order to be

[1] _____ and better than other teams. No team could ever boast a

[2] _____ season, such as winning the World Series, with players who [3]

_____ from the idea of cooperation as the foundation of the game. That was

true in [4] _____ times, and it still is true today. As a fan, it is exciting and

[5] _____ to watch a player do something terrific, such as hit a home run,

especially at a [6] _____ moment, such as when the bases are loaded. How-

ever, the [7] _____ of a great play, such as getting players out at two bases

in succession, requires thinking like a team. A well-trained [8] _____ player

knows that it takes nine individuals to win.

Exercise B *Revise each sentence so the underlined vocabulary word is used in a logical way.*
Be sure to keep the vocabulary word in your revision.

Example: The underline{importance} of this mistake is evident in how easy it is to fix.
The underline{importance} of this mistake is evident in how difficult it is to fix.

1. One of the fundamentals of any game is having snacks available for the fans.

   _____

2. If I duplicate the photo of my dog and me, you will see my cat's unusual markings.

   _____

3. It is a wise philosophy to concentrate on the negative things in life.

   _____

4. If you made the maximum effort, you hardly tried at all.

   _____

5. If your ultimate goal is college, it is the least important reason to do well now.

   _____

6. Kate's determination to succeed showed when she stopped doing her best.

   _____

7. I will refresh my iced tea from the pitcher that I left in the sun.

   _____

8

Name _____ Date _____

"Play Hard; Play Together; Play Smart" *from* **The Carolina Way**
by Dean Smith with John Kilgo
Reading Warm-up A

Read the following passage. Pay special attention to the underlined words. Then, read it again, and complete the activities. Use a separate sheet of paper for your written answers.

Basketball has a fascinating beginning. Unlike many games that developed over time, basketball was actually invented in 1891. The inventor was James Naismith, a physical education teacher. He had a <u>strategic</u> reason to do so. He deliberately designed the game to give athletes a good workout.

Naismith taught at the YMCA training school in Springfield, Massachusetts. The school, which later became known as Springfield College, had a football team in the fall and a baseball team in the spring. In <u>previous</u> years, before Naismith's creation, the school's athletes kept in shape during the cold New England winter by doing gymnastics. However, that plan never worked well. The older students would lose interest quickly. As they wandered away from the training activities, too often they would <u>stray</u> into mischief and bad behavior.

Finally Naismith's boss at the school had enough. He assigned Naismith the task of developing an <u>enjoyable</u> game that the students would like to play. It also needed to be challenging and <u>competitive</u> so that the students would have to play hard to win and keep in shape.

Naismith placed a peach basket on a pole that was ten feet in height and gave his players a soccer ball. He formed two teams of nine players each and read them thirteen rules. Then, he guided his students through the correct <u>execution</u> of the basic plays of basketball. The act of throwing a ball into a basket was then—and still is—the foundation of the game.

Over one hundred years later, basketball now attracts millions of courtside and television fans for college and <u>professional</u> games. Each season ends with <u>championship</u> tournaments. Then, the best teams are honored with trophies.

Naismith never made any money from his invention. He did, however, live to see it become an Olympic sport in 1936.

1. Circle the word clue for <u>strategic</u>. Underline Naismith's **strategic** reason for inventing basketball.

2. Circle the word clue for <u>previous</u>. Underline how Naismith's **previous** students stayed in shape before basketball.

3. Underline the phrase that explains <u>stray</u>. Tell what **stray** into mischief means.

4. Circle the word clue for <u>enjoyable</u>. Describe a sport you find **enjoyable** and explain why.

5. Underline what a team has to do to be <u>competitive</u>. Circle a word that describes what a **competitive** sport is like.

6. Underline the phrase that describes the <u>execution</u> of a key play in basketball. What happens when the **execution** is successful?

7. Give an antonym for <u>professional</u>. Explain the difference between college and **professional** basketball players.

8. Circle a word clue for <u>championship</u>. Underline the rewards of winning **championship** tournaments.

"Play Hard; Play Together; Play Smart" *from* **The Carolina Way**
by Dean Smith with John Kilgo
Reading Warm-up B

Read the following passage. Pay special attention to the underlined words. Then, read it again, and complete the activities. Use a separate sheet of paper for your written answers.

Teamwork is the key to playing sports. It brings together a group of players who must work to achieve the <u>maximum</u> result, which is a winning team. The <u>importance</u> of teamwork can be seen in many other endeavors as well.

One amazing example of teamwork by a family is found at Thunderhead Mountain in South Dakota. There, the Ziolkowski family has created the massive Crazy Horse Memorial. They have worked on this <u>ultimate</u> statue of a horse and rider for over 50 years. When completed, the granite rendering of the famous Native American chief will be the largest monument in the world.

The story of the monument begins with their father, Korczak, now deceased. He learned the basic <u>fundamentals</u> of carving stone through a range of experiences. He taught himself to be a sculptor and then worked on the faces of the presidents on Mount Rushmore.

In 1939, the Lakota Sioux, the tribe of Crazy Horse, asked Korczak to carve a monument to the chief in the Black Hills mountains. It would be nearly 10 years before he would start. World War II began and he served in the U.S. Army and was wounded. Returning home, the mountain air helped to <u>refresh</u> and energize him.

Korczak Ziolkowski worked daily on the statue from 1947 until his death in 1982. During that time, he and his wife, Ruth, raised ten children. Everyone in the family pitched in to support the large homestead while Korczak carved. He also taught his family everything he knew about the monument, including the <u>determination</u> to keep working on it year after year.

After his death, Ruth took over supervising the monument. Seven of their ten children have worked on it. They follow their father's vision, shaping and grinding the granite to <u>duplicate</u> the exact statue he had in mind. They also follow his <u>philosophy</u>: "Go slowly, so you do it right." The wisdom of that belief can be seen in the magnificent monument they have worked together to carve.

1. Underline the phrase that describes the <u>maximum</u> results of teamwork in sports. Explain what *maximum* results means.

2. Circle a word that is a clue to <u>importance</u>. Give a synonym for *importance*.

3. Circle a word that is a clue to <u>ultimate</u>. Underline what makes this the *ultimate* monument.

4. Circle a word clue to <u>fundamentals</u>. Describe what one of the *fundamentals* of carving stone might be.

5. Circle a word that is a clue to <u>refresh</u>. Underline what happened so that he needed a setting that would *refresh* him.

6. Underline a phrase that gives a clue to <u>determination</u>. Explain what *determination* means.

7. Underline the phrase that is a clue to <u>duplicate</u>. Give a synonym for *duplicate*.

8. Circle the word that is a clue to <u>philosophy</u>. In your own words, explain the *philosophy* quoted in the passage.

Dean Smith
Listening and Viewing

Segment 1: Meet Dean Smith
- What is the meaning of "the Carolina way"?
- How do you think Dean Smith's philosophy of "play hard, play smart, play together" also applies to life off of the basketball court?

_____

_____

_____

_____

Segment 2: Themes in Literature
- Why do you think sports writing is an important form of literature?
- What can Dean Smith and John Kilgo's book *The Carolina Way* teach its readers?

_____

_____

_____

_____

Segment 3: The Writing Process
- How did Dean Smith and John Kilgo work together to write books?
- What benefits and challenges exist when writing a book with a coauthor?

_____

_____

_____

_____

Segment 4: The Rewards of Writing
- How has writing been personally rewarding for both Dean Smith and John Kilgo?
- Have you ever read a piece of sports literature that has had a memorable impact on you as a reader? Explain.

_____

_____

_____

_____

Learning About Themes in Literature

Before there was written literature, stories and poems were passed down by **oral** tradition—from generation to generation by word of mouth. Many tales expressed basic human emotions and explored **universal themes,** or insights into life that are true for many different times and cultures. Among such themes are the importance of heroism, the power of love, the strength of loyalty, and the dangers of greed.

Storytellers explored such themes by means of **archetypes.** An archetype is a situation, a character, an image, or a symbol that appears in the tales of various cultures. For example, the hero's quest, the struggle between good and evil, and tricksters appear in the stories of many different cultures and times. The circle is another archetype, a symbol of loyalty, protection, and completion, as in Odysseus' return to his homeland, Ithaca. The **historical context** (the social and cultural background of a particular tale) influences the presentation of archetypes.

The following are important narrative forms that express universal themes. A **myth** is a tale explaining the actions of gods and the humans who interact with them. Myths explain the causes of a natural phenomenon. **Folk tales** are brief stories focusing on human or animal heroes and are not primarily concerned with gods or the creation of the world. A **legend** recounts the adventures of a human hero and may be based on historical fact. **Tall tales** are legends told in an exaggerated way, intended for entertainment. An **epic** is a long narrative poem about a larger-than-life hero who goes on a dangerous journey or quest that is important to the history of a group or culture.

DIRECTIONS: *Circle the letter of the answer that best matches each numbered item.*

1. historical context
   A. author's biography
   B. story's cultural background
   C. story's theme

2. archetype
   A. story element in many cultures
   B. universal theme
   C. hero

3. tall tale
   A. epic
   B. exaggerated folk tale
   C. story featuring monsters

4. epic
   A. factual narrative
   B. legend
   C. long narrative poem

5. the power of love
   A. universal theme
   B. oral tradition
   C. historical context

6. quest
   A. hero's journey
   B. story that explains
   C. opposing person or force

7. main character in a folk tale
   A. historical figure
   B. human or animal hero
   C. god or goddess

"Play Hard; Play Together; Play Smart" *from* **The Carolina Way**
by Dean Smith with John Kilgo

Model Selection: Themes in Literature

Stories, poems, and essays often offer **themes,** or central insights into human life or behavior. The theme of a work may be directly stated by the author. More often, however, it is implied or suggested indirectly. The reader must use clues from the writer's choice of details, as well as from the style and tone of the work, to infer the theme.

Narratives, poems, and essays usually express the **values,** ideals, and behaviors cherished by the society in which they are produced. **Shared values** are held in common by people across cultures, and literary works give voice to them by exploring **universal themes**. In contrast, **culturally distinct values** are specific to a group. In a literary work, **cultural details** are the beliefs, traditions, and customs that reflect a particular society. Modern fiction and nonfiction, though written by individuals rather than fashioned by a group, can also express universal themes.

DIRECTIONS: *Use the space provided to answer the following questions about "Play Hard; Play Together; Play Smart."*

1. What are three cultural values stressed by Dean Smith in the essay?

   _____

   _____

   _____

   _____

2. Dean Smith coached American college basketball in the second half of the twentieth century. Do you think the values he emphasizes in his essay are culturally distinct, or are they shared values found in cultures around the world, in the past and present? Explain your answer in a few sentences.

   _____

   _____

   _____

   _____

   _____

3. Do Smith's main ideas in the essay suggest one or more universal themes? Write a paragraph in which you give your opinion about whether or not his essay contains universal themes. Use reasons and examples to support your position.

   _____

   _____

   _____

   _____

   _____

Name _____ Date _____

Open-Book Test

Short Answer *Write your responses to the questions in this section on the lines provided.*

1. Universal themes are insights into life that are true for many different times and cultures. Which of the following is an example of a universal theme: the central conflict in a work, the absolute importance of success, the power of love, or the appeal of television mysteries?

   _____

   _____

2. What are three symbolic meanings of the circle as an archetype?

   _____

   _____

3. Which of these terms best identifies the passing of stories, poems, and sayings by word of mouth from one generation to the next: archetype, symbol, universal theme, or oral tradition?

   _____

   _____

4. You are reading a tale about a human hero that is based on historical fact. How would you classify this narrative: as a tall tale, a myth, an epic, or a legend?

   _____

   _____

5. Reread the opening paragraphs of the essay from *The Carolina Way*. Briefly explain how Dean Smith's philosophy of coaching differs from a system.

   _____

   _____

6. From details in the essay from *The Carolina Way*, what can you conclude that Dean Smith believes about winning in competitive situations? Whom does Smith cite to support his belief?

   _____

   _____

7. In the middle of the excerpt from *The Carolina Way*, Dean Smith tells about the "young man who shot every time he touched the ball." What theme is strengthened by the telling of this anecdote? How?

   _____

   _____

8. Use three words or phrases from the box below to fill out the cluster diagram with the values that Dean Smith emphasizes in his essay from *The Carolina Way*.

loyalty	commitment to winning	becoming a champion scorer	dedicated effort
publicity	personal ambition	mastery of fundamentals	

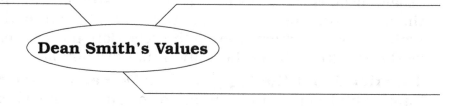

Dean Smith's Values

9. In the selection from *The Carolina Way*, Dean Smith appears to regard his role as that of a teacher. What evidence at the end of the selection supports this idea?

_____

_____

_____

_____

Essay

Write an extended response to the question of your choice or to the question or questions your teacher assigns you.

10. In the selection from Dean Smith's book *The Carolina Way,* Smith uses a number of specific examples and anecdotes to support his main ideas about playing hard, together, and smart. Write an essay in which you discuss one example for each of the three elements in Dean Smith's philosophy. In your essay, evaluate Smith's use of specific details and examples to illustrate his main ideas.

11. In this selection from *The Carolina Way*, Dean Smith discusses the three elements of his philosophy of coaching. In an essay, identify and discuss what Smith means by playing "hard, together, and smart." What do these elements have in common? How do they work together to produce success? In what other areas of life might you apply Smith's philosophy?

12. How would you relate Dean Smith's coaching philosophy, as told in *The Carolina Way*, to universal truths in the oral tradition or in written works of literature? In an essay, discuss the ways in which the "Carolina Way" is linked to such universal themes as the importance of heroism and the strength of loyalty. Support your main ideas with references to the selection and with examples from other literary works and from the oral tradition that are familiar to you.

13. **Thinking About the Big Question: Do heroes have responsibilities?** Dean Smith's philosophy and winning record made him a hero to many of his players and to the fans of North Carolina basketball. In an essay, discuss how in this selection from *The Carolina Way*, Smith encouraged a sense of team responsibility on the part of his players. Support your main ideas with specific references to the selection.

Oral Response

14. Go back to question 7, 8, 9, or to the question that your teacher assigns you. Take a few minutes to expand your answer and to prepare an oral response. Find additional details in this selection from *The Carolina Way* that support your points. If necessary, make notes to guide your oral response.

"Play Hard; Play Together; Play Smart" *from* **The Carolina Way**
by Dean Smith with John Kilgo
Selection Test A

Learning About Themes in Literature *Identify the letter of the choice that best answers the question.*

____ 1. Which of the following best defines a universal theme?
  A. a long narrative poem about a larger-than-life hero
  B. the goal of a hero's quest
  C. the symbol of the circle
  D. an insight into life that is true for many different times and cultures

____ 2. Which of the following is an example of a universal theme?
  A. the power of love
  B. the fear of falling
  C. the absolute importance of success
  D. the appeal of television mysteries

____ 3. Which of the following best defines **antagonist**?
  A. the central conflict in a work
  B. a person or force opposing the protagonist
  C. the hero of a tall tale
  D. a culturally distinct value

____ 4. What is the term for a tale about a human hero that is based on historical fact?
  A. tall tale
  B. myth
  C. epic
  D. legend

____ 5. Which of the following best defines an **archetype**?
  A. the long and dangerous journey of a hero
  B. the trickster figure
  C. the circle as a symbol
  D. a recurring element in world literature

Critical Reading

____ 6. In the first two paragraphs, what does Dean Smith emphasize most strongly?
  A. the importance of winning
  B. the contributions of his assistants
  C. the difficulty in recruiting talented players
  D. the necessity of adapting to change

____ 7. From details in the essay, you can conclude that for Smith "the Carolina Way" sums up which of the following?
A. a philosophy of coaching and playing basketball
B. North Carolina's long string of victories
C. a series of plays that have not changed over the years
D. an unrealistic philosophy of life

____ 8. According to Smith, which of the following lie(s) beyond the control of the players and coaches?
    I. the talent and experience of other teams
    II. the effort and dedication of the North Carolina team
    III. injuries and bad luck
    IV. bad calls by officials
A. I only
B. I and II
C. I and III
D. I, III, and IV

____ 9. What can you conclude that Dean Smith believes about winning?
A. Winning is not important.
B. Winning is the byproduct of his philosophy.
C. Not everybody is a winner.
D. Winning depends on luck.

____ 10. According to Smith, which of the following is most important to the success of a basketball team?
A. togetherness
B. speed
C. physical strength
D. natural talent

____ 11. Dean Smith uses this anecdote to stress the importance of which of the following?

> There was one young man who shot every time he touched the ball. Exasperated from watching him, I pulled his four teammates off the court. He asked who would throw the ball inbounds to him. "You understand that it takes at least one more player," I said to him.

A. precise execution
B. dedication and effort
C. unselfishness
D. obedience to the coach's orders

_____ 12. By "playing hard," Dean Smith means that a good player has to do which of the following?

A. get plenty of rest before a big game

B. put out maximum effort

C. not be afraid to go one-on-one against opponents

D. shoot accurately

_____ 13. Which of these values relates most closely to the element of "playing together" in Dean Smith's philosophy?

A. determination

B. trust

C. courage

D. mastery of fundamentals

_____ 14. In his essay, Dean Smith seems proudest of which of the following?

A. He was able to make his philosophy work at North Carolina.

B. He heeded the advice of coach Tom Osborne.

C. A very high percentage of his players earned their college degrees.

D. His trophy case was full.

_____ 15. The tone of a work is the author's attitude toward the subject, the characters, or the audience. Which of the following best describes the tone of "Play Hard; Play Together; Play Smart"?

A. harsh and pessimistic

B. objective and neutral

C. upbeat and inspirational

D. sad and resigned

Essay

16. In this selection, Dean Smith uses a number of specific examples and anecdotes to support his main ideas about playing "hard, together, and smart." Write an essay in which you discuss one example that Smith uses for each of the three elements in his philosophy. In your essay, evaluate Smith's use of specific details and examples to illustrate his main ideas.

17. Dean Smith relates coaching very closely to teaching. Assume that you are a teacher attempting to apply Smith's philosophy to academic course work. Your class is your team, and you are trying to get your students to "study hard, study together, and study smart." In an essay, discuss some specific ways in which you might encourage your students and put them on the path to success.

18. **Thinking About the Big Question: Do heroes have responsibilities?** Dean Smith's philosophy and winning record made him a hero to many of his players and to the fans of North Carolina basketball. But he gave the responsibility of working as a team to his players. In an essay, give one or two examples from *The Carolina Way* that illustrate how Smith encouraged a sense of team responsibility.

"**Play Hard; Play Together; Play Smart**" *from* **The Carolina Way**
by Dean Smith with John Kilgo
Selection Test B

Learning About Themes in Literature *Identify the letter of the choice that best completes the statement or answers the question.*

____ 1. Which of the following best identifies the passing of stories, poems, and sayings by word of mouth from one generation to the next?
   A. archetype
   B. symbol
   C. universal theme
   D. oral tradition

____ 2. A theme is universal when it
   A. involves the destiny of heroes.
   B. concerns romantic love.
   C. is true for many different times and cultures.
   D. is true for a specific time and culture.

____ 3. All of the following are symbolic meanings of the circle *except*
   A. completion.
   B. protection.
   C. quest.
   D. loyalty.

____ 4. Which of the following best defines a **myth**?
   A. a long narrative poem
   B. a story explaining the interactions of gods and humans
   C. a story about the adventures of a human hero
   D. a set of values shared by a culture

____ 5. Which of the following identifies a legend told in an exaggerated way?
   A. tall tale   C. folk tale
   B. myth   D. epic

____ 6. The monster and the trickster figures are examples of which of the following?
   A. legends   C. archetypes
   B. epics   D. universal themes

Critical Reading

____ 7. What best identifies Dean Smith's attitude toward change?
   A. Change is troublesome, but we must learn to deal with it.
   B. Change is inevitable, so it should not be feared.
   C. You should do everything possible to avoid change.
   D. Change will happen only once in a while, so do not worry about it too much.

_____ 8. By "play hard," Smith means which of the following?
    A. Do not be afraid to be ruthless in your effort to win.
    B. Stay in top physical condition.
    C. Play with effort, determination, and courage.
    D. Do not hesitate to break the rules if you can get away with it.

_____ 9. What did the North Carolina players seldom hear Smith or his assistants talk about?
    A. referees
    B. spectators
    C. winning
    D. losing

_____ 10. For Dean Smith, a system differs from a philosophy primarily in that
    A. a system is more reliable than a philosophy.
    B. a philosophy is less rigid and more open to change than a system is.
    C. a philosophy is more abstract than a system.
    D. a system is more realistic than a philosophy.

_____ 11. Which of the following did Dean Smith coach at North Carolina?
    A. football
    B. baseball
    C. basketball
    D. lacrosse

_____ 12. In his essay, which of the following best explains why Smith includes the anecdote about the young man at the Air Force Academy who shot every time he touched the ball?
    A. Smith wants to underline his own inexperience as a coach at that time.
    B. Smith wants to show how important it is to recruit unselfish players.
    C. Smith wants to show that good players listen to the coach.
    D. Smith wants to stress that players need to feel driven to become top scorers.

_____ 13. According to Smith, a player can control all of the following *except*
    A. his dedication.
    B. his effort.
    C. his unselfishness.
    D. the talent and experience of opposing teams.

_____ 14. If a player did not give maximum effort, how did Smith and his coaches react?
    A. They lectured the player in front of the whole team.
    B. They cut the player from the starting line-up for the next game.
    C. They stopped practice and had the entire team run sprints.
    D. They had the offending player sit out the rest of the practice drills.

_____ 15. After he retired from coaching, Smith missed all of the following *except*
    A. competitive games.
    B. recruiting players.
    C. late-game situations.
    D. his relationship with the players.

____ 16. Which of the following best identifies what Smith means by "playing smart"?
A. researching opponents in advance
B. knowing how to shoot well
C. poise and mastery of fundamentals
D. looking for and obeying Smith's signals

____ 17. Overall, during his coaching career Smith regarded himself as which of the following?
A. a military commander
B. a master strategist
C. a teacher in a leadership role
D. a preacher delivering sermons

____ 18. In his approach to coaching, Smith places emphasis on all of the following values *except*
A. loyalty.
B. mastery of fundamentals.
C. dedicated effort.
D. personal ambition.

____ 19. Which of the following universal themes receives the most emphasis in Smith's essay?
A. the dangers of greed
B. the importance of heroism
C. the strength of loyalty
D. the power of love

Essay

20. In this selection, Dean Smith discusses the three elements of his philosophy of coaching. In an essay, identify and discuss what Smith means by playing "hard, together, and smart." What do these elements have in common? How do they work together to produce success? In what other areas of life might you apply Smith's philosophy?

21. According to Smith, "making winning the ultimate goal usually isn't good teaching." In an essay, discuss the theme of teaching and learning in Smith's essay. How does the philosophy of the "Carolina way" emphasize parallels between the player-coach and the student-teacher relationship? Support your ideas with specific references to the selection.

22. How would you relate Smith's coaching philosophy to universal themes in the oral tradition or in written works of literature? In an essay, discuss the ways in which the "Carolina way" is linked to such universal themes as the importance of heroism and the strength of loyalty. Support your main ideas with references to the selection and with examples from other literary works or from the oral tradition.

23. **Thinking About the Big Question: Do heroes have responsibilities?** Dean Smith's philosophy and winning record made him a hero to many of his players and to the fans of North Carolina basketball. In an essay, discuss how in this selection from *The Carolina Way*, Smith encouraged a sense of team responsibility on the part of his players. Support your main ideas with specific references to the selection.

Vocabulary Warm-up Word Lists

Study these words from the "Odyssey," Part I. Then, complete the activities that follow.

Word List A

companions [kuhm PAN yuhnz] *n.* friends
Marcy and three <u>companions</u> walked to the park together every day.

compelled [kuhm PELD] *v.* forced
The storm <u>compelled</u> us to turn back.

entreat [in TREET] *v.* plead
I <u>entreat</u> you to give me another chance.

immortal [i MAWR tuhl] *adj.* living or continuing forever
Sometimes, people take great risks, thinking that they are <u>immortal</u>.

penalty [PEN uhl tee] *n.* a loss or punishment resulting from some action
One <u>penalty</u> of fame is the lack of privacy.

plucked [PLUHKT] *v.* pulled something off or out quickly
Marguerite <u>plucked</u> the petals from a daisy.

shepherd [SHEP uhrd] *n.* a person who watches over sheep
The <u>shepherd</u> was worried over the one lost sheep.

urged [ERJD] *v.* strongly recommended or encouraged
The inspector <u>urged</u> the homeowners to repair the roof.

Word List B

anguish [ANG gwish] *n.* great suffering caused by pain or worry
Stan suffered great <u>anguish</u> over injuring the driver of the car he hit.

cavern [KAV ern] *n.* a large deep cave
Bushes hid the entrance to the <u>cavern</u>.

formidable [FAWR muh duh buhl] *adj.* causing fear or dread; very powerful
The boxer was not afraid, despite the <u>formidable</u> size of his opponent.

indifferent [in DIF er uhnt] *adj.* not caring; unconcerned or uninterested
The cold-hearted miser was <u>indifferent</u> to the pleas of the beggar.

realm [RELM] *n.* a region or an area; a kingdom
David stood on the balcony, looking out over his <u>realm</u>.

refused [ri FYOOZD] *v.* rejected; said no
Glenda <u>refused</u> to lend her pearls to Rebecca.

tempt [TEMPT] *v.* to do something that might cause problems
The child knew that she would <u>tempt</u> her parents' anger if she threw her food at the cat.

tranquil [TRANG kwuhl] *adj.* calm, quiet, and peaceful
We sat on the porch and enjoyed the <u>tranquil</u> evening.

from the Odyssey, Part I by Homer
Vocabulary Warm-up Exercises

Exercise A *Fill in each blank in the paragraph with an appropriate word from Word List A. Use each word only once.*

"I have [1] _____ the last feather from my last chicken," declared

Otis passionately to his fellow workers in the chicken-packing factory. "I feel

[2] _____ to quit this job right now! I am going to get a job as a

[3] _____! At least I will be outdoors, getting some fresh air every day."

Otis's [4] _____ on the factory floor tried to calm him down.

They strongly [5] _____ him to reconsider his decision. "I

[6] _____ you, Otis, to think twice about this. If you quit now, I am sure

the [7] _____ will be that you will not ever be rehired," said Estelle.

"I do not care!" said Otis. "I know I am not [8] _____, and I also know

that life is short. I must do what makes me happy."

Exercise B *Find a synonym for each word in the following list. Then, use each synonym in a sentence that makes its meaning clear. Refer to a thesaurus if you need help finding a synonym.*

Example: tempt **Synonym:** *attract*
   Sentence: *To attract customers into its showroom, the car manufacturer displays its newest, flashiest models.*

1. anguish   **Synonym:** _____

   _____

2. cavern   **Synonym:** _____

   _____

3. formidable   **Synonym:** _____

   _____

4. indifferent   **Synonym:** _____

   _____

5. realm   **Synonym:** _____

   _____

6. refused   **Synonym:** _____

   _____

7. tranquil   **Synonym:** _____

   _____

Name _____ Date _____

from **the Odyssey, Part I** by Homer
Reading Warm-up A

Read the following passage. Pay special attention to the underlined words. Then, read it again, and complete the activities. Use a separate sheet of paper for your written answers.

A desire to do well often <u>compelled</u> ancient storytellers and poets to begin their work with a call to three Greek goddesses known as the Muses. The Greeks believed that the Muses had the power to inspire people. They also thought that the Muses could prompt the memory. Because no books existed at the time, early storytellers had to rely on their memories, so they would <u>entreat</u> the Muses for their help.

According to legend, the Muses were the daughters of Zeus, the chief god, and Mnemosyne (Memory). Before Hera became Zeus' wife, Zeus took the form of a <u>shepherd</u>. He tended a flock of sheep in the hills where Mnemosyne lived. He stayed with Mnemosyne for nine nights. Mnemosyne later gave birth to nine daughters.

The Muses were supposedly born in this order: Calliope, Clio, Melpomene, Euterpe, Erato, Terpsichore, Urania, Thalia, and Polymnia. Like their father, they were <u>immortal</u>, meaning they could never die. They lived on Mount Olympus, the home of all the gods and goddesses. Here they had many <u>companions</u>, such as the three Charities, goddesses of grace.

Each of the Muses is said to preside over a different branch of the arts or sciences. Calliope is associated with epic poetry, Clio with history, and Melpomene with tragedy. Euterpe is associated with lyric poetry, Erato with love poetry, and Terpsichore with choral dance and song. Urania is associated with astronomy, Thalia with comedy, and Polyhymnia with sacred poetry.

One myth about the Muses involves Hera, queen of the gods. One day, Hera spoke to the Sirens, who had the bodies of birds and the heads of beautiful women. She <u>urged</u> them to compete in a singing contest with the Muses. When the Muses won, they demanded a <u>penalty</u> from the Sirens. They <u>plucked</u> out all of the Sirens' feathers and used them to make crowns for themselves.

Next time you need to be creative, try calling upon the Muses. Perhaps you will hear them singing just to you.

1. Underline the words that tell what <u>compelled</u> storytellers and poets to address the Muses. Tell about something you felt **compelled** to do.

2. Circle the words that explain for what early poets would <u>entreat</u> the Muses. What does **entreat** mean?

3. Underline the words in the next sentence that describe the job of a <u>shepherd</u>. What might be the most important aspect of a **shepherd's** job?

4. Circle the words that tell what <u>immortal</u> means. Use **immortal** in a sentence.

5. Circle the words in the next sentence that name some of the Muses' <u>companions</u>. Name a few of your favorite **companions**.

6. Underline the words that explain what Hera <u>urged</u> the Sirens to do. Describe something that someone **urged** you to do lately.

7. Underline the words that tell who had to pay a <u>penalty</u>. Describe a **penalty** you once had to pay.

8. Circle the words that tell what the Muses <u>plucked</u> out. What else might be **plucked** out?

Name _____ Date _____

from the Odyssey, Part I by Homer
Reading Warm-up B

Read the following passage. Pay special attention to the underlined words. Then, read it again, and complete the activities. Use a separate sheet of paper for your written answers.

According to Greek mythology, Calypso was a sea nymph. As such, she shared many of the attributes of the goddesses, including eternal life and certain <u>formidable</u>, awe-inspiring powers.

Calypso lived on the island Ogygia. Her home was a spacious <u>cavern</u> covered in luxurious green vines. Near this large cave sat four fountains that added to the <u>tranquil</u>, peaceful mood of her <u>realm</u>. All around the cavern were meadows of soft green vegetation covered with violets.

The name *Calypso* means "the concealer" or "the hider," which is fitting considering what she did to Odysseus. When the Greek was washed ashore after a shipwreck, she welcomed him warmly and entertained him lavishly. As time passed, she grew to love him. Wanting to keep him there with her forever, she offered him a promise of everlasting life if he would give up his quest to return home. He <u>refused</u> this offer, wishing to return to his wife, Penelope, and their son, Telemachus, who had been an infant when he left.

<u>Indifferent</u> to Odysseus' own wishes, Calypso held him captive for seven years. She thought that, given enough time, she could convince him to stay. All that time, Odysseus longed to return home but had no way to leave the island.

Finally, Zeus sent Hermes, the messenger of the gods, to help Odysseus. Hermes told Calypso that Zeus had commanded Odysseus' release, and he persuaded her to let Odysseus go. Very reluctantly, Calypso carried out Zeus' wishes. Unwilling to <u>tempt</u> Zeus' anger, she gave Odysseus the supplies he needed to construct a raft, and she gave him the provisions he would need for his trip. Then, she provided the winds he would need to sail away.

According to legend, after Odysseus departed from her island, Calypso's grief caused her so much pain and <u>anguish</u> that she died.

1. Circle the word that helps define <u>formidable</u>. Write a sentence describing a *formidable* character about whom you have read or heard.

2. Underline the words in the next sentence that define <u>cavern</u>. Use *cavern* in a sentence.

3. Circle the word that means about the same as <u>tranquil</u>. Describe a *tranquil* spot that you like to visit.

4. Underline the words and phrases in the paragraph that describe Calypso's <u>realm</u>. Describe a *realm* that you would want to reign over.

5. Underline the words that tell why Odysseus <u>refused</u> Calypso's offer. When was the last time you *refused* a generous offer?

6. Circle the words that show that Calypso was <u>indifferent</u> to Odysseus' wishes. How does someone who is *indifferent* act?

7. Circle the words that tell what Calypso did not want to <u>tempt</u>. Explain what *tempt* means.

8. Underline two words that help you to understand the meaning of <u>anguish</u>. Describe another situation that would cause *anguish*.

from the Odyssey, *Part 1* by Homer
Writing About the Big Question

Do heroes have responsibilities?

Big Question Vocabulary

character	choices	hero	honesty	identify
imitate	intentions	involvement	justice	morality
obligation	responsibility	serve	standard	wisdom

A. *Use one or more words from the list above to complete each sentence.*

1. The _____ made by a(n) _____ in a literary work often determine the outcome of the plot.

2. A(n) _____ is usually someone who embodies the values of an entire culture or society.

3. _____ and _____ are two values that a(n) _____ typically upholds.

4. By any measure, Odysseus in Homer's *Odyssey,* lives up to a heroic _____.

5. It is usually easy to _____ the hero of an epic poem.

B. *Follow the directions in responding to each of the items below.*

1. List two different times that you became aware of a **responsibility.**

_____

_____

2. Write two sentences to explain one of these experiences, and describe how it made you feel. Use at least two of the Big Question vocabulary words.

_____

_____

C. *Complete the sentences below. Then, write a short paragraph in which you connect the sentences to the Big Question.*

A **hero** has an **obligation** to _____. The **choices** he or she makes

must _____.

_____

_____

_____

_____

Name _____ Date _____

from **the Odyssey,** *Part 1* by Homer
Literary Analysis: Epic Hero

An **epic hero** is the larger-than-life central character in an epic—a long narrative poem about important events in the history or folklore of a nation or culture. Through adventurous deeds, the epic hero demonstrates traits—such as loyalty, honor, and resourcefulness—that are valued by the society in which the epic originates.

Many epics begin *in medias res* ("in the middle of things"), meaning that much of the important action in the story occurred before the point at which the poem begins. Therefore, an epic hero's adventures are often recounted in a **flashback,** a scene that interrupts the sequence of events in a narrative to relate earlier events. Flashbacks also allow the poet to provide a more complete portrait of the epic hero's character.

DIRECTIONS: *Consider the adventures shown in the left column of the following chart. Then, determine what evidence is contained in each adventure to support the position that Odysseus has the superior physical and mental prowess to be an epic hero. Write your answers in the chart.*

Adventure	Evidence of Mental Prowess	Evidence of Physical Prowess
1. The Lotus-Eaters		
2. The Cyclops		
3. The Sirens		
4. Scylla and Charybdis		

from **the Odyssey,** *Part 1* by Homer
Reading: Analyze the Influence of Historical and Cultural Context

The **historical and cultural context** of a work is the backdrop of details of the time and place in which the work is set or in which it was written. These details include the events, beliefs, and customs of a specific culture and time. When you read a work from another time and culture, **use background and prior knowledge** to analyze the influence of the historical and cultural context.

- Read the author biography, footnotes, and other textual aids to understand the work's historical and cultural context.
- Note how characters' behavior and attitudes reflect that context.

DIRECTIONS: *Answer the following questions on the lines provided.*

1. What does the common noun *odyssey* mean? Use a dictionary, if necessary, to look up this word and identify its meaning. How does this word relate to Homer's epic and the hero Odysseus?

   _____

   _____

   _____

2. What does the word *Homeric* mean? How does this word relate to the ancient Greek epics the *Iliad* and the *Odyssey*?

   _____

   _____

   _____

3. About when were the Homeric epics composed, or when did they assume their final form after centuries of development in the oral tradition?

   _____

4. Reread Odysseus' description of the Cyclopes in Part 1, lines 109–120. What does this passage imply about ancient Greek values and beliefs? Explain your answer in a brief paragraph.

   _____

   _____

   _____

   _____

   _____

   _____

from the Odyssey, *Part 1* by Homer
Vocabulary Builder

Word List

ardor   assuage   bereft   dispatched   insidious   plundered

A. DIRECTIONS: *In each of the following items, think about the meaning of the italicized word and then answer the question.*

1. If you regard someone as *insidious,* do you like or dislike that person? Why?

   _____

2. Historically, when do people tend to *plunder*—during wartime or peacetime?

   _____

3. If Maria *dispatched* her assignment, did it take her a long time or a short time to finish?

   _____

4. Would you use gentle words or provocative words to *assuage* someone's anger or demands? Explain.

   _____

5. If you were *bereft* of sleep, would you feel fatigued or well-rested?

   _____

B. WORD STUDY: *The Old English prefix* be-, *meaning "around," "make," or "covered with," can sometimes be added to a noun or an adjective to create a transitive verb. Examples include* beheld *and* begone. *Match the word in Column A with its meaning in Column B by writing the correct letter on the line provided.*

___ 1. bemoan   A. be on one's guard

___ 2. bewilder   B. lament

___ 3. beware   C. signify

___ 4. betoken   D. confuse

___ 5. bereft   E. deprived

from **the Odyssey, *Part 1*** by Homer
Enrichment: Geography

The term *odyssey,* meaning a long voyage or wandering, comes from the name Odysseus. Indeed, Zeus' winds send Odysseus and his men to the farthest reaches of the Mediterranean Sea. Scholars have traced many of the locations in Homer's epic to actual places in and around the Mediterranean.

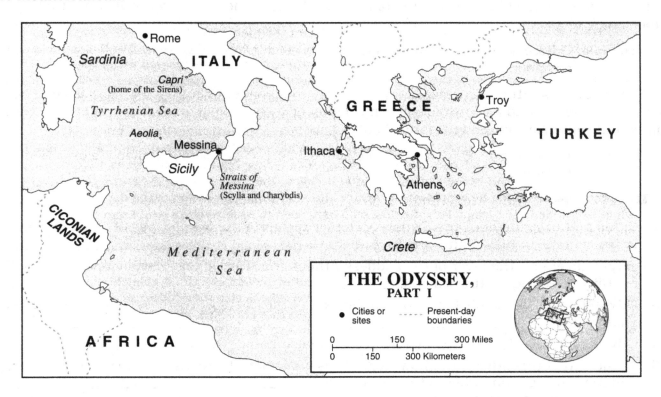

DIRECTIONS: *Use details from the map and the* Odyssey *to find out more about Odysseus' travels.*

1. After the war ends at Troy, Odysseus sets sail for Ithaca. What is the exact location of Odysseus' beloved home?

   _____

2. Between the time that he drags his men away from the Lotus-Eaters in the land of the Cicones and the time that he reaches Aeolia, Odysseus encounters the Cyclops. Where might the land of the Cyclops have been located?

   _____

3. Scholars have named the Strait of Messina as the home of Scylla and Charybdis. Why might these watery threats be attributed to this geographical feature?

   _____

4. The Italian island of Capri has been traditionally thought to be the home of the Sirens. After escaping the Sirens, in which direction does Odysseus sail?

   _____

5. On the map, chart the route that Odysseus travels from Troy until his first encounter with Scylla and Charybdis.

Name _____ Date _____

from the Odyssey, *Part 1* by Homer
Integrated Language Skills: Grammar

Simple and Compound Sentences

A **simple sentence** consists of a single independent clause. Although a simple sentence is just one independent clause with one subject and verb, the subject, verb, or both may be compound. A simple sentence may have modifying phrases and complements. However, it cannot have a subordinate clause.

> **Example:** Odysseus returned to Ithaca and took his revenge on the suitors. (simple sentence with compound verb)

A **compound sentence** consists of two or more independent clauses. The clauses can be joined by a comma and a coordinating conjunction or by a semicolon. Like a simple sentence, a compound sentence contains no subordinate clauses.

> **Example:** The suitors reveled in the hall; in the meantime, Penelope questioned the disguised Odysseus.

A. DIRECTIONS: *Identify each sentence as simple or compound.*

1. In his monumental epic, the *Odyssey,* Homer recounts the wanderings of Odysseus on his journey home to Ithaca after the Trojan War. _____

2. Odysseus enjoys the favor of the goddess Athena, but his safe return is jeopardized by the hostility of Poseidon, the sea god. _____

3. Odysseus foolishly leads his men into the cave of the Cyclops; there, several of them meet a ghastly fate. _____

4. Odysseus tricks the Cyclops by telling him a false name: "Nohbdy." _____

5. At the end of this adventure, however, Odysseus boastfully reveals his true name, thereby making himself vulnerable to the Cyclops' curse. _____

B. WRITING APPLICATION: *On the following lines, write a paragraph in which you describe what you would wish for if you had three wishes. In your writing, use both simple and compound sentences. Be prepared to identify each type of sentence.*

_____

_____

_____

_____

_____

_____

_____

_____

_____

_____

Name _____ Date _____

Integrated Language Skills:
Support for Writing an Everyday Epic

Use a chart like the one below to jot down notes for your everyday epic.

Everyday Event:

_____

Epic Dimensions (adventure, bravery, life-and-death challenges): _____

_____

_____

_____

_____

_____

Multiple Points of View: _____

_____

_____

Supernatural/Fantastic Elements: _____

_____

_____

_____

_____

_____

Ideas for Performance/Recitation: _____

_____

_____

_____

_____

_____

from **the Odyssey,** *Part 1* by Homer
Integrated Language Skills: Support for Extend Your Learning

Listening and Speaking

Use the following lines to make notes for your everyday conversation.

Odysseus' Exploits

The Lotus-Eaters: _____

_____

The Cyclops: _____

_____

The Land of the Dead: _____

_____

The Sirens: _____

_____

Scylla and Charybdis: _____

_____

The Cattle of the Sun God: _____

_____

Ancient Greek Values Shown in the *Odyssey*

Courage: _____

_____

Intelligence: _____

_____

Respect for the Gods: _____

_____

Leadership: _____

_____

Name _____ Date _____

from the **Odyssey, Part 1,** by Homer
Open-Book Test

Short Answer *Write your responses to the questions in this section on the lines provided.*

1. In the opening verses of the *Odyssey*, Part 1, Homer describes Odysseus, the epic hero. Reread lines 1–9. Which specific phrase best calls attention to the portrayal of Odysseus as clever and able to meet challenges? Briefly support your choice.

   _____

   _____

   _____

   _____

2. According to Odysseus, in the *Odyssey*, Part 1, what is the cause of the doom he and his men face on the island of Cicones? Explain the events leading up to the doom.

   _____

   _____

   _____

   _____

3. Return to lines 101–105 of the *Odyssey*, Part 1, in which Odysseus saves his men from the Lotus Eaters. What is heroic about Odysseus' actions?

   _____

   _____

   _____

4. Explain lines 110–112 from the *Odyssey*, Part 1, that describe the Cyclopes. How does this description of the Cyclopes relate to the historical and cultural context of the epic—that is, to the Greek concept of a civilized society?

   _____

   _____

   _____

   _____

5. What characteristics lead Odysseus to put his men in danger during the episode with the Cyclops? Name two instances in the *Odyssey*, Part 1, in which he risks the group's safety by his actions.

   _____

   _____

   _____

6. Who is Tiresias in the Land of the Dead? What is his purpose in the plot of the *Odyssey*, Part 1, and to Odysseus?

_____

_____

_____

7. In the *Odyssey*, Part 1, what does Odysseus mean when he describes being at sea and "letting the wind and steersman work the ship" (line 683)? Use background and prior knowledge to explain these words.

_____

_____

_____

8. Scylla and Charybdis are located in a strait, which is a narrow channel of water, between Italy and Sicily. Explain why the story of the sea monster and the whirlpool in the *Odyssey*, Part 1, may have developed.

_____

_____

_____

9. According to the *Odyssey*, Part 1, what type of person would *plunder* a city like Troy? Use the meaning of *plunder* in your answer.

_____

_____

10. As an epic hero in the *Odyssey*, Part 1, Odysseus is a larger-than-life character. In the chart, list Odysseus' strengths and weaknesses.

Odysseus' Strengths	Odysseus' Weaknesses

Essay

Write an extended response to the question of your choice or to the question or questions your teacher assigns you.

11. Choose an adventure from the *Odyssey*, Part 1, and in an essay, retell the story in your own words. Reread the passage to be clear on all the details. Include the location of Odysseus and his men, the difficulty they face, and the way they manage to solve the problem and escape.

12. Based on the episode of the Land of the Dead in the *Odyssey*, Part 1, explain in a brief essay what you have learned of the Greek view of the afterlife. In your essay, explain how Odysseus and his men traveled there, what they did to talk with the dead, and what the dead wanted from them. What knowledge could they gain from the dead?

13. At the beginning of the epic, Homer speaks to the Muse, asking for help in relating the adventures of Odysseus. In an essay, explain why you think Homer asks for help from a goddess in creating the *Odyssey*. In your essay, cite examples from the *Odyssey*, Part 1, to support your opinion.

14. **Thinking About the Big Question: Do heroes have responsibilities?** In an essay, describe Odysseus' character. Cite strengths and weaknesses from the chart you made for question 10, and cite examples from the *Odyssey*, Part 1, that reveal these characteristics. How is Odysseus a brave hero who fulfills his responsibility to his men? In what ways does he let his weaknesses cause him trouble or lead him to fall short of his responsibilities?

Oral Response

15. Go back to question 4, 5, 6, or to the question your teacher assigns you. Take a few minutes to expand your answer and prepare an oral response. Find additional details in the *Odyssey*, Part 1, that will support your points. If necessary, make notes to support your answer.

from **the Odyssey,** *Part 1* by Homer
Selection Test A

Critical Reading *Identify the letter of the choice that best answers the question.*

___ 1. Which of the following characters is the father of Odysseus?
   A. Polyphemus
   B. Helios
   C. Poseidon
   D. Laertes

___ 2. Which of the following best defines an *epic*?
   A. a long narrative poem based on actual historical events
   B. a long narrative poem about important events in the history or folklore of a nation or culture
   C. a dramatic poem that includes fantastic and supernatural elements
   D. a prose narrative in which the hero embarks on a long journey in search of something

___ 3. What danger to Odysseus' men do the Lotus-Eaters pose?
   A. Eating the lotus will make the men forget about returning home.
   B. Making friends with the Lotus-Eaters is dangerous because they are cannibals.
   C. The Lotus-Eaters may deliberately mislead the crew about the route home.
   D. The Lotus-Eaters may cause the winds to subside.

___ 4. Read the following lines from the *Odyssey:*
   In the next land we found were Cyclopes,
   giants, louts, without a law to bless them.

   By implication, what cultural value in ancient Greece is Odysseus emphasizing in this passage?
   A. physical strength
   B. mental intelligence
   C. civilized life in a law-abiding society
   D. the benefits of travel

___ 5. When the Cyclops asks Odysseus' name, what does the hero tell him?
   A. Odysseus says that he is the son of Poseidon.
   B. Odysseus claims that his mother is rosy-fingered Dawn.
   C. Odysseus tells the Cyclops his real name.
   D. Odysseus lies, telling the Cyclops that he is called "Nohbdy."

___ 6. Why does Odysseus blind the Cyclops rather than kill him when the giant is asleep?

    A. His men convince him that they will all be cursed by the powerful god Poseidon if they kill the Cyclops.

    B. Odysseus is moved by compassion for the Cyclops.

    C. Odysseus realizes that he and his men need the Cyclops to roll aside the huge stone that blocks the cave's entrance.

    D. Odysseus and his men lack the physical strength to kill the giant.

___ 7. In which of these episodes does Odysseus lose all his men?

    A. the Cyclops

    B. the Lotus-Eaters

    C. the Cattle of the Sun God

    D. the Sirens

___ 8. Which of the following correctly defines a *flashback*?

    A. a scene that interrupts the sequence of events in a narrative to relate earlier events

    B. a sudden realization on the part of the epic hero

    C. a scene that foreshadows an epic hero's destiny

    D. an extended comparison or contrast between present events and past events

___ 9. Read the following lines from the *Odyssey:*

                Men hold me
    formidable for guile in peace and war:
    this fame has gone abroad to the sky's rim.

    What quality of the epic hero does Odysseus emphasize in this passage?

    A. arrogance

    B. craftiness

    C. compassion

    D. modesty

___ 10. At the end of the Cyclops adventure, what does Polyphemus do that has an important impact on future events in the epic?

    A. He destroys Odysseus' ship.

    B. He prophesies that Odysseus will visit Hades.

    C. He begs his father Poseidon to curse Odysseus.

    D. He tells Odysseus that the hero will return safely home to Ithaca.

___ 11. What personality trait does Odysseus reveal when he devises a plan to listen to the Sirens' song and yet escape destruction?

A. irritability

B. loyalty

C. curiosity

D. generosity

Vocabulary and Grammar

___ 12. Which of the following is the best synonym for *assuage*?

A. influence

B. pacify

C. antagonize

D. imitate

___ 13. Which of the following is most nearly opposite in meaning to *insidious*?

A. enormous

B. deceitful

C. straightforward

D. harmful

___ 14. Which of the following statements about a simple sentence is correct?

A. It always has a compound subject.

B. It always has a compound verb.

C. It may contain a subordinate clause.

D. It consists of a single independent clause.

Essay

15. As an epic hero, Odysseus is a larger-than-life character. In an essay, identify and discuss Odysseus' characteristics—both his strengths and his weaknesses. Be sure to support your main ideas with specific examples or quotations from the epic.

16. Choose an adventure from Part 1 of the *Odyssey*, and retell the story in your own words. Reread the passage carefully in order to be clear on all the details. In your retelling, include the location of Odysseus and his men, the difficulty or challenge that they face, and the way they manage to solve the problems and escape.

17. **Thinking About the Big Question: Do heroes have responsibilities?** Odysseus is brave, crafty, cunning, clever, and obedient to the gods and the laws. In an essay, describe one event from the *Odyssey*, Part 1, that shows how these strengths help Odysseus be a responsible hero.

from **the Odyssey,** *Part 1* by Homer
Selection Test B

Critical Reading *Identify the letter of the choice that best completes the statement or answers the question.*

____ 1. Part 1 of the *Odyssey* is mainly about Odysseus'
   A. influence with the gods.
   B. love of travel.
   C. heroic deeds.
   D. loyalty to Helios.

____ 2. Which of the following quotations describes an act typical of an epic hero?
   A. "Now I let go with hands and feet, plunging / straight into the foam beside the timbers, / pulled astride, and rowed hard with my hands / to pass by Scylla."
   B. "I rather dwelt on this part of the forecast, / while our good ship made time, bound outward down / the wind for the strange island of Sirens."
   C. "In the next land we found were Cyclopes, / giants, louts, without a law to bless them."
   D. "We beached her, grinding keel in the soft sand, / and waded in, ourselves on the sandy beach."

____ 3. The epithet "Laertes' son," which is frequently applied to Odysseus, emphasizes
   A. Laertes' high standards for Odysseus.
   B. Laertes' trust in Odysseus.
   C. Odysseus' lack of maturity.
   D. Odysseus' loyalty to his family.

____ 4. Which statement most accurately describes the role of Zeus in Odysseus' adventures?
   A. Zeus encourages Odysseus' crew.
   B. Zeus controls the weather by which Odysseus sails.
   C. Zeus strengthens Odysseus' enemies.
   D. Zeus protects Odysseus' crew from harm.

____ 5. Read the following passage from the *Odyssey:*

   Cyclopes have no muster and no meeting,
   no consultation or old tribal ways,
   but each one dwells in his own mountain cave,
   dealing out rough justice to wife and child,
   indifferent to what the others do. . . .

   In this description, what ancient Greek cultural value does Odysseus imply that the Cyclopes lack?
   A. ambition to achieve success
   B. artistic and literary talent
   C. structured life in a well-organized society
   D. loyalty to the gods

____ 6. Although Odysseus' men want to steal the Cyclops' cheese and animals and depart immediately, Odysseus wishes "to see the cave man, what he had to offer." Considering Odysseus' character, what might he be hoping the Cyclops will offer?
A. an exciting challenge
B. a faster ship
C. a place to stay
D. a good meal

____ 7. Which is the best rephrasing of the following lines?
> When the young Dawn with fingertips of rose
> lit up the world, the Cyclops built a fire. . . .

A. When young Dawn's fingertips turned rosy and lit up the world, the Cyclops built a fire.
B. At daybreak, the Cyclops built a fire.
C. The Cyclops built a fire whenever he saw a pinkish or rosy-colored sky.
D. The sun rises. The Cyclops builds a fire.

____ 8. Which character trait does Odysseus demonstrate when he lies about his name to the Cyclops?
A. ruthlessness   C. cleverness
B. loyalty   D. stubbornness

____ 9. What is the meaning of Polyphemus' words in the following lines?
> Let him lose all companions, and return
> under strange sail to bitter days at home.

A. Let Odysseus return home without his companions.
B. Odysseus and some of his crew will sail home in a strange type of sailing vessel.
C. Let Odysseus return home in a stranger's boat, alone and troubled.
D. Curse Odysseus with a difficult journey home.

____ 10. Which of the following correctly defines an *epic*?
A. a lengthy narrative that alternates sections in prose with sections in verse
B. a narrative whose central character experiences a conflict with nature
C. a long narrative poem about important events in the history or folklore of a nation or culture
D. a lengthy narrative whose plot features romantic love

____ 11. The epic hero Odysseus most clearly demonstrates the realistic, human side of his character when he
A. resists the temptations of Calypso and Circe.
B. refuses to taste the honeyed Lotus plant.
C. ties his men beneath the Cyclops' rams.
D. weeps upon meeting Elpenor's ghost in Hades.

____ 12. What is meant by the expression *in medias res*?
A. on the Mediterranean Sea   C. in the middle of things
B. according to law   D. in conformity with fate

____ 13. What is demonstrated by Odysseus' failure to wake up and prevent his men from slaughtering the sun god's cattle?
A. Eurylochus' skills as a leader
B. Odysseus' exhaustion
C. the power of the gods
D. the disloyalty of the crew

____ 14. To understand the historical and cultural context of a literary work, which of the following is most helpful?
A. Skim the work first, and then read it slowly and carefully.
B. Consider how the work has affected subsequent poems, novels, or essays.
C. Read the author biography, footnotes, and other textual aids.
D. Consider how you would set the work to music.

Vocabulary and Grammar

____ 15. Which word best completes the following sentence?
Despite Calypso's _____ for him, Odysseus insists on returning to Ithaca.
A. ardor
B. bereft
C. assuage
D. insidious

____ 16. Odysseus would probably respond to an *insidious* member of his crew by
A. rewarding him.
B. trying to befriend him.
C. punishing him.
D. ignoring him.

____ 17. A simple sentence *cannot* have which of the following?
A. a comma
B. a compound subject
C. a compound verb
D. a subordinate clause

____ 18. Which of the following correctly describes the following sentence?
Odysseus' men tie him to the mast, and the hero listens to the song of the Sirens.
A. simple sentence
B. compound sentence
C. complex sentence
D. compound-complex sentence

Essay

19. How do the men of Odysseus' crew feel about him? Do you think they regard him as a hero? Why or why not? In an essay, state your opinion and then support it with evidence from the epic.

20. An epic hero possesses the character traits most valued by the society in which the epic originated. Based on this portion of the *Odyssey*, write a brief essay describing the character traits most valued in ancient Greece. Support your main ideas with specific references to the epic.

21. In general, does Odysseus control his own destiny, or is his fate determined by the gods? Explore this question in a brief essay, supporting your conclusions with evidence from the selection.

22. **Thinking About the Big Question: Do heroes have responsibilities?** In an essay, describe strengths and weaknesses in Odysseus' character. Cite examples from the *Odyssey*, Part 1, that reveal these characteristics. How is Odysseus a brave hero who fulfills his responsibility to his men? In what ways does he let his weaknesses cause him trouble or lead him to fall short of his responsibilities?

Vocabulary Warm-up Word Lists

Study these words from the "Odyssey," Part II. Then, complete the activities that follow.

Word List A

faithful [FAYTH fuhl] *adj.* loyal and true
Carly could depend on Michael, a <u>faithful</u> friend.

fame [FAYM] *n.* state of being well known
<u>Fame</u> did not change Matthew's down-to-earth character.

intend [in TEND] *v.* to have in mind as a purpose; plan
What do you <u>intend</u> to do about this problem?

marvel [MAR vuhl] *v.* to feel surprise or admiration
I <u>marvel</u> at how anyone is able to survive when lost in the wilderness.

presence [PREZ uhns] *n.* being in a particular place
Marcia's <u>presence</u> was a comfort to Alex.

serene [suh REEN] *adj.* peaceful or very calm
Misha gave us a <u>serene</u> smile, indicating that all was well.

throngs [THRAHNGZ] *n.* crowds; a very large number of people
<u>Throngs</u> of men, women, and children came to the new stadium.

vessel [VES uhl] *n.* a ship or large boat
The <u>vessel</u> we bought was a large sailboat.

Word List B

combat [KAHM bat] *n.* a battle or fight, usually in war
Darryl was injured in <u>combat</u> just before his term of duty ended.

contemptible [kuhn TEMP tuh buhl] *adj.* not deserving any respect
Walter was a <u>contemptible</u> bully and everyone avoided him.

guise [GYZ] *n.* outward appearance
The <u>guise</u> of bravery often masks fear.

handiwork [HAN dee werk] *n.* something made by hand
Brenda displayed her <u>handiwork</u> at the fair, and her quilting won first prize.

outrage [OWT rayj] *n.* extreme anger or an act that is violent
Dylan displayed his <u>outrage</u> by stamping his foot.

pride [PRYD] *n.* a strong sense of one's worth and importance
Her great <u>pride</u> made it difficult for her to make friends.

shield [SHEELD] *n.* a broad piece of armor carried by warriors to protect themselves
Athena is usually pictured with a <u>shield</u> to help her in battle.

wrath [RATH] *n.* extreme anger; rage
Amber controlled her <u>wrath</u> by counting to ten.

from the **Odyssey, Part II** by Homer
Vocabulary Warm-up Exercises

Exercise A *Fill in each blank in the paragraph with an appropriate word from Word List A. Use each word only once.*

"Where do you [1] _____ to go for your vacation this year?" asked Jason.

"We might go camping," said Amanda. "It is so [2] _____ by the quiet lake where we pitch our tent. We can rent a fishing [3] _____ this year, too, and I can take along my [4] _____ dog, Oscar."

"Do you not worry about the [5] _____ of [6] _____ of bears near that lake?" asked Jason.

"Not really," said Amanda, "but last year, one bold bear achieved a certain amount of [7] _____ by searching the campgrounds for food."

"I [8] _____ at your bravery," Jason replied. "You would not catch me anywhere near that lake!"

Exercise B *Revise each sentence so that the underlined vocabulary word is used in a logical way. Be sure to keep the vocabulary word in your revision.*

Example: Olivia welcomed the absolutely <u>contemptible</u> Rosa into her home.
Olivia banished the absolutely <u>contemptible</u> Rosa from her home.

1. Darryl's <u>pride</u> made him seem very friendly and fun to be with.

   _____

2. Because she was using a <u>shield</u>, Diana was hit by several arrows.

   _____

3. During <u>combat</u>, Nathan took a nap.

   _____

4. In the <u>guise</u> of an old woman, young Ashton did not fool any of his friends.

   _____

5. In great <u>outrage</u>, Helen urged everyone to remain calm.

   _____

6. Jon's <u>wrath</u> led him to thank Janet for her helpful comments.

   _____

7. Brett's wonderful <u>handiwork</u> could not have been accomplished without expensive machines.

   _____

from the Odyssey, Part II by Homer
Reading Warm-up A

Read the following passage. Pay special attention to the underlined words. Then, read it again, and complete the activities. Use a separate sheet of paper for your written answers.

Ithaca is a small Greek island off the west coast of mainland Greece. Located in the Ionian Sea, it is one of the seven islands called the Ionian Islands.

Travelers to Ithaca are drawn to it because of its <u>fame</u> as the home of Odysseus, the hero of Homer's _Odyssey_. It was here that the <u>faithful</u> Penelope, Odysseus's wife, waited patiently for her husband's return from the Trojan War.

Ithaca is named for Ithacis, a character of Greek myth. Legend has it that Ithacis was the son of a king of Kefallonia, one of the larger Ionian islands. After moving to Ithaca, Ithacis and his brother built a fountain. With the <u>presence</u> of this fountain, the entire island would always have enough water.

Evidence indicates that the island has probably been inhabited for about 2,200 years. Odysseus, if he really existed, would have been its king at the time of the Trojan War, 1500 B.C., ruling over <u>throngs</u> of people.

A terrible earthquake in 1953 destroyed most of the buildings on the island. Therefore, if you visit Ithaca today, you will not see many old buildings. If you do <u>intend</u> to tour the island, plan to take a ferry or some other <u>vessel</u> to get there. Ithaca has no airport.

Ambitious hikers who visit Ithaca enjoy the east coast of the island, which is steep and mountainous. Sunbathers like the west coast. It has lush green countryside with gentle hills and both sand and pebble beaches. Snorkelers <u>marvel</u> over the many enchanting coves with crystal-clear waters.

Ithaca, however, is not the destination of choice for those seeking an exciting nightlife or crowded beaches. Instead, it is a beautiful, peaceful, and <u>serene</u> destination. It is a perfect setting for outdoor activities and relaxing. It is also a perfect place to gaze out to sea and imagine, far off in the distance, Odysseus slowly approaching the island home to which he longed to return.

1. Circle the words that explain the <u>fame</u> of Ithaca. What do you think you might be able to do that would bring you _fame_?

2. Underline the words that indicate Penelope was a <u>faithful</u> wife. Use _faithful_ in a sentence.

3. Underline the words that tell why the <u>presence</u> of the fountain was important. Explain what _presence_ means.

4. Circle the word that gives a hint to the meaning of <u>throngs</u>. Where have you seen _throngs_ of something?

5. Circle the word that means about the same as <u>intend</u>. What do you _intend_ to do this weekend?

6. Underline the word that names a type of <u>vessel</u>. On what kind of _vessel_ would you most like to travel or spend an afternoon?

7. Circle the words that tell what makes snorkelers <u>marvel</u>. Describe something that made you _marvel_.

8. Underline the word that means about the same as <u>serene</u>. Describe a place that you think is _serene_.

Name _____ Date _____

from the **Odyssey, Part II** by Homer
Reading Warm-up B

Read the following passage. Pay special attention to the underlined words. Then, read it again, and complete the activities. Use a separate sheet of paper for your written answers.

According to Greek mythology, the goddess Athena was the favorite child of Zeus, the chief god. The legend of her birth is particularly interesting. Zeus became enamored with Metis (Wisdom); together, he and Metis conceived a child. Zeus had been advised that any child he had by Metis would eventually overthrow him.

Wishing to avoid such an outcome, he swallowed the pregnant Metis. Soon, he developed a terrible headache. To relieve Zeus' excruciating pain, Hephaestus (the god of fire and the forge) split his skull with an ax, and Athena sprang from the wound fully armed and holding a <u>shield</u>.

The goddess of war, Athena participated in <u>combat</u> only in defense of the state and home. She was also the goddess of the arts of peace, such as weaving.

Athena, like all the gods, did not like humans who exhibited too much <u>pride</u>. She thought they were <u>contemptible</u> and not worthy of any respect. She heard that Arachne, a proud woman famous for her weaving skills, boasted constantly about her <u>handiwork</u>. "I weave the finest cloth in the world," Arachne had declared haughtily. "I am even more adept than Athena!"

One day, Athena, in the <u>guise</u> of an old beggar, visited Arachne and advised her to change her prideful ways. Arachne refused, saying that she would win any contest against Athena. Then Athena assumed her true appearance and stood before Arachne as a beautiful goddess.

"You shall have your contest," the goddess said. The two set up their looms and began weaving. Both were master weavers. Athena's design told of the wonderful deeds of the gods. Arachne's work also showed stories of the gods, but at their worst behavior.

Athena became filled with <u>wrath</u> as she looked at Arachne's work and, in her anger and <u>outrage</u>, destroyed Arachne's loom. Then, she turned her into a spider, declaring, "Now you and your descendants may spin and weave all you wish."

1. Underline the word that tells what Athena was doing with the <u>shield</u>. What is a *shield*?

2. Circle the words that explain why Athena would participate in <u>combat</u>. Use *combat* in a sentence.

3. Underline the words that tell how Athena felt about people with too much <u>pride</u>. How would a person with too much *pride* behave?

4. Circle the words that define <u>contemptible</u>. Describe one type of behavior that you find *contemptible*.

5. Circle the words in a nearby sentence that are an example of <u>handiwork</u>. Tell about some *handiwork* that you or someone whom you know does.

6. Underline the words that tell what <u>guise</u> Athena assumed. If you could assume the *guise* of an animal, which animal would you choose and why?

7. Underline the words that mean about the same as <u>wrath</u>. If you ever felt *wrath*, what would you do to control it?

8. Circle the words that tell what Athena's <u>outrage</u> led her to do. Explain whether you would like to be around someone who is full of *outrage*.

Unit 6 Resources: Themes in Literature

from the Odyssey, **Part II** by Homer
Writing About the Big Question

Do heroes have responsibilities?

Big Question Vocabulary

character	choices	hero	honesty	identify
imitate	intentions	involvement	justice	morality
obligation	responsibility	serve	standard	wisdom

A. *Use one or more words from the list above to complete each sentence.*

1. One definition of a(n) _____ is that he or she is someone whom large numbers of people would like to _____.

2. Many epics focus on a hero's _____ in a journey or quest.

3. Our _____ were good, but we could not steer the project to a successful outcome.

4. In epic narratives, heroes often profit from the _____ of a god, sage, or prophet.

5. Responsible politicians usually feel a(n) _____ to the voters who elected them.

B. *Follow the directions in responding to each of the items below.*

1. List two different times when you had to decide between two very different **choices.**

   _____

   _____

2. Write two sentences to explain one of these experiences, and describe how it made you feel. Use at least two of the Big Question vocabulary words.

   _____

   _____

C. *Complete the sentence below. Then, write a short paragraph in which you connect the sentences to the Big Question.*

The true **character** of a **hero** can be seen in _____.

   _____

   _____

   _____

   _____

from the Odyssey, *Part 2* by Homer
Literary Analysis: Epic Simile

An **epic simile** is an elaborate comparison that may extend for several lines. Epic similes may use the words *like, as, just as,* or *so* to make the comparison. Unlike a normal simile, which draws a comparison to a single, distinct image, an epic simile is longer and more involved. It might recall an entire place or story. Epic similes are sometimes called Homeric similes.

DIRECTIONS: *Read the epic similes that follow. Then, circle the letter of the answer that best completes each sentence.*

A. But the man skilled in all ways of contending,
    satisfied by the great bow's look and heft,
    like a musician, like a harper, when
    with quiet hand upon his instrument
    he draws between his thumb and forefinger
    a sweet new string upon a peg: so effortlessly
    Odysseus in one motion strung the bow.

  1. In the passage, what extended comparison does Homer use to complete this analogy: *archer : bow* ::
    A. composer : instrument.
    B. peg : string.
    C. musician : harp.
    D. hand : forefinger.

  2. The comparison suggests that, like the musician, Odysseus
    A. is nervous before he begins.
    B. works with a stringed instrument.
    C. is proficient in music.
    D. knows his instrument and where to get good strings.

B. Think of a catch that fishermen haul in to a half-moon bay
    in a fine-meshed net from the whitecaps of the sea:
    how all are poured out on the sand, in throes for the salt sea,
    twitching their cold lives away in Helios' fiery air:
    so lay the suitors heaped on one another.

  1. In the passage, what comparison does Homer use to complete this analogy: *Odysseus : suitors* ::
    A. big fish : little fish.
    B. hunter : catch.
    C. Odysseus : enemies.
    D. fisherman : fish.

  2. The comparison suggests that
    A. Odysseus was also a good fisherman.
    B. the suitors had as much chance against Odysseus as fish have when they are caught in a net.
    C. something fishy was going on in Ithaca, and Odysseus had to correct it.
    D. the setting of much of the epic is the Greek isles, where fishing is an important industry.

from the Odyssey, *Part 2* by Homer
Reading: Analyze the Influence of Historical and Cultural Context

The **historical and cultural context** of a work is the backdrop of details of the time and place in which the work is set or in which it was written. These details include the events, beliefs, and customs of a specific culture and time. When you **identify influences on your own reading and responses,** the historical and cultural context reflected in a work becomes more apparent.

- As you read a work from another time and culture, keep your own beliefs and customs in mind.
- Notice the ways in which your reactions to ideas and situations in the work differ from the reactions of the characters.
- Consider whether your reactions reflect your own cultural values.

DIRECTIONS: *For each of the following events or elements in Part 2 of the* Odyssey, *write a few notes on the historical and cultural context. Pay special attention to whether the event or element seems to reflect a universal value or belief or whether it seems specifically rooted in the cultural context of ancient Greece.*

1. Odysseus' reunion with Telemachus

   _____

   _____

   _____

2. the episode focusing on Odysseus' dog, Argus

   _____

   _____

   _____

3. the laziness and arrogance of the suitors

   _____

   _____

   _____

4. Odysseus' and Penelope's testing of each other

   _____

   _____

   _____

5. Odysseus' slaughter of the suitors

   _____

   _____

   _____

Name _____ Date _____

from **the Odyssey, *Part 2*** by Homer
Vocabulary Builder

Word List

bemusing   contempt   dissemble   equity   incredulity   maudlin

A. DIRECTIONS: *In each of the following items, think about the meaning of the italicized word and then answer the question.*

1. From whom would you reasonably expect *equity*—a judge or a thief?

   _____

2. Would you treat someone whom you admire with *contempt*? Why or why not?

   _____

3. Does being *maudlin* involve your intelligence or your emotions? Explain your answer.

   _____

4. Are the intentions of people who *dissemble* likely to be good or bad?

   _____

5. What kind of story or report would inspire *incredulity* in you? Explain.

   _____

6. Would you react to a long, *bemusing* lecture with enthusiasm or with annoyance?

   _____

B. DIRECTIONS: *Use the context of the sentences and what you know about the Latin prefix* dis- *to explain your answer to each question.*

1. If one high school football team *displaces* another in the league rankings, what happens?

   _____

   _____

2. If you *disentangle* a complex problem, what have you done: solved it, or made it worse?

   _____

   _____

3. If two plays or novels are *dissimilar*, are they more notable for their likenesses or their differences?

   _____

   _____

from **the Odyssey,** *Part 2* by Homer
Enrichment: Greek Divinities

As they are portrayed in Homer's epics and in other works of ancient Greek literature, the Greek divinities sometimes appear to be petty, judgmental, meddling, and prone to favoritism. However, these divinities are also described as all-powerful, life-preserving champions of humans. In Greek myths, humans are seldom left to their own devices. Odysseus is a perfect example of a human being who has the disfavor of one god (Poseidon) and the favor of another (Athena). The following information on Greek divinities will explain why certain gods favor Odysseus and why others wish him ill.

According to Greek myth, high atop a mountain peak in northeastern Greece is Olympus, the home of **Zeus,** father of the gods, and of his wife and children. He is the sky god who is associated with thunder and lightning. Zeus is the defender of all that is just and right in the Greeks' concept of a "civilized" world. Though Zeus occasionally meddles in individual struggles during the Trojan War—as recounted in Homer's other epic poem, the *Iliad*—he tries hard to stay neutral.

Poseidon, Zeus' brother, is the primary god of the waters—and of the sea in particular. Instead of a thunderbolt, Poseidon carries a trident—a three-pronged fork resembling a fisherman's spear. In the myths, Poseidon is called the "earth-shaker"; he is the god of earthquakes, by which he expresses his anger. Little does Odysseus dream of the consequences when he blinds the Cyclops Polyphemus, who is Poseidon's son. From this point on, Poseidon is relentless in stopping Odysseus' efforts to return to Ithaca.

One of Zeus' children is the goddess **Athena,** who acts as Odysseus' helper throughout Homer's narrative. Athena is the goddess of wisdom and is also known for her prowess in war. She shares a connection to warfare, in fact, with her brother **Ares,** the god of war. In addition to this military connection, however, she is also the goddess of a range of specific crafts and skills. She is a tamer of horses, interested in ships, and patroness of women's household arts, especially spinning and weaving. Animals often depicted with Athena are the owl and the snake.

DIRECTIONS: *Answer these questions based on the information you have just read.*

1. What qualities or characteristics does Zeus have that help to characterize him as the king of the gods? Why do you think so?

   _____

   _____

   _____

2. What action by Odysseus causes Poseidon to turn against him?

   _____

   _____

3. At the end of the *Odyssey*, Athena arranges a peaceful agreement between Odysseus and the families of the slain suitors. Which of Athena's characteristics leads her to act as peacekeeper in this situation? Explain your answer.

   _____

   _____

   _____

from the Odyssey, *Part 2* by Homer
Integrated Language Skills: Grammar

Complex and Compound-Complex Sentences

A **complex sentence** consists of one independent clause, which can stand by itself as a sentence, and at least one subordinate clause, which cannot stand by itself as a sentence. A **compound-complex sentence** consists of two or more independent clauses and one or more subordinate clauses.

Complex sentence:	After Odysseus gave Telemachus the signal, Telemachus removed the weapons from the hall.
Compound-complex sentence:	Scholars, who live throughout the world, disagree about whether the epics were composed by the same person, and they also wonder about Homer's historical existence.

A. DIRECTIONS: *Identify each sentence as complex or compound-complex.*

1. Although Odysseus is in disguise, his old dog Argus recognizes him instinctively.

   _____

2. The suitors, who have competed to marry Penelope, behave arrogantly, and they conspire to murder Odysseus' son and heir, Telemachus.

   _____

3. Odysseus becomes anxious when Penelope questions him about the marriage bed.

   _____

4. The *Odyssey,* which has entertained audiences for thousands of years, contains many universal themes; its broad appeal can be explained by Homer's profound understanding of human nature.

   _____

B. WRITING APPLICATION: *On the following lines, write a paragraph in which you describe a gift that you would like to present to a loved one. In your writing, use all four types of sentences that have been mentioned: simple, compound, complex, and compound-complex. Be prepared to identify each type of sentence.*

_____

_____

_____

_____

_____

_____

_____

_____

from **the Odyssey,** *Part 2* by Homer
Integrated Language Skills: Support for Writing a Biography

Use a chart like the one shown to make notes for your biography of Odysseus.

Events That Reveal Odysseus' Character

1. _____
_____
_____

2. _____
_____
_____

3. _____
_____
_____

4. _____
_____
_____

5. _____
_____
_____

Quotations From the Epic

1. _____
_____
_____

2. _____
_____
_____

3. _____
_____
_____

from **the Odyssey, *Part 2*** by Homer
Integrated Language Skills: Support for Extend Your Learning

Listening and Speaking

Use a chart such as the one shown to make notes for your debate on the prosecution of Odysseus for killing Penelope's suitors.

Debate Teams: _____

Arguments for the Prosecution

1. _____
_____
_____

2. _____
_____
_____

3. _____
_____
_____

Arguments for the Defense

1. _____
_____
_____

2. _____
_____
_____

3. _____
_____
_____

from the **Odyssey, Part 2,** by Homer
Open-Book Test

Short Answer *Write your responses to the questions in this section on the lines provided.*

1. In lines 1059–1065 in Homer's *Odyssey*, Part 2, Odysseus reveals himself to Telemachus, and father and son weep. What is the epic simile Homer uses to describe their crying?

   _____

   _____

2. In lines 1112–1116 of the *Odyssey*, Part 2, why does Telemachus, Odysseus' son, doubt that Athena and Zeus will help them in their fight against the suitors?

   _____

   _____

3. Return to lines 1163–1208. What member of the household recognizes Odysseus in the disguise of a beggar? Describe what happens to the one who recognizes Odysseus. Tell why Homer may have included this scene in the *Odyssey*, Part 2.

   _____

   _____

   _____

4. In "The Suitors" in the *Odyssey*, Part 2, Antinous, thinking Odysseus is a beggar, throws a stool and hits him when Odysseus asks for food. Use your own reading and responses, as well as the historical and cultural context, to explain why one of the other suitors rebukes Antinous for his action.

   _____

   _____

5. In the *Odyssey*, Part 2, Penelope calls the beggar in and asks him to tell about himself. She ends up confiding in him. Fill in the diagram with details of Penelope's unfortunate situation, as she describes it to the beggar, who in reality is Odysseus in disguise. Then answer the question below the diagram.

   Penelope's Situation

   Is Penelope loyal, or truly devoted, to Odysseus? Why or why not?

   _____

6. In "The Challenge," lines 1370–1378, in the *Odyssey*, Part 2, Odysseus takes his turn in the contest to string the bow and shoot an arrow through twelve axhandle sockets. What simile describes Odysseus' stringing the bow?

_____

_____

7. In "The Challenge," line 1398, in the *Odyssey*, Part 2, what does Odysseus mean by saying, "The hour has come to cook their lordships' mutton"? Use your reading and responses, as well as the historical and cultural context, to explain this line.

_____

_____

_____

8. What does Telemachus throw to save Odysseus when Amphinomus tries to attack him in "Odysseus' Revenge" in the *Odyssey*, Part 2? What happens? What does this action show about Telemachus' character?

_____

_____

_____

9. Identify the simile Homer uses in lines 1615–1623 of the *Odyssey*, Part 2, to describe how Odysseus has longed for Penelope during the years he has been away. Explain why the simile is an excellent comparison.

_____

_____

_____

_____

10. Toward whom does Odysseus show his contempt in the *Odyssey*, Part 2? Base your answer on the meaning of *contempt*.

_____

_____

Essay

Write an extended response to the question of your choice or to the question or questions that your teacher assigns you.

11. In the *Odyssey*, Part 2, Odysseus returns home, but he must proceed carefully in order to defeat the suitors and get his home and family back. In an essay, identify the important steps Odysseus takes to accomplish his goal.

12. Look through the story of Odysseus' return in the *Odyssey*, Part 2, and find an epic simile that appeals to you. Write the simile and explain its meaning in a brief essay, telling why you consider (or do not consider) it appropriate for the context in which the comparison is placed.

13. Consider Part 2 of the *Odyssey* as a set of problems and solutions. After an absence of twenty years, Odysseus faces a number of problems when he returns to Ithaca. In an essay, identify three problems that Odysseus faces. Explain how he solves each problem and describe the consequences of his actions.

14. **Thinking About the Big Question: Do heroes have responsibilities?** Think of an example from Part 2 of the *Odyssey* in which Odysseus displays a strong sense of responsibility to his family. How does Homer portray the epic hero as highly aware of his responsibilities to his wife and son? Support your main ideas in an essay with references to the text of the epic.

Oral Response

15. Go back to question 5, 8, 9 or to the question your teacher assigns you. Take a few minutes to expand your answer and prepare an oral response. Find additional details in the *Odyssey*, Part 2, that support your points. If necessary, make notes to support your oral response.

from the Odyssey, _Part 2_ by Homer
Selection Test A

Critical Reading _Identify the letter of the choice that best answers the question._

___ 1. In Part 2 of the _Odyssey_, who is Eumaeus?
   A. one of Penelope's suitors
   B. a minor god
   C. Odysseus' loyal swineherd
   D. Odysseus' faithful dog

___ 2. What does Odysseus order Telemachus to do when Odysseus gives him a signal?
   A. remove the weapons from the hall
   B. reveal Odysseus' identity to Penelope
   C. leave Ithaca and set sail for Pylos
   D. string the great bow

___ 3. The brief episode involving Argus, Odysseus' dog, closes with which of the following?
   A. Eumaeus removes Argus from the hall.
   B. Odysseus fails to recognize Argus.
   C. After Argus recognizes Odysseus, the dog dies.
   D. The suitors object to Argus' presence in the hall.

___ 4. Which of the following strategies is most helpful when you try to understand the historical and cultural context of a literary work?
   A. Read the end of the work first, and then go back and start reading from the beginning.
   B. Compare and contrast your reactions to ideas and situations with the characters' reactions.
   C. Write a short summary of the work that covers all of the characters and plot events.
   D. State the theme of the work—its message or insight about life or people.

___ 5. Which of the following is involved in Penelope's deception of the suitors?
   A. a great bow
   B. a death shroud for Laertes
   C. a precious ring
   D. a lengthy dispute over land

___ **6.** Which of the following is an example of a *simile?*

    A. In one motion, Odysseus strung the bow.

    B. Odysseus stood watching the unruly suitors like a captain surveying a rough sea.

    C. The suitors, both strong and weak, tried and failed to string the bow.

    D. The setting of Odysseus' final challenge is his native island of Ithaca.

___ **7.** Which of Odysseus' traits allows him to triumph in the bow-and-arrow challenge that Penelope sets for her suitors?

    A. his love for Penelope

    B. his loyalty to the gods

    C. his pride in his bow

    D. his skill as a marksman

___ **8.** Read the following passage about Odysseus from Part 2 of the *Odyssey:*

    But the man skilled in all ways of contending,
    satisfied by the great bow's look and heft,
    like a musician, like a harper, when
    with quiet hand upon his instrument
    he draws between his thumb and forefinger
    a sweet new string upon a peg: so effortlessly
    Odysseus in one motion strung the bow.

    This epic simile compares what to what?

    A. Odysseus to a musician

    B. a musician to a harper

    C. Odysseus to an archer

    D. a bow string to sweet music

___ **9.** Why does Penelope test Odysseus toward the end of Part 2?

    A. She wants to see if he is still as intelligent as he was in his youth.

    B. She wants him to demonstrate to the people that he is really their king.

    C. She wants to know more details about the Trojan War.

    D. She wants to know if he is really her husband.

___ **10.** Which of the following best describes the tone at the end of the *Odyssey?*

    A. melancholy

    B. reflective

    C. triumphant

    D. ironic

Vocabulary and Grammar

___ 11. Which of the following is the best synonym for *contempt?*
A. scorn   C. admiration
B. complaint   D. permission

___ 12. Which of the following is most nearly *opposite* in meaning to *equity?*
A. equivalence   C. violence
B. unfairness   D. prudence

___ 13. Which item correctly identifies the following sentence:
   After Odysseus returned to Ithaca, Athena disguised him.
A. simple sentence   C. complex sentence
B. compound sentence   D. compound-complex sentence

___ 14. Which of the following statements about a subordinate clause is correct?
A. There must be at least one subordinate clause in every compound sentence.
B. A subordinate clause cannot stand by itself as a sentence.
C. A subordinate clause must always have a single subject and a single verb.
D. A sentence cannot contain two subordinate clauses.

Essay

15. Suspense is a feeling of tension or uncertainty about what will happen next in a narrative. Write an essay in which you discuss how Homer creates and maintains suspense in Part 2 of the *Odyssey*. In your essay, identify which characters and events involve the element of suspense, and comment on how effectively you think Homer uses this technique. Be sure to support your main ideas with specific references to the selection.

16. **Thinking About the Big Question: Do heroes have responsibilities?** In Part 2 of the *Odyssey*, Odysseus displays a strong sense of responsibility to his family and to their welfare. In an essay, tell how the suitors threaten his ability to be responsible. Tell how Odysseus regains his responsible role.

from **the Odyssey, Part 2** by Homer
Selection Test B

Critical Reading *Identify the letter of the choice that best completes the statement or answers the question.*

____ 1. Odysseus' comment to Telemachus, "This is not princely, to be swept / away by wonder at your father's presence," implies which of the following about ancient Greek cultural values?
  A. People expected that princes would be easily amazed.
  B. People looked up to princes as men of imagination.
  C. Princes commonly believed in miracles.
  D. Princes were not expected to display emotion.

____ 2. An *epic simile* is different from a normal simile in that an epic simile
  A. is not limited to a single, distinct image, but is more complex.
  B. is used only in connection with the epic hero.
  C. begins with the words *like, as, just as,* or *so.*
  D. contains personification.

____ 3. In Part 2 of the *Odyssey,* the hero appears disguised as which of the following?
  A. a suitor
  B. Eumaeus
  C. a beggar
  D. a priest of Zeus

____ 4. The episode about Argus, Odysseus' dog, is important to the plot because it emphasizes
  A. the length of Odysseus' absence from home.
  B. Eumaeus' awareness of Odysseus' disguise.
  C. the epic's main theme of loyalty vs. treachery.
  D. the qualities that people and animals have in their youth.

____ 5. Which of Telemachus' actions best demonstrates his obedience to his father?
  A. his journey through Pylos and Sparta in search of Odysseus
  B. his suspicion that the beggar is a god
  C. the tears he sheds when Odysseus reveals his true identity
  D. his silence when Antinous confronts Odysseus

____ 6. What is one result of Odysseus' initial exchange with the suitor Antinous?
  A. Telemachus removes all the shields and weapons from the hall.
  B. Penelope summons the "beggar" Odysseus and questions him.
  C. The swineherd Eumaeus discovers Odysseus' true identity.
  D. Argus is killed.

____ 7. The episode in which Penelope invites the old beggar to her room is important because it
  A. allows suspense to build.
  B. explains Penelope's sadness.
  C. explains Telemachus' sadness.
  D. reveals Odysseus' identity.

_____ 8. Why does the disguised Odysseus make up a story and tell Penelope that her husband will be home soon?
   A. to give himself a few days to figure out what to do
   B. to see whether her reaction to the news is one of joy or disappointment
   C. to prepare Penelope emotionally for recognizing and welcoming her husband
   D. to make the surprise of his true identity all the greater

_____ 9. Which of the following character traits does Penelope reveal in Part 2 of the *Odyssey*?
   A. stubbornness and fear
   B. weakness and longing
   C. prudence and loyalty
   D. indecision and panic

_____ 10. Choose the phrase that best defines an *epic simile*.
   A. a figure of speech in which one thing is spoken of as if it were something else
   B. a literary technique that involves differences between meaning and intention
   C. a work created in imitation of another
   D. a long, elaborate comparison between two dissimilar actions or objects

_____ 11. Which of the following is an important theme in Part 2 of the *Odyssey*?
   A. Good triumphs over evil.
   B. Separation weakens relationships.
   C. The quest for power never ends.
   D. Old age triumphs over youth.

_____ 12. Toward the end of Part 2, how does Penelope test Odysseus?
   A. She disguises herself to see if he will recognize her.
   B. She tells him that she almost married one of the suitors.
   C. She pretends that she has moved their marriage bed.
   D. She challenges him to string the great bow a second time.

_____ 13. Odysseus' slaughter of the suitors shows that ancient Greece held which of the following cultural values?
   A. Violence is never justified.
   B. Even heroes sometimes allow their emotions to get the better of them.
   C. Intelligence is more highly prized than physical strength.
   D. Revenge is sometimes justified, even if it involves killing.

Vocabulary and Grammar

_____ 14. Upon his return home, Athena instructs Odysseus, saying ". . . *dissemble* to your son no longer now." What is she telling him to do?
   A. conceal his appearance from his son
   B. instruct his son to disguise himself as well
   C. reveal his disguise to the trusted swineherd
   D. reveal his identity to Telemachus

_____ 15. When Odysseus says to Penelope, ". . .or you might think—/ I had got *maudlin* over cups of wine," he means that Penelope may think he is acting
    A. loud and annoying.
    B. violently angry.
    C. foolishly sentimental.
    D. preoccupied by foolish thoughts.

_____ 16. Which of the following is most nearly *opposite* in meaning to *contempt*?
    A. scorn
    B. disloyalty
    C. admiration
    D. hesitation

_____ 17. A complex sentence contains which of the following?
    A. a compound subject and a compound verb
    B. one independent clause and one or more subordinate clauses
    C. a sentence fragment
    D. two or more independent clauses and one or more subordinate clauses

Essay

18. Consider Part 2 of the *Odyssey* as a set of problems and solutions. After an absence of twenty years, Odysseus must face a number of problems when he returns to Ithaca. In an essay, identify three problems that Odysseus faces. Explain how he solves each problem, and describe the consequences of his actions.

19. In literature, as in life, people must decide from among alternative courses of action. Think of an example from the *Odyssey* in which the story might have ended differently if a character had acted differently. Cite examples to support your speculation.

20. **Thinking About the Big Question: Do heroes have responsibilities?** Think of an example from Part 2 of the *Odyssey* in which Odysseus displays a strong sense of responsibility to his family. How does Homer portray the epic hero as highly aware of his responsibilities to his wife and son? Support your main ideas in an essay with references to the text of the epic.

Poetry by Edna St. Vincent Millay, Margaret Atwood, Derek Walcott, Constantine Cavafy
Vocabulary Warm-up Word Lists

Study these words from the selections. Then, complete the activities that follow.

Word List A

ancient [AYN shuhnt] *adj.* happening far back in history; very old
This work of art dates back to <u>ancient</u> Egypt.

boring [BAWR ing] *adj.* always the same; dull; not interesting
Walter thought that knitting was a <u>boring</u> activity.

design [di ZYN] *n.* pattern or arrangement
The <u>design</u> on the wallpaper consisted of flowers and vines.

merchandise [MER chuhn dys] *n.* things that are for sale
Carter sold fine <u>merchandise</u> made in Italy and Spain.

purchase [PER chis] *v.* to buy something
Abigail will <u>purchase</u> green silk at the fabric store today.

shuttle [SHUHT uhl] *n.* a device used in making cloth that pulls a thread back and forth
The invention of the <u>shuttle</u> was a great aid to those who made cloth.

valuable [VAL yoo uh buhl] *adj.* worth a great deal
Dean's most <u>valuable</u> possession is his computer.

weaving [WEEV ing] *n.* the making of cloth or baskets
The workers spent all their time <u>weaving</u> baskets.

Word List B

fierce [FEERS] *adj.* violent or angry and ready to attack
The wolves' <u>fierce</u> fight determined which one would lead the pack.

gesture [JES cher] *n.* a motion that shows or communicates feelings
The host's <u>gesture</u> indicated that we should be seated.

irresistible [ir i ZIS tuh buhl] *adj.* unstoppable; cannot be resisted
Her <u>irresistible</u> charm had us all under her spell.

mythical [MITH i kuhl] *adj.* existing only in myths or legends
The Sirens are <u>mythical</u> creatures whose singing caused sailors to die at sea.

siege [SEEJ] *n.* being surrounded by an army for a long time
Inside the walled city, people were starving during the long <u>siege</u>.

squadrons [SKWAHD ruhnz] *n.* military units of troops or planes
Four <u>squadrons</u> of soldiers left the base and headed for the battle.

tradition [truh DISH uhn] *n.* like something made or done in the past
Sheila danced in the classic <u>tradition</u> of Russian ballerinas.

trials [TRY uhlz] *n.* difficult experiences and troubles
The child's illnesses were great <u>trials</u> for his family.

Name _____ Date _____

Poetry by Edna St. Vincent Millay, Margaret Atwood, Derek Walcott, and Constantine Cavafy
Vocabulary Warm-up Exercises

Exercise A *Fill in each blank in the paragraph with an appropriate word from Word List A.*
Use each word only once.

Jake thought attending the Renaissance fair was a [1] _____ experi-
ence not to be missed. He felt that it gave him a better understanding of history and of
some [2] _____ arts and practices. One of the participants at the fair
was busy [3] _____ a beautiful rug. Jake stopped to admire the intricate
[4] _____ she was creating. Jake had always thought such work must
be dull and [5] _____, but he was changing his mind. Watching the
woman move the [6] _____ back and forth, he realized that the art could
be very rewarding. He could see that some of the [7] _____ the weaver
had created was for sale. He did not have enough money to [8] _____ a
rug, but he could afford a scarf. Considering the amount of work that went into it, Jake
thought he got a bargain.

Exercise B *Answer the questions with complete explanations.*

Example: Would you expect <u>trials</u> to be pleasant or unpleasant?
I would expect <u>trials</u> to be unpleasant because they are difficult and cause suffering.

1. Would you be scared of a <u>fierce</u> dog?
   _____

2. What kind of a <u>gesture</u> might you make toward a person to whom you had just
   been introduced?
   _____

3. If a temptation were <u>irresistible</u>, would you be able to walk away from it?
   _____

4. Would you be afraid of a <u>mythical</u> creature, such as a fire-breathing dragon?
   _____

5. Would you want to be inside a walled city during a <u>siege</u>?
   _____

6. If several <u>squadrons</u> of armed soldiers were protecting your city, would you feel safe?
   _____

7. If someone ran a circus in the <u>tradition</u> of old-time circuses, would he or she use all
   kinds of new technology?
   _____

Name _____ Date _____

Poetry by Edna St. Vincent Millay, Margaret Atwood, Derek Walcott, and Constantine Cavafy
Reading Warm-up A

Read the following passage. Pay special attention to the underlined words. Then, read it again, and complete the activities. Use a separate sheet of paper for your written answers.

No one knows exactly when or where people started underline{weaving} thread into cloth. Evidence proves that people were practicing this ancient art in Mesopotamia and Turkey as long as 10,000 years ago. Pieces of fabric from that time have not survived. However, we do have other proof, such as a centuries-old piece of clay pottery. It has the imprints of the woven basket in which it was formed.

Historians believe that people first got the idea of weaving from beavers' dams, birds' nests, and spiders' webs. Looking at these objects probably gave early humans the idea of interlacing twigs and vines to make netting. Such netting was quite valuable. It could be used to catch fish and trap game.

Before long, humans began weaving fibers. They created mats, rugs, clothing, baby carriers, blankets, and pouches. There is evidence that early peoples added various elements of design to their weavings. Natural dyes and different sizes of fibers helped create patterns.

The loom is the framework used for interweaving yarn or threads into a fabric. A series of threads, called the warp, is laid lengthwise across the frame. Then, another series of threads is woven in and out of the warp. These threads are called the weft, woof, or filling.

This process was very boring. By hand, a person had to lift each warp thread to pass the weft under and over it. The development of the shuttle speeded up the process. This tapered device holds the weft thread. It passes between warp threads, pushing, or beating, the threads into place.

Other inventions, all the way up to today's computers, have improved the process of weaving. Today, merchandise that used to take days or weeks to create can be made much faster. Yet, woven items that you might purchase in shops today are made according to the same principles that were used by early humans.

1. Underline the words that tell what early people started weaving. What could you make by **weaving**?

2. Circle the words that prove weaving is an ancient art. Which **ancient** civilization would you like to learn more about?

3. Underline the sentence that tells why the netting was valuable. Name a possession you have or want that is **valuable**.

4. Circle the word in the next sentence that is a synonym for design. Describe a **design** that you like.

5. Underline the sentence that tells why the weaving process was boring. Name a **boring** activity.

6. Circle the words that tell what a shuttle does. Use **shuttle** in a sentence.

7. Underline the words that identify the merchandise. What type of **merchandise** might you want to make for sale?

8. Circle the word that tells where you might purchase things today. Name three things you want to **purchase**.

Poetry by Edna St. Vincent Millay, Margaret Atwood, Derek Walcott, and Constantine Cavafy
Reading Warm-up B

Read the following passage. Pay special attention to the underlined words. Then, read it again, and complete the activities. Use a separate sheet of paper for your written answers.

Have you heard the expression "Achilles' heel"? People use this expression in the <u>tradition</u> of the Greeks.

According to Greek legend, Achilles was the son of Thetis, a <u>mythical</u> sea goddess, and Peleus, a human. She was so beautiful that even Jupiter, the father of the gods, found her <u>irresistible</u> and had wanted to marry her. However, when Jupiter learned that a son of Thetis would become greater than his father, Jupiter changed his mind. He decreed that Thetis should marry a mortal. After some difficult <u>trials</u>, Peleus was able to win Thetis for his bride.

Of course, Thetis wanted to give her son, Achilles, all the protection she possibly could. In a dramatic <u>gesture</u>, she dipped the baby Achilles into the magic waters of the River Styx, the river that divides the world of the living from the world of the dead. Her goal was to cover his body with a magic shield that would protect him from injuries and fatal wounds caused by any weapon. Because she held him by the heel, it did not get wet. His heel, then, was the only part of his body that weapons could penetrate.

Years later, when Achilles was a great warrior, he led his <u>fierce</u> fighters into battle during the Trojan War. He was among those who participated in the <u>siege</u> of Troy. This war, of course, was fought because Paris, the son of the king of Troy, had wooed Helen and taken her to Troy. Helen's husband—King Menelaus of Sparta—along with <u>squadrons</u> of his supporters in Greece, went to Troy to get Helen back.

Paris learned of the secret of Achilles' weak spot. During a battle, Paris shot a poisoned arrow into Achilles' heel. Aiming for this unprotected part of his foot was the only way to kill Achilles. To this day, when we refer to a person's "Achilles' heel," we are talking about his or her weak, or vulnerable, spot.

1. Circle the word that tells in whose <u>tradition</u> the expression "Achilles' heel" is used. Explain what *tradition* means.

2. Underline the words that support the idea that Thetis was a <u>mythical</u> sea goddess. Describe a *mythical* creature that you have read about or seen in a movie.

3. Underline the words that tell why Jupiter found Thetis so <u>irresistible</u>. Name something that you find *irresistible*.

4. Circle the word that gives a hint to the meaning of <u>trials</u>. Describe some *trials* that you or someone whom you know has had to face.

5. Underline the words that describe the dramatic <u>gesture</u> Thetis performed. What is one friendly *gesture* that you use often?

6. Circle the word that tells who is <u>fierce</u>. Describe something else that is *fierce*.

7. Circle the name of the city that was under <u>siege</u>. Explain what happens to a city when it is under *siege*.

8. Underline the words that tell who made up the <u>squadrons</u> that went to Troy. What skills would those in *squadrons* need?

Poetry by Edna St. Vincent Millay, Margaret Atwood,
Derek Walcott, and Constantine Cavafy

Writing About the Big Question

 Do heroes have responsibilities?

Big Question Vocabulary

character	choices	hero	honesty	identify
imitate	intentions	involvement	justice	morality
obligation	responsibility	serve	standard	wisdom

A. *Use one or more words from the list above to complete each sentence.*

1. A person's individual _____, or code of ethics, is often apparent in the _____ that he or she makes at moments of decision.

2. During the civil rights movement of the 1950s and 1960s, Dr. Martin Luther King, Jr., was one of our nation's most stirring spokesmen for social _____.

3. Since heroes usually embody values we all admire, most of us would like to _____ them.

4. In the legends of King Arthur, Merlin was an elderly sage whose good advice made him famous for his _____.

B. *Follow the directions in responding to each of the items below.*

1. List two occasions on which you felt that you, or someone you know, failed to receive **justice.**

   _____

   _____

2. Write two sentences to explain one of these experiences. Use at least two of the Big Question vocabulary words.

   _____

   _____

C. *Complete the sentences below. Then, write a short paragraph in which you connect the experience to the Big Question.*

In my own life, I know I am responsible for _____. If I do not live up to this **obligation,** one consequence might be _____. When I make responsible **choices,** one positive result is _____.

_____

_____

_____

Poetry by Edna St. Vincent Millay, Margaret Atwood, Derek Walcott, and Constantine Cavafy
Literary Analysis: Contemporary Interpretations

The characters and events of Homer's *Odyssey* are timeless and universal in their appeal and meaning and have inspired many contemporary interpretations. A **contemporary interpretation** of a literary work is a new piece of writing, such as a poem, story, or play, that a modern-day author bases on an ancient work. An **allusion** is a reference to a well-known person, place, event, literary work, or work of art. By reinventing Homer's tales or by making allusions to them, modern-day writers shed new light on Homer's ancient words. Contemporary interpretations may allude to any aspects of Homer's epic, including plot, characters, settings, imagery and language, and theme.

Even when they are based on the same work, contemporary interpretations can differ widely in purpose and theme. The cultural and historical backgrounds, ideas, attitudes, and beliefs of the contemporary writers profoundly affect their perceptions of the ancient work and the new writings that result.

DIRECTIONS: *Circle the letter of the answer that best completes the sentence.*

1. In Edna St. Vincent Millay's "An Ancient Gesture," the speaker focuses most closely on
   A. Odysseus' travels and the hero's relationships to the gods.
   B. the anguish of Odysseus' son Telemachus.
   C. Penelope's inner grief and frustration at Odysseus' long absence.
   D. the devastation wrought by the Trojan War.

2. In "Siren Song," Margaret Atwood's interpretation of the Sirens suggests that
   A. women are much more complex than they have been given credit for.
   B. the poet herself is not very clever.
   C. men are more clever than they think they are.
   D. women enjoy the roles they play.

3. In "Prologue" and "Epilogue" to the *Odyssey,* Derek Walcott suggests that Billy Blue
   A. has confused the chronological sequence of Odysseus' adventures.
   B. is a modern-day version of Homer, singing the adventures of a "main-man" hero.
   C. believes that we are all capable of behaving as heroically as Odysseus did.
   D. has misinterpreted the character of Penelope.

4. In "Ithaca," Constantine Cavafy sees the wanderings of Odysseus as representing
   A. a grand vacation to exotic places.
   B. the journey through life itself.
   C. a voyage of discovery made possible by such modern conveniences as a credit card.
   D. a trip without a real purpose.

5. In "Ithaca," the lines "Always keep Ithaca fixed in your mind, / . . . But do not hurry the voyage at all" suggest that
   A. the journey is more important than the destination.
   B. we need to know where we are going in life.
   C. everyone should have a home.
   D. some places always remain the same, no matter how other places may change.

Poetry by Edna St. Vincent Millay, Margaret Atwood, Derek Walcott, and Constantine Cavafy
Vocabulary Builder

Word List
authentic   defrauded   lofty   picturesque   siege

A. DIRECTIONS: *Revise each sentence so that the underlined vocabulary word is used logically. Be sure not to change the vocabulary word.*

1. They refused to buy the old silver coin because they believe it is <u>authentic</u>.

   _____

2. Because the landscape was so <u>picturesque</u>, we did not bother to take any photographs.

   _____

3. The <u>siege</u> of the city was successful, so the soldiers outside the walls retreated.

   _____

4. Because he is a person of <u>lofty</u> ideals, we criticize him harshly.

   _____

5. As a merchant with great integrity, he always <u>defrauds</u> his customers.

   _____

B. DIRECTIONS: *On the line, write the letter of the choice that is the best synonym for each numbered word.*

___ 1. defrauded
   A. rejected
   B. praised
   C. cheated
   D. promoted

___ 2. lofty
   A. illusory
   B. pretentious
   C. drafty
   D. noble

___ 3. authentic
   A. genuine
   B. antique
   C. practical
   D. sentimental

___ 4. siege
   A. strong grip
   B. armed blockade
   C. military alliance
   D. crisis intervention

___ 5. picturesque
   A. grotesque
   B. paradoxical
   C. prevalent
   D. charming

Poetry by Edna St. Vincent Millay, Margaret Atwood, Derek Walcott, and Constantine Cavafy

Support for Writing to Compare Literary Works

For each poem in this section, use a chart like the one shown to make prewriting notes for an essay focusing on ways in which Homer's epic poem the *Odyssey* provides worthwhile material for a modern-day writer.

Title of Work: _____   _____
Author's purpose: _____   _____   _____   _____   _____
Contemporary conflict/situation addressed: _____   _____   _____   _____   _____
Additions by contemporary writer: _____   _____   _____   _____   _____
My personal response: _____   _____   _____   _____   _____

"An Ancient Gesture" by Edna St. Vincent Millay
"Siren Song" by Margaret Atwood
from The Odyssey: A Stage Version by Derek Walcott
"Ithaca" by Constantine Cavafy

Open-Book Test

Short Answer *Write your responses to the questions in this section on the lines provided.*

1. In Edna St. Vincent Millay's poem "An Ancient Gesture," what ancient gesture does the speaker share with Penelope, Odysseus' wife in the *Odyssey*?

   _____

2. What timeless theme does Edna St. Vincent Millay find in the *Odyssey* by Homer and then emphasize in "An Ancient Gesture"?

   _____

   _____

3. The speaker in Edna St. Vincent Millay's poem says the ancient gesture is authentic. What would the gesture be if it were not authentic? Base your answer on the meaning of *authentic.*

   _____

   _____

4. In Margaret Atwood's "Siren Song," who or what is the speaker? What is the speaker's objective?

   _____

   _____

5. Margaret Atwood puts the Siren in "Siren Song" into a bird suit or costume. What contemporary belief might this image express?

   _____

   _____

   _____

6. In Derek Walcott's *The Odyssey: A Stage Version,* whom does Billy Blue allude to as his "main man"?

   _____

   _____

7. How do the journeys in Constantine Cavafy's poem "Ithaca" and the hero's journey in the *Odyssey* by Homer differ?

   _____

   _____

   _____

8. Other than length, explain why a reader today might find Derek Walcott's *The Odyssey: A Stage Version* easier to read than the *Odyssey* by Homer?

   _____

   _____

   _____

9. Use the chart below to list three allusions to the *Odyssey* made by the speaker in Constantine Cavafy's "Ithaca." Then answer the question that follows.

Allusions to the *Odyssey* in "Ithaca"

   Do the allusions you chose refer to plot, characters, or setting of the *Odyssey*?

   _____

10. In Cavafy's poem "Ithaca," why is the journey to Ithaca so important?

    _____

    _____

    _____

Essay

Write an extended response to the question of your choice or to the question or questions your teacher assigns you.

11. The poems in this collection take a contemporary or new look at the old *Odyssey* by Homer. Choose either "An Ancient Gesture" by Edna St. Vincent Millay or "Ithaca" by Constantine Cavafy. Then, in an essay, discuss the new message or new point of view the poet brings to today's reader. Include examples from the poem to support your ideas.

12. The following lines are from the end of Cavafy's poem "Ithaca." In an essay, explain the comparison Cavafy makes and respond to these questions: What does Ithaca mean to the speaker? Why is the journey to Ithaca so important? Support your ideas with specific references to the text of the poem.

> And if you find her poor, Ithaca has not defrauded you. / With the great wisdom you have gained, with so much experience, / You must surely have understood by then what Ithaca means.

13. In an essay, explain how "An Ancient Gesture," "Siren Song," *The Odyssey: A Stage Version* and "Ithaca" incorporate ideas and events from Homer's *Odyssey*. Include in your discussion the ideas and themes from the original epic that remain the same in the modern pieces and also what new interpretations, such as point of view of the speaker, each poet presents.

14. **Thinking About the Big Question: Do heroes have responsibilities?** Consider the portrayals of heroism in the poems by Millay, Atwood, Walcott, and Cavafy. Do any of the poems imply that heroism requires responsibility as well as outstanding achievement? Discuss this issue in a brief essay, supporting your main ideas with references to the selections.

Oral Response

15. Go back to question 5, 7, 8, or to the question your teacher assigns you. Take a few minutes to expand your answer and prepare an oral response. Find additional details in the poems by Millay, Atwood, Walcott, and/or Cavafy that support your points. If necessary, make notes to guide your oral response.

Poetry by Edna St. Vincent Millay, Margaret Atwood,
Derek Walcott, and Constantine Cavafy
Selection Test A

Critical Reading *Identify the letter of the choice that best answers the question.*

____ 1. In "An Ancient Gesture," what part of Penelope's life does the poet describe?
   A. her childhood
   B. the years she spent weaving Laertes' shroud
   C. her reunion with Odysseus
   D. the last two years before her death

____ 2. According to "An Ancient Gesture," what is the difference between the gesture made by Penelope and the gesture made by Ulysses (Odysseus)?
   A. Penelope really has an apron, but Ulysses does not.
   B. Penelope's gesture is authentic, but Ulysses' is deliberately planned.
   C. Penelope represents all women, while Ulysses represents all men.
   D. Penelope's gesture is ancient, and Ulysses' is modern.

____ 3. Compare the presentation of Penelope in Millay's poem with Homer's portrait of her in the *Odyssey*. Which of the following is an important difference between the two?
   A. In "An Ancient Gesture," Penelope is not faithful to Odysseus.
   B. In Millay's poem, the speaker alludes to Penelope, but Penelope does not actually appear.
   C. The tone in Millay's poem is more upbeat than Homer's tone in the *Odyssey*.
   D. In "An Ancient Gesture," Odysseus ignores Penelope's wishes.

____ 4. Who is the speaker in "Siren Song"?
   A. Odysseus
   B. Homer
   C. one of the Sirens
   D. one of the men whom the Sirens threaten to destroy

____ 5. How does the speaker in Atwood's "Siren Song" contrast with Homer's Sirens in the *Odyssey*?
   A. She is more destructive.
   B. She sings more sweetly.
   C. She wants to be friends with Odysseus.
   D. She claims to be in a bird costume.

____ 6. In "Siren Song," what message do the Sirens sing to persuade sailors to leap overboard?

A. a cry for help

B. a promise of rich rewards

C. a hymn to the power of the sea

D. a prayer to the gods

____ 7. The following lines are from Walcott's "Prologue" to the *Odyssey*. In which line does Billy Blue, the narrator, allude to Odysseus' many dangerous adventures?

A. "Gone sing 'bout that man because his stories please us"

B. "Who saw trials and tempests for ten years after Troy"

C. "I'm Blind Billy Blue, my main man's sea-smart Odysseus"

D. "Slow-striding Achilles, who put the hex on Hector"

____ 8. In Walcott's "Epilogue," how does Billy Blue comment on the story of Odysseus?

A. He says that Homer should have paid more attention to Penelope.

B. He says that the story of Odysseus has changed over the centuries.

C. He says that people continue to tell Odysseus' story long after Homer first told it.

D. He says that the story of Odysseus will eventually fade away.

____ 9. What is an important difference between Walcott's poem and Homer's *Odyssey*?

A. Walcott's portrait of Odysseus is less than heroic.

B. Walcott ignores Penelope's role in the story.

C. Walcott's language is less solemn and dignified than Homer's.

D. Walcott's poem is intended for an audience of children.

____ 10. In "Ithaca," why does the speaker tell the reader to pray that the road to Ithaca will be long?

A. The journey to Ithaca symbolizes the journey of life.

B. The speaker knows that the reader admires Odysseus.

C. The speaker hopes that the reader will want to lead a heroic life.

D. The speaker feels that everyone needs to be challenged.

____ 11. Compare the journey in Cavafy's "Ithaca" with Odysseus' journey to Ithaca in the *Odyssey*. How do the journeys differ?

A. In "Ithaca," reaching the destination is much less important than making the journey.

B. In "Ithaca," the speaker feels that the journey will never end.

C. In "Ithaca," the speaker feels that modern life is boring, but Odysseus enjoys many exciting adventures.

D. Ithaca, the destination in Cavafy's poem, has changed greatly over time.

Vocabulary

____ 12. Which of the following might be appropriately described as *picturesque*?

A. a seaside village   C. a blank piece of paper

B. an emergency room   D. a garbage dump

____ 13. Which of the following is the best synonym for *authentic*?

A. cautious   C. genuine

B. angry   D. silent

Essay

14. The authors of the four poems in this group draw on Homer's *Odyssey*, but each author has a different purpose for writing. Choose one of the four poems. Then, in an essay, discuss what you think the author's purpose is. Be sure to support your statements with specific references to the poem.

15. Choose either Millay's "An Ancient Gesture" or Atwood's "Siren Song." Then, write an essay in which you compare the modern work with the corresponding part of Homer's *Odyssey*.

    If you choose "An Ancient Gesture," compare and contrast the descriptions of Penelope in Millay's poem and Homer's epic (in the section titled "Penelope"). Explain your response.

    If you choose "Siren Song," compare it to the song of the Sirens in the *Odyssey*, Part 1. In your essay, explore the following questions: To whom are the Sirens singing in the two works? What aspects of their songs are similar? How are they different?

16. **Thinking About the Big Question: Do heroes have responsibilities?** Consider the portrayal of a hero, or heroine, in the poem "An Ancient Gesture" by Edna St. Vincent Millay. Who does the poet say is the heroine? What does the heroine do that is heroic? What responsible action makes her admirable? Answer these questions in a brief essay. Support your main ideas with a reference to the poem.

Poetry by Edna St. Vincent Millay, Margaret Atwood,
Derek Walcott, and Constantine Cavafy

Selection Test B

Critical Reading *Identify the letter of the choice that best completes the statement or answers the question.*

____ 1. In "An Ancient Gesture," why does Penelope cry?
  A. She has no one to protect her from the suitors.
  B. She is exhausted from all the weaving she has done and undone.
  C. Her husband has been gone for years, and she does not know where he is.
  D. Nobody ever visits her as she sits alone weaving day after day.

____ 2. In "An Ancient Gesture," what is the "ancient gesture" to which the speaker refers?
  A. singing
  B. tying an apron
  C. weaving
  D. crying

____ 3. What is the timeless theme that the poet Edna St. Vincent Millay finds in Homer's *Odyssey* and then emphasizes in "An Ancient Gesture"?
  A. the importance of fighting for one's beliefs
  B. the beauty of practicing and working hard at a craft, such as weaving
  C. differences in the experiences and emotions of men and women
  D. the ways in which war tears families and relationships apart

____ 4. According to the speaker in "Siren Song," why would everyone want to learn her song?
  A. It is beautiful and entertaining.
  B. It is powerful and irresistible.
  C. It is mythical.
  D. It is lengthy and complex.

____ 5. Margaret Atwood's poem "Siren Song" differs most from the *Odyssey* in the
  A. effect of the Sirens' song.
  B. Sirens' appeal to men on ships.
  C. attitude of the Siren toward her job.
  D. attitude of Odysseus toward the Sirens.

____ 6. What is the main idea of "Siren Song"?
  A. People can learn valuable lessons from the secrets of birds.
  B. Love founded on pity is the only true love.
  C. Women who stand up for themselves are the most attractive to men.
  D. Men cannot resist women who seem helpless.

____ 7. In Margaret Atwood's poem "Siren Song," the Sirens' song is a
  A. beautiful melody.
  B. mother's plea.
  C. love song.
  D. cry for help.

_____ 8. Margaret Atwood's Sirens resemble the Sirens in Homer's *Odyssey* because their songs are
A. irresistible to men.
B. difficult to learn.
C. boring to listen to.
D. popular among women.

_____ 9. Which of the following makes Derek Walcott's "Prologue" and "Epilogue" a very contemporary version of Homer's *Odyssey*?
A. Walcott changes the names of Homer's main characters.
B. Walcott focuses on Achilles and Hector.
C. Walcott refers often to the sea.
D. Walcott uses contemporary, vernacular language.

_____ 10. In Derek Walcott's "Epilogue," how does Billy Blue regard Penelope?
A. She is angry and bitter about Odysseus' long journey.
B. She is flighty and unfaithful to Odysseus while he is gone.
C. She is faithful, strong, and dependable.
D. She cares more about her weaving than she does about Odysseus' trials at sea.

_____ 11. Who is the "first blind singer" mentioned in Walcott's "Epilogue"?
A. Homer
B. Odysseus
C. Penelope
D. Billy Blue

_____ 12. To whom is the speaker in "Ithaca" addressing his advice?
A. travelers leaving on vacation
B. old people getting ready to die
C. Odysseus, king of Ithaca, and the Greek gods
D. young people with their lives ahead of them

_____ 13. The Ithaca in Cavafy's poem is similar to Homer's Ithaca in that both
A. are impossible to reach.
B. represent final destinations.
C. hold the promise of great riches.
D. can be easily reached.

_____ 14. What is the major difference between the Ithaca in Cavafy's poem and the Ithaca in Homer's *Odyssey*?
A. Cavafy's Ithaca is a symbolic place rather than a real location.
B. It takes longer to reach Cavafy's Ithaca than it does to reach Homer's Ithaca.
C. The journey to Cavafy's Ithaca is more difficult than the journey to Homer's.
D. Travelers are less interested in reaching Cavafy's Ithaca than visiting Homer's Ithaca.

_____ 15. In Cavafy's poem "Ithaca," why is the "journey to Ithaca" so important?
A. Ithaca is a place filled with great wonders.
B. The journey teaches people about fighting angry monsters.
C. The journey provides people with wisdom and experience.
D. The journey makes people wealthy.

Vocabulary

___ 16. Which of the following would best describe an *authentic* account of an incident or event?
   A. genuine   C. obscure
   B. problematic   D. petty

___ 17. If you felt *defrauded* by someone, of what would you feel that person is guilty?
   A. underestimating   C. slapping
   B. cheating   D. tripping

___ 18. Which of the following best defines the word *siege*?
   A. capture of an enemy   C. encirclement by an armed force
   B. false arrest   D. fortification of a city

___ 19. Which of the following words is most nearly *opposite* in meaning to *lofty*?
   A. ideal   C. ignoble
   B. impractical   D. probable

Essay

20. In an essay, explain the following passage from Cavafy's poem "Ithaca":

    And if you find her poor, Ithaca has not defrauded you. / With the great wisdom you have gained, with so much experience, / You must surely have understood by then what Ithaca means.

    What does Ithaca mean to the speaker? Why is the journey to Ithaca so important? Support your main ideas with specific references to the text of the poem.

21. In an essay, explain how "An Ancient Gesture," "Siren Song," "Ithaca," and "Prologue" and "Epilogue" to the *Odyssey* incorporate ideas and events from Homer's *Odyssey*. Include in your discussion the ideas and themes from the original epic that remain the same in the modern pieces and what new interpretation each writer presents.

22. **Thinking About the Big Question: Do heroes have responsibilities?** Consider the portrayals of heroism in the poems by Millay, Atwood, Walcott, and Cavafy. Do any of the poems imply that heroism requires responsibility as well as outstanding achievement? Discuss this issue in a brief essay, supporting your main ideas with references to the selections.

Writing Workshop
Technical Document: Manual for Meeting Minutes

Prewriting: Identifying Information

Think about the information to be presented in the minutes of any meeting. Complete the following chart with questions to guide someone gathering that information. (Several questions have been filled in for you.)

Questions to Gather Information about a Meeting

Place/ time/ participants of meeting	1. *When and where did the meeting take place?* 2. _____
Purpose / topic	*Was the meeting specially called or a regular meeting?*
Approval of past minutes	1. *Were the minutes approved as submitted, or corrected?* 2. _____
Agenda	1. _____
Motions and their outcomes	1. *What motions were made?* 2. _____
Conflicts and resolutions	1. _____ 2. _____
Non-agenda interruptions/discussions	1. *What non-agenda items were brought up?* 2. _____
Announcements	1. _____

Drafting: Organizing Minutes

Create a sample outline for the minutes of a meeting of a group familiar to you.

   I. Place, Time, Participants: _____

   _____

  II. Minutes of Previous Meeting: _____

 III. Old business on agenda, with motions (if any)

      A. _____

      B. _____

  IV. New business on agenda, with motions (if any)

      A. _____

      B. _____

      C. _____

   V. Additional discussion

      _____

      _____

      _____

Writing Workshop
Meeting Minutes: Integrating Grammar Skills

Revising Fragments and Run-on Sentences

A **fragment** is a group of words that does not express a complete thought. It is punctuated as if it were a sentence, but it is only part of a sentence. Often, it is missing a subject, a verb, or both. To correct a fragment, build a sentence that has a subject and a verb and that expresses a complete thought.

   Fragment: On a summer evening.   **Corrected**: It was a summer evening.

   A **run-on sentence** is two or more complete thoughts that are not properly joined or separated. They may have no punctuation between or among them, or they may have the wrong punctuation. To correct a run-on sentence, use the proper punctuation, and add a conjunction or a conjunctive adverb if necessary.

Run-on with No Punctuation (Fused Run-on)	The sun set the moon came out.
Run-on with Wrong Punctuation (Comma Splice)	The sun set, the moon came out.
Corrected as Two Sentences	The sun set. The moon came out.
Corrected with Coordinating Conjunction	The sun set, and the moon came out.
Corrected with Semicolon	The sun set; the moon came out.
Corrected with Semicolon and Conjunctive Adverb	The sun set; however, the moon came out.

Identifying Fragments and Run-on Sentences

A. DIRECTIONS: *On the line before each sentence, write* F *if it is a sentence fragment,* R *if it is a run-on sentence, or* S *if it is a complete, properly punctuated sentence.*

____ 1. In summer I always run early in the morning.

____ 2. Too hot to go later.

____ 3. My mom often runs with me, my dad usually goes in the evening.

____ 4. My brother runs with us if he is awake; otherwise, he runs with dad later.

Fixing Fragments and Run-on Sentences

B. DIRECTIONS: *On the lines provided, correct the fragments and run-on sentences. If a sentence is correct as presented, write* correct.

1. I am taking a class in summer school, so is Joanna.

   _____

2. Learning some recent advances in computers.

   _____

3. I would rather be outside, the warm weather is so inviting.

   _____

4. The class starts at ten o'clock.

   _____

Unit 6: Themes in Literature: Heroism
Benchmark Test 11

Literary Analysis

1. Which of these statements most accurately describes an epic?
   A. An epic is a short poem that usually tells an exciting story.
   B. An epic is usually about an ordinary person who faces an extraordinary situation.
   C. An epic is usually about a hero whose traits are valued by his or her society.
   D. An epic is usually narrated in chronological order, with no jumps in time.

2. What does it mean to start an epic *in medias res?*
   A. start with the earliest event in time
   B. start at the end of the action and work backwards
   C. start in the middle of the action
   D. start in ancient times

3. What do you call an elaborate comparison that extends over several lines in an epic?
   A. an epic simile
   B. an epithet
   C. an analysis
   D. a Homeric stanza

Read this retelling of a portion of the Aeneid, *an ancient Roman epic. Then, answer the questions that follow.*

   Aeneas and his men appeared in Dido's rich court. "My lady, I am Aeneas, once prince of Troy and now a wanderer," he said. For six long years, he and his fellow Trojans had sailed the seas seeking a new home. In doing so, they had followed the will of the gods, who had directed Aeneas to leave the devastation of Troy with twenty ships and his loyal men. Yet, despite his goodness and bravery, some of the gods had sided against him and sent troubles his way. It was the goddess Juno who had arranged the fierce storm that sent his fleet to Carthage, where Dido was queen.

   On Aeneas' arrival, Queen Dido welcomed him and said she was willing to share her kingdom with him. However, the time would come when Aeneas would have to continue his journey, for he was destined to do something greater than rule Carthage.

4. What characteristic of this passage most clearly indicates that it is from an epic?
   A. It describes the actions of a larger-than-life hero.
   B. It relates an important conversation.
   C. It explains a central conflict.
   D. It takes place during ancient times.

5. Which answer choice most accurately characterizes Aeneas as an epic hero?
   A. His men are loyal to him even during hard times.
   B. He has been lost at sea and survived a storm.
   C. He suffered losses when Troy was destroyed, so he knows how it feels to fail.
   D. He shows qualities valued by Roman culture, such as bravery and obedience to the gods.

6. What does the selection show about the culture that produced the *Aeneid*?
   A. The ancient Romans thought that noble birth was more important than obedience to the gods.
   B. The ancient Romans viewed women as unsuitable rulers.
   C. The ancient Romans lived in a violent world in which power often shifted.
   D. The ancient Romans knew nothing of sailing or navigating.

7. Through which literary structure do readers learn about Aeneas' past in this passage?
   A. an exclamation
   B. a flashback
   C. a beginning *in medias res*
   D. a simile

Read the following summaries. Then, answer the questions that follow.

The Epic of Gilgamesh

King of Uruk in ancient Mesopotamia, Gilgamesh was a widely praised ruler who built the walls that protected the city from invasion. He was so powerful that the goddess Aruru created Enkidu to fight him. Although he was strong, Enkidu still lost a wrestling match to Gilgamesh. After that, the two became the best of friends. Then, Enkidu died from wounds he received while helping Gilgamesh fight the monster Humbaba. Stricken with grief, Gilgamesh risked his life in a journey to the underworld to try to find his friend.

Gil Gamesh

Mayor of Ulrick, Missouri, Gil Gamesh was a popular politician who oversaw many building projects that brought jobs into the community. Holding the job for many years, Gamesh had grown powerful, but his easy time ended when an environmentalist named Hank Ido came to town. The two men fought many policy battles, but they joined forces to fight expansion plans of the Humber Cement Plant. When Hank fell down the quarry while investigating matters at the cement plant, Gil risked his life to go down into the quarry and save his friend.

8. What do Gilgamesh and Gil Gamesh have in common?
   A. Both are strong rulers who protect citizens from violence.
   B. Both are popular leaders who face challenges.
   C. Both are rugged outdoorsmen who enjoy wrestling.
   D. Both are big city leaders in the Middle East.

9. The character of Hank Ido is an allusion to which detail in the original epic?
   A. a place called Uruk
   B. a goddess named Aruru
   C. a character named Enkidu
   D. a character named Humbaba

10. What is one chief difference between the attitudes and beliefs expressed in the two works?
    A. The original epic shows a strong belief in supernatural forces; the contemporary interpretation does not.
    B. The original epic shows a strong belief in the importance of friendship; the contemporary interpretation does not.
    C. The original epic shows a strong concern for the physical environment; the contemporary interpretation does not.
    D. The contemporary interpretation reflects a rural society; the original epic reflects an urban society.

11. In what way does the contemporary interpretation shed light on the original epic?
    A. By comparing a cement plant to a monster, it shows how powerful the construction industry was in ancient as well as modern times.
    B. By discussing Hank Ido's environmental concerns, it shows how important the environment was in both times.
    C. By having Gil Gamesh go down into the quarry, it shows how unbelievable Gilgamesh's quest in the underworld was.
    D. By stressing common elements, it makes the ancient epic seem more relevant today.

Reading Skill: Historical and Cultural Context

Read the selection. Then, answer the questions that follow.

Mary Hays, known as Molly, went from soldier to soldier with her pitcher of water. She had been a servant before she married John Hays; now she served water to John and his comrades as they fought in the colonial artillery. Traveling with them, she had endured the cruel winter at Valley Forge. Now it was nearly 100 degrees, and the Battle of Monmouth raged all around them. She mopped John's brow as he collapsed to the ground in exhaustion. Then, she began to load and fire the cannon herself. She would do what she could to help the American colonists in their fight against the British.

12. What is the historical context of this selection?
    A. the American Revolution
    B. the American Civil War
    C. the Spanish-American War
    D. World War II

13. What prior knowledge is most valuable for identifying the historical context of the selection?
    A. You need to know that Molly is sometimes a nickname for Mary.
    B. You need to know in which state Monmouth is located.
    C. You need to know in which war Valley Forge played an important role.
    D. You need to know what the term *artillery* means.

14. In order to appreciate the main character's achievements, what difference between your own historical context and that of the selection would it be most important to keep in mind?
   A. In the past, more people worked as servants than today.
   B. In the past, there was no air conditioning as there is today.
   C. In the past, water pollution was not the serious problem that it is today.
   D. In the past, women did not usually help fight in military battles.

Read the selection. Then, answer the questions that follow.

   As Mari walked back from the blacksmith's hut, he passed a baobab tree. Reaching up, he removed several leaves to bring home to his mother. His mother often used them as a condiment in her cooking. He recalled that it was just such a tree that Sundiata, the great lion king of old Mali, had pulled from the ground while still a young boy. Mari knew the story from the *griots*. Sundiata had seemed backward for his age because it took him so long to learn to walk. Others made fun of him for being a weakling and a fool. Yet on that day, Sundiata had shown that he was neither. Later he become a fine ruler of the Mandingo people. Mari was proud to be his descendant.

15. What do the details in the selection show about the historical and cultural context of the work?
   A. In Africa of old, blacksmiths were highly respected.
   B. In Africa of old, the best chefs were usually women.
   C. In Africa of old, people admired physical strength.
   D. In Africa of old, people were afraid of lions.

16. Which text aid would most help you understand the historical and cultural context?
   A. a background section on the old African kingdom of Mali
   B. a vocabulary feature explaining the meaning of the word *condiment*
   C. a footnote telling you how to pronounce the name *Sundiata*
   D. a full color illustration of a baobab tree

17. What prior knowledge can best help you understand the cultural context of the selection?
   A. You need to know that blacksmiths work with metal.
   B. You need to know that *griots* are African oral historians.
   C. You need to know that some tree leaves were used as medicine in Africa.
   D. You need to know that lions are found in Africa.

18. Which contemporary American value seems to be shared by Mari's culture?
   A. a respect for the outdoors
   B. a respect for the elderly
   C. a respect for people who work hard
   D. a respect for people who overcome challenges

Reading Skill: Identify Characteristics of Various Types of Text *Study this application. Then, answer the questions that follow.*

JOB APPLICATION Please print in ink.

1. Name (last name first): _____
2. Address (include ZIP code): _____
3. Phone Number (include area code): _____
4. Date of Birth (month/day/year): _____
5. For what position are you applying? _____

19. What text characteristic is found in this job application?
    A. write-on lines
    B. captions
    C. charts
    D. a bulleted list

20. How should Celia H. Simms write her name on line 1?
    A. Celia H. Simms, printed with a pencil
    B. Celia H. Simms, in script with a pen
    C. Simms, Celia H., in script with a pencil
    D. Simms, Celia H., printed with a pen

21. Which of these dates fits the format requested in item 4?
    A. December 1996
    B. 31/12/1996
    C. December 31
    D. 12/31/1996

Vocabulary: Prefixes

22. The prefix *be-* can mean "around" or "make." Using this knowledge, explain how you make a person feel if you *belittle* him or her.
    A. important
    B. insignificant
    C. confident
    D. exhausted

23. The words *disinterest, disagreement,* and *disadvantage* all share the prefix *dis-*. Using this knowledge, choose the answer that best states the meaning of *dis-*.
    A. like; similar to
    B. ahead of; in front of
    C. together; with
    D. not; away; apart

Grammar

24. Which of these is a simple sentence?
    A. Roland and El Cid are both famous epic heroes of medieval Europe.
    B. Roland appears in a French epic, while El Cid appears in a Spanish one.
    C. Roland was a knight when Charlemagne was emperor.
    D. Roland's epic is long, but El Cid's epic exists only in fragments.

25. Which of these is a compound sentence?
    A. Roland and El Cid are both famous epic heroes of medieval Europe.
    B. Roland appears in a French epic, while El Cid appears in a Spanish one.
    C. Roland was a knight when Charlemagne was emperor.
    D. Roland's epic is long, but El Cid's epic exists only in fragments.

26. What kind of sentence does the following example illustrate?

    The batter ran to first base after she hit the ball.

    A. simple
    B. compound
    C. complex
    D. compound-complex

27. Which of the following is correctly punctuated?
    A. The hero was brave he died in the end.
    B. The hero was brave, he died in the end.
    C. The hero was brave; he died in the end.
    D. The hero was brave; He died in the end.

28. What is the defining characteristic of a run-on sentence?
    A. incorrect or missing punctuation
    B. extremely long length
    C. misuse of a semicolon
    D. ellipses

29. Which of the following is a sentence fragment?
    A. He plays the piano.
    B. Go practice the violin.
    C. She practiced a lot.
    D. A guitar and a drum set.

WRITING

30. Think of a person from everyday life that you consider heroic. Write a brief "everyday epic" in the form of a one-paragraph description of this person. Describe his or her personality and achievements, and explain why you admire him or her.

31. Think of a famous person whose background you know something about. It could be someone alive today or someone who lived long ago. Write a two-paragraph introduction for a biography of this person's life and achievements.

32. Think of a task that you know how to complete, such as wrapping a gift or tying a particular type of knot. Write technical directions that readers can use to help them complete the task.

Unit 6: Themes in Literature: Heroism Skills Concept Map—2

Do heroes have responsibilities?

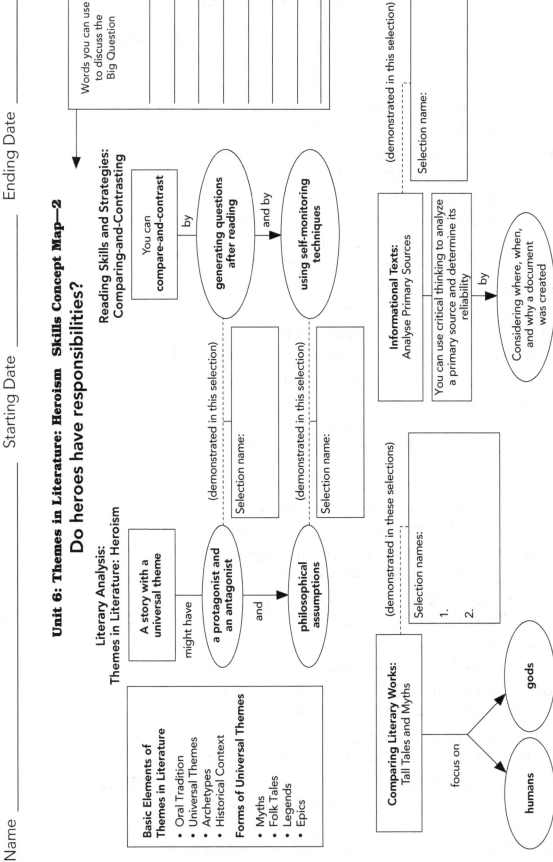

Literary Analysis:
Themes in Literature: Heroism

Reading Skills and Strategies:
Comparing-and-Contrasting

A story with a universal theme — might have → a protagonist and an antagonist — and → philosophical assumptions

You can **compare-and-contrast** — by → **generating questions after reading** — and by → **using self-monitoring techniques**

(demonstrated in this selection)
Selection name:

(demonstrated in this selection)
Selection name:

(demonstrated in this selection)
Selection name:

Informational Texts:
Analyse Primary Sources

You can use critical thinking to analyze a primary source and determine its reliability — by → Considering where, when, and why a document was created

Basic Elements of Themes in Literature
- Oral Tradition
- Universal Themes
- Archetypes
- Historical Context

Forms of Universal Themes
- Myths
- Folk Tales
- Legends
- Epics

Comparing Literary Works:
Tall Tales and Myths

focus on → gods

focus on → humans

(demonstrated in these selections)
Selection names:
1.
2.

Words you can use to discuss the Big Question

Student Log

Complete this chart to track your assignments.

Writing	Extend Your Learning	Writing Workshop	Other Assignments

Study these words from "Three Skeleton Key." Then, complete the activities that follow.

Word List A

descriptions [di SKRIP shuhns] *n.* statements telling what something is like
Her <u>descriptions</u> of the books made us want to read them.

devoured [di VOWRD] *v.* ate quickly, with great hunger
The hungry lions captured their prey and <u>devoured</u> it in no time.

emerged [i MERJD] *v.* came out of; became visible
The children were dripping wet as they <u>emerged</u> from the pool.

exception [ik SEP shuhn] *n.* something not included
I enjoyed the entire concert, with the <u>exception</u> of the last song.

occupied [AHK yuh pyd] *v.* filled up a space
The prisoner's law books <u>occupied</u> almost his whole cell.

reeking [REEK ing] *adj.* giving off a strong bad smell
<u>Reeking</u> with the smell of dirty socks, the hamper had to be emptied.

superior [soo PEER ee er] *adj.* better than other similar things
My sister studied harder, so her grades were usually <u>superior</u> to mine.

vivid [VIV id] *adj.* very clear, almost seeming real
The dream was so <u>vivid</u> that I thought it had really happened.

Word List B

barrier [BA ree uhr] *n.* something that separates things
The fence served as a <u>barrier</u> between our land and our neighbor's.

distraction [di STRAK shuhn] *n.* something that interrupts your focus
The music was a <u>distraction</u> when I was trying to work.

fantastic [fan TAS tik] *adj.* strange and unbelievable; unreal
A tornado transported Dorothy to the <u>fantastic</u> land of Oz.

framework [FRAYM wurk] *n.* a structure supporting something
If the <u>framework</u> is solid, the bridge should last for a very long time.

guardians [GAHR dee uhnz] *n.* ones who watch over or protect
My aunt and uncle are the <u>guardians</u> of our family photos.

nauseating [NAW zee ayt ing] *adj.* sickening to the stomach
We were sickened by the <u>nauseating</u> odor of the garbage dump.

regaining [ree GAYN ing] *n.* getting something back or recovering something
<u>Regaining</u> the use of his hand, he was finally able to type again.

treacherous [TRECH er uhs] *adj.* very dangerous
They steered their raft carefully, hoping to avoid the <u>treacherous</u> rocks.

Name _____ Date _____

"Three Skeleton Key" by George G. Toudouze
Vocabulary Warm-up Exercises

Exercise A *Fill in each blank in the paragraph with an appropriate word from Word List A. Use each word only once.*

I have clear and [1] _____ memories of the apartment building I grew up in as a child. The Millers were a large family that [2] _____ the apartment next to ours. Thanks to our neighbors, who were always making cabbage soup, we had to deal with a [3] _____ hallway. They must have [4] _____ a ton of that soup! With the [5] _____ of my grandmother, no one in my family liked to cook. I could tell you about some of the weird dishes my mother used to make, but my [6] _____ would not do them justice. I still remember the day when one of the Miller children [7] _____ from their apartment carrying a huge bowl of cabbage soup. She handed the bowl to my mother. That soup was far [8] _____ to anything I had ever eaten before! I will always remember that wonderful cabbage soup.

Exercise B *Revise each sentence so that the underlined vocabulary word is used in a logical way. Be sure to keep the vocabulary word in your revision.*

Example: The building collapsed because the <u>framework</u> was very well designed.
The building collapsed because the <u>framework</u> was poorly designed.

1. We were delighted by the <u>nauseating</u> smell of his cigar.

   _____

2. Our mother warned us to play outside during the <u>treacherous</u> weather.

   _____

3. He began <u>regaining</u> weight when he stopped snacking all the time.

   _____

4. As <u>guardians</u> of the secret information, we revealed it to anyone who asked.

   _____

5. The story was set in a <u>fantastic</u> world that was exactly like the real world we live in.

   _____

6. The mountain range was a <u>barrier</u> that sped up the progress of the wagon train.

   _____

7. Our teacher's voice was a <u>distraction</u> when we were trying to listen to our teacher's lesson.

   _____

Name _____ Date _____

Read the following passage. Pay special attention to the underlined words. Then, read it again, and complete the activities. Use a separate sheet of paper for your written answers.

I am a rat and proud of it.

We rats have had a long and noble history. My ancestors came to America by ship more than a hundred years ago. They comfortably <u>occupied</u> the entire lower deck of the ship along with their many friends. The deck, <u>reeking</u> of garbage and rotting fish, delighted my ancestors. Still, they <u>emerged</u> from that ship with great enthusiasm. They had a whole new world to conquer, and conquer it they did.

Rats soon found homes for themselves in barns and neglected buildings all over the country. I have never understood why people are so reluctant to welcome us into their homes. Rats are <u>superior</u> houseguests. We require very little space, and we gladly eat any leftovers we can find. We are always around when needed, too. In fact, our females produce litters of six to twenty-two little rats every month.

People's <u>descriptions</u> of rats are often less than flattering. We have been called filthy vermin and other <u>vivid</u> names that I am too polite to repeat. Humans blame us for destroying crops and spreading disease. Although I have <u>devoured</u> my fair share of farm products, I have never made anyone ill. It is true that fleas carrying typhus and plague will sometime hitch a ride on the back of a rat, but is that our fault?

I have never bitten or scratched a human being, with the <u>exception</u> of a few overly curious individuals who showed insufficient respect for my privacy. On the other hand, I have heard that human scientists sometimes imprison white rats in cages and perform experiments on them. However, I prefer to believe that this is just an urban legend.

It is my fondest hope that rodents and humans can someday live together in peace and harmony.

1. Underline the words that tell what the narrator's ancestors <u>occupied</u>. Name a place you know that rats might have *occupied*.

2. Circle the words that tell what caused the <u>reeking</u>. Tell what would cause a *reeking* kitchen.

3. Underline the words that tell how the rats <u>emerged</u> from the ship. Rewrite the sentence, using a different word or phrase for *emerged*.

4. Circle the word that <u>superior</u> describes. Compare two things—one that is *superior* to the other.

5. Underline the words that tell what people's <u>descriptions</u> of rats are often like. What are *descriptions*?

6. Circle the words that identify a <u>vivid</u> name for rats. What other *vivid* words could describe a rat?

7. Underline the words that tell what the narrator has <u>devoured</u>. Explain how the meanings of *devoured* and ate differ.

8. Underline the words that tell the <u>exception</u> to the narrator's claim of never biting or scratching. What would be an *exception* to the rule that you should not use the word ain't?

Name _____ Date _____

"Three Skeleton Key" by George G. Toudouze
Reading Warm-up B

Read the following passage. Pay special attention to the underlined words. Then, read it again, and complete the activities. Use a separate sheet of paper for your written answers.

Long before the invention of airplanes and steam engines, people relied on wind power to travel great distances over the water in sailing ships.

Every sailing ship has a hull, rigging, and at least one mast to support its sails. The hull is the framework upon which the ship is built. It serves as a barrier between the water on the outside and the people and cargo within. The rigging allows the crew to raise and lower the sails on tall poles called masts. Traditionally, a vessel with fewer than three masts was called a *boat* rather than a *ship*.

Sailing across the ocean has always been a treacherous undertaking, full of possible dangers. A severe storm can blow a sailing ship off course, or even lead to shipwreck. Seasickness can transform an otherwise pleasant ocean crossing into a nauseating experience. Boredom is another hazard of long voyages. Gazing at the beautiful starry sky is a fine distraction on a balmy evening. However, passengers can grow restless on a long and uneventful trip.

The crew of a traditional sailing ship had many jobs to do. A sailor's day was divided into watches. Crew members would alternate hours, working four on and four off around the clock. They would take turns steering the ship and navigating. As guardians of the ship's safety, the sailors in charge of keeping lookout had one of the most important jobs of all.

Keeping the ship in good condition was a constant concern. Rigging and sails needed to be repaired, and the masts needed oiling. Once passengers began questioning a ship's safety, regaining their confidence could be a very difficult task.

After many weeks at sea, sailors sometimes reported seeing such fantastic creatures as mermaids and sea serpents. Often, these sightings would turn out to be whale sharks or giant squid. Other times, they proved to be no more than figments of a bored sailor's imagination.

1. Circle the phrase that tells where the <u>framework</u> is. What does *framework* mean?

2. Underline the words that tell what the <u>barrier</u> separates. Name two other things that often serve as a *barrier*.

3. Circle the word that gives a good clue to the meaning of <u>treacherous</u>. Write a sentence about something that is *treacherous*.

4. Circle the word that tells what can make an ocean crossing <u>nauseating</u>. Describe a *nauseating* experience you have had.

5. Underline the words that tell what makes a fine <u>distraction</u>. Tell about a *distraction* that you have experienced.

6. Circle the word that gives a good clue to the meaning of <u>guardians</u>. What characteristics might good *guardians* possess?

7. Underline the words that tell what sailors would have trouble <u>regaining</u>. Write a sentence about something you had trouble *regaining*.

8. Circle two examples of <u>fantastic</u> creatures. Name some *fantastic* creatures that you know about from books or movies.

"Three Skeleton Key" by George G. Toudouze
Writing About the Big Question

Do heroes have responsibilities?

Big Question Vocabulary

character	choices	hero	honesty	identify
imitate	intentions	involvement	justice	morality
obligation	responsibility	serve	standard	wisdom

A. *Use one or more words from the list above to complete each sentence.*

1. In epic tales, heroes often struggle against opponents who lack a sense of
   _____.

2. In our office, Raymond has the _____ for purchasing supplies.

3. In a dramatic announcement, the president declared that he would not
   _____ a second term.

4. During the debate, the panel of journalists quizzed the candidates about their
   _____ if they were elected.

5. Confucius was an ancient Chinese statesman and philosopher, much respected for
   his _____.

B. *Follow the directions in responding to each of the items below.*

1. List two of your personal heroes.

   _____

   _____

2. Write two sentences to explain your choice of one of these heroes. Use at least two
   of the Big Question vocabulary words.

   _____

   _____

C. *Complete the sentence below. Then, write a short paragraph in which you connect the experience to the Big Question.*

   A **hero** may not choose _____, but he or she must make **choices**

   _____

   _____

   _____

   _____

Name _____ Date _____

"Three Skeleton Key" by George Toudouze
Literary Analysis: Protagonist and Antagonist

The **protagonist** is the chief character in a literary work—the character whose fortunes are of greatest interest to the reader. Some literary works also have an **antagonist**—a character or force that fights the protagonist. The antagonist may be another character or an external force, such as nature, that acts as a character.

Although the protagonist is not always an admirable or even likeable character, readers are interested in what happens to him or her.

- The protagonist's motives may be commonly understood feelings and goals, such as curiosity, the search for love, or the desire to win.
- The protagonist's conflict with the antagonist may represent a larger struggle, such as the conflict between good and evil, success and failure, or life and death.

DIRECTIONS: *Answer the following questions on the lines provided.*

1. Who or what is the protagonist in "Three Skeleton Key"? What is the occupation of the protagonist?

   _____

   _____

2. What qualities or characteristics make the protagonist a bit unusual and attract our interest?

   _____

   _____

   _____

3. Who or what is the antagonist in the story?

   _____

4. How does the author use the technique of personification to make the antagonist seem like a difficult and even dangerous opponent?

   _____

   _____

   _____

5. What parts of the conflict between the protagonist and the antagonist in "Three Skeleton Key" can you identify?

   _____

   _____

Name _____ Date _____

Reading: Compare and Contrast Characters

Comparing and contrasting characters is recognizing and thinking about their similarities and differences. You can compare different characters within a work, characters from different works, or a single character at different points in a particular work. To make a valid, productive comparison, you must examine each character (or the same character at different points in the narrative) in the same way. As you read, ask questions about each character you are comparing in the following general categories. Then, **generate questions after reading** that are specific to the characters and situations in the story.

- What are the character's actions?
- What are the character's reasons for his or her actions?
- What qualities does the character demonstrate?

DIRECTIONS: *Use the space provided to answer these questions about the characters in* "Three Skeleton Key."

1. How does Itchoua contrast with Le Gleo and the narrator?

   _____

2. In the struggle with the rats, how does Le Gleo react differently from the other characters? What does this difference suggest about the ways in which human beings react to extreme pressure or danger?

   _____

   _____

   _____

3. How successful is Toudouze in personifying the ship's rats, making them seem like characters rather than rats?

   _____

   _____

   _____

4. What attitudes does the narrator display about his profession and Three Skeleton Key at the beginning of the story? What attitudes does he display at the end? What does a comparison of his before-and-after outlooks suggest about the narrator's personality?

   _____

   _____

   _____

   _____

   _____

"Three Skeleton Key" by George Toudouze
Vocabulary Builder

Word List

derisive   diminution   incessantly   lurched   monotonous   provisions

A. DIRECTIONS: *Circle the letter of the best answer to each of the following questions.*

1. Which of the following answers is the best synonym for *lurched*?
   A. moved jerkily   B. launched   C. subsided

2. Which of the following answers most nearly means the OPPOSITE of *diminution*?
   A. delay   B. memory   C. increase

3. If you answered someone in a *derisive* fashion, which of the following answers would best describe your tone of voice?
   A. soothing   B. mocking   C. loud

B. DIRECTIONS: *For each of the following items, think about the meaning of the underlined word and then answer the question.*

1. If you wrote a <u>derisive</u> review of a film, would your review be admiring or critical?
   _____

2. If the company for which you worked reported a sharp <u>diminution</u> in sales, would the company's owners feel pleased or concerned?
   _____

3. Would you feel comfortable on a bus that <u>lurched</u> during most of a five-hour journey? Why or why not?
   _____

4. If your kitchen was stocked with <u>provisions</u>, would you likely go hungry in the near future?
   _____

5. If a lecturer's voice is <u>monotonous</u>, would the audience find it easy to pay attention?
   _____

6. If children complain <u>incessantly</u>, would they likely feel satisfied?
   _____

C. WORD STUDY: *The Latin root -min- means "small." Use the context of the sentences and what you know about the Latin root -min- to explain your answer to each question.*

1. If an event has a *minimal* impact on you, has it affected you greatly? Why or why not?
   _____

   _____

2. If there are *minuscule* traces of an element in a chemical compound, can they be described as significant? Why or why not?
   _____

   _____

Name _____ Date _____

"Three Skeleton Key" by George Toudouze
Enrichment: Lighthouses

The history of lighthouses goes back to ancient times. It is believed that the Phoenicians and the Egyptians built lighthouses, but the earliest lighthouse for which we have detailed records is the lighthouse at Pharos, an island in the harbor of Alexandria, Egypt. Built by the Greeks, this structure, which stood about 350 feet high, was one of the Seven Wonders of the Ancient World. It was destroyed by an earthquake in the fourteenth century.

Lighthouse designers have had to figure out many things, including how to build a tall structure in the open sea and how to furnish enough power so that the light can be seen from far off. As technology has improved, lighthouses have improved as well.

DIRECTIONS: *Using an encyclopedia or Internet resources, compile information for an oral report on the development of lighthouses. Select three or four important milestones in lighthouse technology. Use the space provided to make detailed notes about these milestones for your report.*

_____

_____

_____

_____

_____

_____

_____

_____

_____

_____

_____

_____

_____

_____

"Three Skeleton Key" by George G. Toudouze
Open-Book Test

Short Answer *Write your responses to the questions in this section on the lines provided.*

1. Early in the story of "Three Skeleton Key" by George G. Toudouze, the narrator establishes himself as the protagonist with a goal. This goal is his reason for taking the lighthouse job. What is his first goal in the story?

   _____

   _____

2. Who or what is the antagonist in "Three Skeleton Key"?

   _____

3. Reread the paragraph in the middle of "Three Skeleton Key" that begins, "The rats of the sea are fierce, bold animals." How does author George G. Toudouze communicate the power or force of the rats?

   _____

   _____

   _____

4. Reread the paragraph in the middle of "Three Skeleton Key" that begins, "Their teeth grated as they pressed against the glass of the lantern-room. . . ." What do you hear, see, and smell in this paragraph?

   _____

   _____

   _____

5. In "Three Skeleton Key," how does Le Gleo react differently from Itchoua and the narrator as the men retreat into the lantern-room?

   _____

   _____

   _____

6. One conflict in "Three Skeleton Key" is the men's decision to not light the lantern. What is the purpose of not lighting the lantern? What conflict for the protagonists does this decision cause?

   _____

   _____

   _____

   _____

7. At the end of "Three Skeleton Key," the narrator seems to have changed his attitude toward the island. How would you describe this shift in attitude?

_____

_____

_____

8. In "Three Skeleton Key," the protagonist's conflict with the antagonists holds the reader's attention because it is a struggle between two universal elements or forces. Which of the following best identifies these forces: right vs. wrong, good vs. evil, life vs. death, or beauty vs. ugliness?

_____

_____

9. In "Three Skeleton Key," what do the sharks do that is unexpected?

_____

_____

10. At the end of "Three Skeleton Key," the rats are finally defeated by means of a clever trick that the patrol squadron sets for the rats. Use details from the short story to complete the three stages or phases of the trap and the results of each stage. Include the words *lurched* and *diminution* in your explanation.

(1) Tug and barge: _____

_____

(2) Incendiary shell from patrol boat: _____

_____

(3) Shrapnel and sharks: _____

_____

Essay

Write an extended response to the question of your choice or to the question or questions your teacher assigns you.

11. Write an essay in which you discuss the struggle between the protagonist and the antagonists in "Three Skeleton Key." Describe the protagonist and the antagonists. Discuss their struggle and the main parts of the plot. Why is this struggle interesting to the reader? Use at least two examples from the story to support your essay.

12. In "Three Skeleton Key," George Toudouze uses a narrator with the first-person point of view. The narrator is a major participant in the action. In an essay, discuss the ways in which you think the story would have been different if the author had used a third-person point of view, standing outside the action. Would the events have been so gripping and suspenseful? How might our impressions of the protagonist (the narrator) have been different? Support your main ideas with at least two examples from the story.

13. The conflict between protagonist and antagonists in this story pits the narrator against a force of nature. Toudouze goes to considerable lengths to personify the rats, giving them a degree of intelligence and a decision-making capacity that make them seem almost human. In an essay, discuss this aspect of the story. Use at least two examples from "Three Skeleton Key" to discuss how the author exaggerates the rats' behavior to make them strong and frightening antagonists.

14. **Thinking About the Big Question: Do heroes have responsibilities?** What evidence can you find in "Three Skeleton Key" to show that the narrator is, or is not, characterized by a sense of responsibility toward his fellow human beings? Respond to this question in an essay, supporting your main ideas with at least two examples from the story.

Oral Response

15. Go back to question 3, 4, 6, or to the question your teacher assigns you. Take a few minutes to expand your answer and to prepare an oral response. Find additional details in "Three Skeleton Key" that support your points. If necessary, make notes to guide your oral response.

Unit 6 Resources: Themes in Literature
103

"Three Skeleton Key" by George Toudouze
Selection Test A

Critical Reading *Identify the letter of the choice that best answers the question.*

____ 1. The setting of a story is the time and place of the action. Which of the following is the setting for "Three Skeleton Key"?
   A. a building in the center of Paris, France
   B. on board a fishing boat on the Atlantic Ocean
   C. a lighthouse on an island off the coast of Guiana
   D. a sugar plantation in the United States

____ 2. What kind of story do these opening lines from "Three Skeleton Key" lead you to expect?"
   > My most terrifying experience? Well, one does have a few in thirty-five years of service in the Lights. . . .
   A. a suspenseful tale of adventure
   B. a story of romantic love
   C. an introduction to lighthouse keeping
   D. an amusing tale about childhood

____ 3. In "Three Skeleton Key," which of the following are characters who work with the narrator?
   A. the three skeletons
   B. Itchoua and Le Gleo
   C. the whaleboat captain
   D. Le Gleo and three convicts

____ 4. Which of the following best defines the term *antagonist*?
   A. a force that opposes the protagonist
   B. an outsider whom no one likes
   C. a joker who makes fun of people
   D. an author who writes stories

____ 5. In "Three Skeleton Key," which of the following is a "derelict"?
   A. a two-masted ship
   B. an abandoned ship
   C. a lonely island
   D. an insane crew

___ **6.** In "Three Skeleton Key," which of the following turns out to be the antagonist?
   A. the Flying Dutchman
   B. *Cornelius de Witt*
   C. Itchoua
   D. the rats

___ **7.** Read the following passage from "Three Skeleton Key":

> The rats of the sea are fierce. . . . Large, strong, and intelligent, clannish and seawise, able to put the best of mariners to shame with their knowledge of the sea, their uncanny ability to foretell the weather.

How has the author managed to communicate the power of the rats in these sentences?
   A. by making them sound like animals
   B. by making them crawl like animals
   C. by making them seem like people
   D. by making them talk like people

___ **8.** How does Le Gleo react to the main conflict in "Three Skeleton Key"?
   A. He experiences nightmares and then cracks under the strain.
   B. He boldly challenges the rats by leaping out to fight them.
   C. He does not care about what happens to the other characters.
   D. He predicts that the rats will leave them alone after a while.

___ **9.** In "Three Skeleton Key," what do the sharks do that is unexpected?
   A. The sharks turn out to be larger than expected.
   B. The sharks are actually peace-loving creatures.
   C. The sharks help the men by eating some of the rats.
   D. The sharks send a signal to the mainland.

___ **10.** At the beginning of "Three Skeleton Key," the narrator refers to "my most terrifying experience." In what surprising way does the narrator think about the island at the end of the story?
   A. with hatred
   B. with terror
   C. with affection
   D. with disgust

___ **11.** When does the lighthouse keepers' problem become solved in "Three Skeleton Key"?
   A. when the ship arrives on the island
   B. when the narrator slaps Le Gleo in the face
   C. when the rats are finally destroyed
   D. when Itchoua becomes infected

Vocabulary and Grammar

___ 12. If a ship *lurched* as it rode on the waves, which of the following would be another way to describe its movement?
  A. It slid inside of something.   C. It sailed steadily.
  B. It moved awkwardly.   D. It went underwater.

___ 13. If there was a *diminution* in your interest in a project, how could you describe your interest?
  A. as increased   C. as unchanged
  B. as lessened   D. as canceled

___ 14. Where should commas be added in the following sentence?
  "Three Skeleton Key" got its name as the narrator tells us from three escaped convicts.
  A. after *got* and *us*   C. after *as*
  B. after *name* and *us*   D. after *three*

___ 15. Which of the following sentences needs correction in its use of commas?
  A. The lighthouse keeper said, "Watch out for the rats!"
  B. His companion, a man from France, grew afraid.
  C. Later, all three men struggled to stay sane.
  D. One of them became, extremely frightened.

Essay

16. Write an essay in which you discuss the struggle between the protagonist and the antagonist in "Three Skeleton Key." Describe the protagonist and the antagonist. Discuss their struggle and the main parts of the plot. Why is this struggle interesting to the reader? Use at least two examples from the story to support your essay.

17. In "Three Skeleton Key," George Toudouze uses a narrator with the first-person point of view. He uses words like "I, me, my," and so on, and he is a participant in the action. In an essay, discuss the ways in which you think the story would have been different if the author had used a third-person point of view, standing outside the action. Would the events have been as gripping and suspenseful? How might our impressions of the protagonist (the narrator) have been different? Support your main ideas with at least two examples from the story.

18. **Thinking About the Big Question: Do heroes have responsibilities?** The narrator of "Three Skeleton Key" is a hero with a sense of responsibility for his fellow human beings. Tell how the decision to not light the lantern or the narrator's action of striking Le Gleo supports this idea of being responsible. Provide your explanation in an essay. Support your main ideas with specific information from the story.

"Three Skeleton Key" by George Toudouze
Selection Test B

Critical Reading *Identify the letter of the choice that best completes the statement or answers the question.*

_____ 1. The term *protagonist* is used for which of the following?
A. a heroic character who undertakes a quest
B. a character with internal conflicts
C. a surprise ending in a story
D. the main character in a literary work

_____ 2. Which of the following is the setting for "Three Skeleton Key"?
A. a cemetery in France
B. a small island off the coast of Guiana
C. a training school for lighthouse keepers
D. on board a Dutch ship

_____ 3. Point of view is the perspective from which a story is told. Which of the following sentences shows the point of view used by the author in "Three Skeleton Key"?
A. I was one of three men on the island.
B. He thought the rats were dead.
C. He looked at the rats with dismay.
D. The three men stood together.

_____ 4. In "Three Skeleton Key," what do the men on the island gradually realize about why the *Cornelius de Witt* has become a derelict ship?
A. The ship was old and badly needed maintenance.
B. Rats had forced the crew to abandon the ship.
C. An epidemic of smallpox had killed the ship's crew.
D. A mutiny had broken out and the men had all been killed.

_____ 5. In "Three Skeleton Key," who or what is the antagonist?
A. Itchoua
B. Le Gleo
C. the rats
D. the narrator

_____ 6. Which of the following best describes the reactions of the lighthouse men to their situation?
A. They all react the same way: with panic and fright.
B. Two men remain calm, but the third cracks under the strain.
C. An angry argument erupts between two of the men.
D. The narrator resents the other characters' behavior.

_____ 7. In "Three Skeleton Key," how do the men signal to the mainland for help?
A. They send a wireless message.
B. They hail a passing ship.
C. They hoist a large flag in plain view.
D. They decide not to light the lantern.

_____ 8. How did the island in "Three Skeleton Key" get its name?
  A. Three lighthouse keepers were once killed there by rats.
  B. Three escaped convicts died there of hunger and thirst.
  C. Three sailors thought they were going to die there.
  D. Three men were attacked by sharks and died.

_____ 9. How were the men eventually saved from the rats in "Three Skeleton Key"?
  A. The rats died of starvation on the island.
  B. The men were able to shoot the rats.
  C. The rats were killed on a fiery barge.
  D. The rats were all eaten by sharks.

_____ 10. The narrator changes his attitude from the beginning of the story to the end. Which of the following best describes this contrast?
  A. First, he recalls a terrifying experience; then, he regrets leaving Three Skeleton Key.
  B. First, he is aware of the dangers of service; then, he is relieved that his career is over.
  C. First, he is friendly with his fellow lighthouse keepers; then, he is angry at their behavior.
  D. First, he admires the ship's rats; then, he is terrified by their attack on the lighthouse.

_____ 11. Which of the following best describes the overall atmosphere, or mood, in "Three Skeleton Key"?
  A. amusing
  B. suspenseful
  C. relaxed
  D. tragic

_____ 12. In "Three Skeleton Key," the protagonist's conflict with the antagonist holds our attention because it is a struggle between which of the following?
  A. right against wrong
  B. culture against nature
  C. life against death
  D. beauty against ugliness

Vocabulary and Grammar

_____ 13. Which of the following is the best synonym for *derisive*?
  A. mocking
  B. laughing
  C. exaggerating
  D. playing

_____ 14. If a ship *lurches* this way and that, how might you describe its movements?
  A. consistent
  B. unpredictable
  C. slow
  D. smooth

___ **15.** Where should a comma or commas be added in the following sentence?

In his career of thirty-five years the narrator a lighthouse keeper had lived through some strange experiences.

    A. after *career* and *years*

    B. after *years, narrator,* and *keeper*

    C. after *narrator* and *keeper*

    D. after *narrator*

Essay

16. How would you describe the personality of the narrator in "Three Skeleton Key"? What character traits do you see in the story's protagonist based on his words, actions, and reactions? In an essay, discuss your impressions of the narrator, supporting your main ideas with at least two examples from the story.

17. The conflict between protagonist and antagonist in this story pits the narrator against a force of nature. Toudouze goes to considerable lengths to personify the rats, giving them a degree of intelligence and a decision-making capacity that make them almost seem human. In an essay, discuss this aspect of the story. Use at least two examples from "Three Skeleton Key" to discuss how the author exaggerates the rats' behavior to make them a strong and frightening antagonist.

18. **Thinking About the Big Question: Do heroes have responsibilities?** What evidence can you find in "Three Skeleton Key" to show that the narrator is, or is not, characterized by a sense of responsibility toward his fellow human beings? Respond to this question in an essay, supporting your main ideas with at least two examples from the story.

Vocabulary Warm-up Word Lists

Study these words from "The Red-headed League." Then, complete the activities that follow.

Word List A

advertisement [ad ver TYZ muhnt] *n.* words or pictures that tell about some product or service
   We found the apartment through a newspaper <u>advertisement</u>.

bizarre [bi ZAHR] *adj.* very unusual and strange
   Everyone was shocked by his <u>bizarre</u> behavior.

despair [di SPAIR] *n.* complete loss of hope
   I felt <u>despair</u> when I saw the big red *F* on my paper.

exceedingly [eks SEE ding lee] *adv.* extremely
   It is <u>exceedingly</u> rare to see an armadillo this far north of Texas.

interfere [in ter FEER] *v.* to get involved when you are not wanted
   The camera crew asked the crowd not to <u>interfere</u> with their filming.

obvious [AHB vee uhs] *adj.* easy to see or understand
   It was <u>obvious</u> to everyone that our team was going to win.

occupation [ahk yuh PAY shuhn] *n.* job or profession
   Nursing is an <u>occupation</u> that involves helping others.

vulnerable [VUL ner uh buhl] *adj.* easy to harm, hurt, or attack
   Their computer was <u>vulnerable</u> to a virus attack.

Word List B

commerce [KAHM ers] *n.* the buying and selling of goods
   After the war, merchants in the two nations resumed normal <u>commerce</u>.

deference [DE fuh ruhns] *n.* behavior showing respect for
   In <u>deference</u> to your wishes, I will do as you ask.

effective [i FEK tiv] *adj.* producing a desired result
   The new medicine was highly <u>effective</u> in treating the disease.

intuition [in too ISH uhn] *n.* knowing something through feelings or instincts
   Her <u>intuition</u> told her that something bad would happen at the party.

misgivings [mis GIV ings] *n.* doubts or fears
   I have certain <u>misgivings</u> about the plan you have proposed.

narrative [NAR uh tiv] *n.* a description of events told as a story
   We listened closely as he began his lengthy <u>narrative</u>.

relentless [ri LENT lis] *adj.* determined and persistent
   A successful researcher must be <u>relentless</u> in his or her pursuit of the facts.

unique [yoo NEEK] *adj.* one of a kind; unusual
   Her <u>unique</u> personality set her apart from the crowd.

Name _____ Date _____

Exercise A *Fill in each blank in the paragraph with an appropriate word from Word List A.*
Use each word only once.

When I lost my job, I decided to seek an entirely new [1] _____. I
knew that changing jobs could be [2] _____ difficult, but I refused to let
anything [3] _____ with my search for a new career. Nothing would
stop me. So, I opened the newspaper to the "help wanted" page and carefully read each
[4] _____. It soon became [5] _____ to me that finding
a new job was going to be impossible! Each position I saw listed in the paper seemed
more [6] _____ than the one before. Suddenly, I felt all alone and
[7] _____. My enthusiasm had turned to [8] _____.
Then, I knew I had to snap out of it. After all, I was not even out of the ninth grade yet!

Exercise B *Write a complete sentence to answer each question. For each answer, use a*
word from Word List B to replace each underlined word or group of words without changing its
meaning.

1. Where in your town does <u>business</u> take place?

   _____

2. Why should you show <u>respect</u> to older people?

   _____

3. What would be a <u>useful</u> way to prepare for an important exam?

   _____

4. Should people always trust their <u>feelings about something</u>?

   _____

5. Would you go somewhere with a friend if you had <u>doubts</u> about the plans?

   _____

6. What would you do if a close friend were telling you a long and boring <u>story</u> about
   her vacation?

   _____

7. Under what circumstances might it be a bad idea to be <u>persistent</u>?

   _____

8. If someone said you were <u>one of a kind</u>, would you feel complimented or insulted?

   _____

Name _____ Date _____

"The Red-headed League" by Sir Arthur Conan Doyle

Reading Warm-up A

Read the following passage. Pay special attention to the underlined words. Then, read it again, and complete the activities. Use a separate sheet of paper for your written answers.

Arthur Conan Doyle began practicing medicine in Scotland in 1882. When it became <u>obvious</u> to him that his practice was not attracting very many patients, Doyle turned to writing. He soon discovered that this <u>occupation</u> suited him much better than the medical profession.

In 1886, Doyle decided to try his hand at a detective story. Detective stories were <u>exceedingly</u> rare at that time. Edgar Allen Poe had created the first fictional detective little more than 40 years before.

Doyle's Sherlock Holmes first appeared in 1887 in a novel called *A Study in Scarlet*. A second novel, then a series of short stories, followed. In 1894, an image of Holmes was used in a newspaper <u>advertisement</u> for Beechams' pills.

Readers loved Holmes, but Doyle did not want the success of his detective series to <u>interfere</u> with his ambition to be recognized as a writer of serious fiction. In a story called "The Final Problem," written in 1893, Doyle made the somewhat <u>bizarre</u> decision to let his beloved hero plunge to his death.

The public was outraged, but Doyle ignored his readers' cries of <u>despair</u>. He wrote for 8 more years before bringing Holmes back. Then, Doyle featured the detective in *The Hound of the Baskervilles*, in which the events took place before Holmes's death. The novel was a huge success when it appeared in 1901.

Holmes was revived for good in 1903. In "The Empty House," readers learned that Holmes had not been so <u>vulnerable</u> after all. In fact, he had miraculously survived the fall that was believed to have killed him. Fans around the world rejoiced!

By the time Doyle died in 1930, Holmes had appeared in four novels and fifty-six short stories. His adventures have been translated into more than fifty languages. The character has already appeared in over 200 movies. Today, people who know nothing about Sir Arthur Conan Doyle still recognize the familiar image of Holmes with his cape, deerstalker's cap, and magnifying glass.

1. Underline the words that tell what became <u>obvious</u> to Doyle. Tell about something that is **obvious** to you.

2. Circle the word that is a synonym for <u>occupation</u>. What **occupation** do you think might suit you?

3. Circle the words that tell what was <u>exceedingly</u> rare. Give a synonym for **exceedingly**.

4. Circle the word that tells where the <u>advertisement</u> appeared. Why would an **advertisement** use an image of Holmes?

5. Underline the words that tell with what Doyle thought his success might <u>interfere</u>. Explain what **interfere** means.

6. Circle the word that tells what is <u>bizarre</u>. Why might this be described as **bizarre**?

7. Circle the word that gives a hint to the meaning of <u>despair</u>. Write a sentence about something else that might cause **despair**.

8. Circle the word that shows that Holmes was not so <u>vulnerable</u>. Write a sentence using **vulnerable**.

"The Red-headed League" by Sir Arthur Conan Doyle
Reading Warm-up B

Read the following passage. Pay special attention to the underlined words. Then, read it again, and complete the activities. Use a separate sheet of paper for your written answers.

So you want to be a detective?

Many things about being a detective have changed since the fictional Sherlock Holmes prowled the streets of London. The basic principles of detection, however, remain the same.

Perhaps the most important quality that any detective must possess is <u>intuition</u> about human nature. Detectives rely on their natural instincts to know when people are lying and when they are telling the truth. They observe a suspect closely and listen carefully to his or her <u>narrative</u>. In this way, they pick up important clues that an untrained observer would be unlikely to recognize.

Detectives must conceal any <u>misgivings</u> they may be having. They must behave as if they have no doubts at all about the truthfulness of a suspect's story. By showing <u>deference</u> to the suspect, a detective can sometimes get him or her to reveal secrets never meant to be spoken aloud!

Each case is <u>unique</u> and distinctive. Detectives investigate everything from murders to missing persons. Detectives may be hired to locate witnesses or track down old friends. Business owners may seek their help with thefts and other crimes related to <u>commerce</u>.

Unlike Holmes, modern detectives rely on computer skills to be fully <u>effective</u> in their work. Databases allow them to quickly gather information that was beyond the reach of detectives just a few decades ago.

Detectives must also be skilled in the art of surveillance. Whether in a car or on foot, a detective must know how to watch someone without that person knowing he or she is being watched. Detectives now have access to electronic spying devices that Holmes and real-life detectives in the past could never have imagined.

Above all, detectives must be <u>relentless</u> in their search for the truth. Like Holmes, a good detective is driven by natural curiosity to pursue each case to its inevitable conclusion.

1. Circle the words that mean about the same as <u>intuition</u>. Do you think that *intuition* is more useful to a detective than reasoning ability? Explain.

2. Circle a word in the next paragraph that means about the same as <u>narrative</u>. Which do you enjoy more: a written *narrative* or a spoken one? Explain.

3. Circle a word in the next sentence that means about the same as <u>misgivings</u>. Tell about something you have had *misgivings* about.

4. Why might suspects reveal secrets if they are shown <u>deference</u>?

5. Circle a word that means about the same as <u>unique</u>. Describe something that makes you *unique*.

6. Circle a word that means about the same as <u>commerce</u>. Why would criminals be interested in the world of *commerce*?

7. Underline the words that tell how detectives can be <u>effective</u>. Describe a way in which you are *effective*.

8. Underline the words that tell in what a good detective is <u>relentless</u>. Write a sentence using *relentless*.

"The Red-headed League" by Sir Arthur Conan Doyle
Writing About the Big Question

Do heroes have responsibilities?

Big Question Vocabulary

character	choices	hero	honesty	identify
imitate	intentions	involvement	justice	morality
obligation	responsibility	serve	standard	wisdom

A. *Use one or more words from the list above to complete each sentence.*

1. In Massachusetts during the 1600s, laws passed by the Puritans were evidence of their stern _____.

2. When you take out a bank loan for a house, your mortgage is a formal document stating your _____ to repay the money.

3. Can you _____ the rhyme scheme of this brief lyric poem?

4. Merchants known for their _____ will never knowingly sell a defective product.

5. Patricia promised that, if she were elected to the student council, she would _____ the sophomore class with dedication.

B. *Follow the directions in responding to each of the items below.*

1. List two ways in which you might like to **serve** your community.

_____

_____

2. Write two sentences to explain one of your **choices** of community service. Use at least two of the Big Question vocabulary words.

_____

_____

C. *Complete the sentences below. Then, write a short paragraph in which you connect the experience to the Big Question.*

When a crime is being committed, a **hero** will _____. The hero's **involvement** may _____

_____

_____

_____

_____

"**The Red-headed League**" by Sir Arthur Conan Doyle
Literary Analysis: Protagonist and Antagonist

The **protagonist** is the chief character in a literary work—the character whose fortunes are of greatest interest to the reader. Some literary works also have an **antagonist**—a character or force that fights the protagonist. The antagonist may be another character or an external force, such as nature, that acts as a character.

Although the protagonist is not always an admirable or even likeable character, readers are interested in what happens to him or her.

- The protagonist's motives may be commonly understood feelings and goals, such as curiosity, the search for love, or the desire to win.
- The protagonist's conflict with the antagonist may represent a larger struggle, such as the conflict between good and evil, success and failure, or life and death.

DIRECTIONS: *Answer the following questions on the lines provided.*

1. Who or what is the protagonist in "The Red-headed League"? What is the occupation of the protagonist?

   _____

2. What qualities or characteristics make the protagonist somewhat unusual and attract our interest?

   _____

   _____

   _____

3. Who or what is the antagonist in the story?

   _____

   _____

4. What parts of the conflict between the protagonist and the antagonist in "The Red-headed League" can you identify?

   _____

   _____

   _____

   _____

   _____

   _____

   _____

   _____

Name _____ Date _____

"**The Red-headed League**" by Sir Arthur Conan Doyle
Reading: Compare and Contrast Characters

Comparing and contrasting characters is recognizing and thinking about their similarities and differences. You can compare different characters within a work, characters from different works, or a single character at different points in a particular work. To make a valid, productive comparison, you must examine each character (or the same character at different points in the narrative) in the same way. As you read, ask questions about each character you are comparing in the following general categories. Then, **generate questions after reading** that are specific to the characters and situations in the story.

- What are the character's actions?
- What are the character's reasons for his or her actions?
- What qualities does the character demonstrate?

DIRECTIONS: *Use the space provided to answer these questions about the characters in "The Red-headed League."*

1. How does Sherlock Holmes compare and contrast with Dr. Watson?

_____

_____

_____

2. How does Sherlock Holmes contrast with Peter Jones, the police agent from Scotland Yard?

_____

_____

_____

3. How would you compare Sherlock Holmes with his antagonist, the murderer and thief John Clay?

_____

_____

_____

4. How does Holmes's outlook on life at the beginning of "The Red-headed League" compare or contrast with his outlook at the end of the story?

_____

_____

_____

Name _____ Date _____

Vocabulary Builder

Word List

embellish   endeavored   formidable   introspective   tenacious   vex

A. DIRECTIONS: *Circle the letter of the best answer to each question.*

—— 1. Which of the following answers is the best synonym for *vex*?
    A. predict   **B.** annoy   **C.** promise

—— 2. Which of the following answers most nearly means the OPPOSITE of *introspective*?
    A. outgoing   **B.** exhausted   **C.** optimistic

—— 3. Which of the following answers is the best synonym for *formidable*?
    A. bashful   **B.** lively   **C.** awe-inspiring

—— 4. Which of the following answers is the best synonym for *embellish*?
    A. demand   **B.** encourage   **C.** decorate   **D.** replace

—— 5. Which of the following answers is the best synonym for *endeavored*?
    A. attempted   **B.** analyzed   **C.** suspected   **D.** traversed

—— 6. Which of the following answers is the best synonym for *tenacious*?
    A. realistic   **B.** gallant   **C.** translucent   **D.** persistent

B. DIRECTIONS: *In each of the following items, think about the meaning of the underlined word and then answer the question.*

1. If you faced a <u>formidable</u> enemy, would you face an easy or a difficult challenge?

    _____

2. If you found a situation <u>vexing</u>, would you be pleased or annoyed?

    _____

3. Would a person in an <u>introspective</u> mood be feeling thoughtful, bored, or excited?

    _____

C. WORD STUDY: *The Latin root -spec(t)- means "see" or "look." For example, a retrospective looks back at past events; a spectater is a person who views an event. Using what you know about the root -spec(t)-, match the word in Column A with its meaning in Column B by writing the correct letter on the line provided.*

____ 1. introspective   **A.** general view or survey

____ 2. respective   **B.** point of view

____ 3. perspective   **C.** looking inward; reflective

____ 4. conspectus   **D.** as relates individually to each of two persons

Name _____ Date _____

"The Red-headed League" by Sir Arthur Conan Doyle
Enrichment: Investigative Careers

Sherlock Holmes demonstrates specific skills as he solves the mystery of the Red-headed League. For example, he is good at deductive reasoning, or reasoning that moves from evidence to a conclusion. He also has excellent listening skills and is good at solving problems. What is more, he keeps himself in excellent physical shape, as shown in the climax of "The Red-headed League."

Although Sherlock Holmes is a fictional detective, his skills suggest some real-life requirements for people who make their careers as investigators. One investigative career is that of serving as an agent with the Federal Bureau of Investigation (FBI).

To be a candidate for the FBI, one must have a college degree and three years of work experience. Candidates must also be in excellent physical condition. FBI agents go through a fifteen-week training program, studying crime detection, evidence, law, and methods of investigation. Prospective agents also learn about self-defense and weaponry.

DIRECTIONS: *Imagine that you are a hiring director for an investigative agency such as the FBI. On a separate page, prepare a questionnaire for people you might want to hire. Your questions should try to find out how well suited the candidate is for investigative work. For example, you might ask the candidate to describe the hardest problem he or she has ever had to solve and the way he or she solved it. The answer would help you learn how well the person solves problems.*

After you complete your questionnaire, work with a classmate. Respond to each other's questions. Discuss your responses with your partner to see how well suited you may be for a career in investigative work.

_____

_____

_____

_____

_____

_____

_____

_____

_____

_____

_____

_____

_____

"Three Skeleton Key" by George Toudouze
"The Red-headed League" by Sir Arthur Conan Doyle
Integrated Language Skills: Grammar

Using Commas Correctly

Study the following list, which contains helpful suggestions on correct comma usage.

- Use a comma before the coordinating conjunction to separate two independent clauses in a compound sentence.

   We wanted to attend the concert, but our friends wanted to stay home.

- Use commas to separate three or more words, phrases, or clauses in a series.

   She bought onions, tomatoes, and peas.

- Use a comma after an introductory word, phrase, or clause.

   At the end of our day at the beach, we returned home.

- Use commas to set off parenthetical and nonessential expressions.

   His painting, which I saw yesterday, is difficult to understand.

- Use commas with places, dates, and titles.

   Edgar Allan Poe was raised in Richmond, Virginia.

- Use a comma to set off a direct quotation.

   Teresa asked, "Has everyone had enough salad?"

A. DIRECTIONS: *Rewrite the following sentences, adding commas where they are needed.*

1. Sir Arthur Conan Doyle the creator of Sherlock Holmes first studied to be an eye doctor.

   _____

2. When Doyle was in medical school he became aware of a certain professor.

   _____

3. This doctor who could diagnose illnesses that puzzled his colleagues may have been the model for the great Sherlock Holmes.

   _____

B. WRITING APPLICATION: *On the following lines, write a paragraph in which you tell what you like or dislike about detective stories. Use a variety of sentence structures, and be sure you use commas correctly.*

   _____

   _____

   _____

   _____

   _____

"Three Skeleton Key" by George Toudouze
"The Red-headed League" by Sir Arthur Conan Doyle
Integrated Language Skills: Support for Writing Journal Entries

For your journal entries, use the following chart to jot down notes.

Timeline: (1) _____
_____

(2) _____
_____

(3) _____
_____

(4) _____
_____

(5) _____
_____

(6) _____
_____

Choice of Days for Journal Entries: (1) _____
_____

(2) _____
_____

(3) _____
_____

As you write, remember to stay in character and make sure that your journal entries reflect any changes that the character experiences in the course of the story.

"Three Skeleton Key" by George Toudouze
"The Red-headed League" by Sir Arthur Conan Doyle
Support for Extend Your Learning

Research and Technology: "Three Skeleton Key"

Use the following lines to jot down notes for your **oral report** on ship rats.

Physical Appearance: _____

Other Possible Names: _____

Location/Diet/Survival Rates: _____

_____

_____

_____

_____

Comparisons with Toudouze's Descriptions: _____

_____

_____

_____

_____

Research and Technology: "The Red-headed League"

Use the following lines to jot down notes for your **oral report** on the science of detective work.

Fingerprinting: _____

Lie Detectors: _____

Police Sketches: _____

Other Techniques Used to Gather Information: _____

_____

_____

_____

_____

Comparisons with Holmes's Methods: _____

_____

_____

_____

_____

Name _____ Date _____

"The Red-headed League" by Sir Arthur Conan Doyle
Open-Book Test

Short Answer *Write your responses to the questions in this section on the lines provided.*

1. In "The Red-headed League" by Sir Arthur Conan Doyle, which character is the protagonist? Which character is the antagonist?

   _____

   _____

2. In "The Red-headed League," Dr. Watson says that his medical practice is "never very absorbing." Why does Watson enjoy working with Sherlock Holmes?

   _____

3. Reread the passage in the middle of "The Red-headed League" in which Holmes and Watson walk around Saxe-Coburg Square. What two significant details in this passage point toward Holmes's solution of the mystery?

   _____

   _____

   _____

4. Near the end of the story Mr. Jabez Wilson tells Sherlock Holmes in "The Red-headed League," Mr. Wilson reveals that the Red-headed League was suddenly dissolved. What was the real reason that the League ended? When does Holmes reveal his deduction?

   _____

   _____

   _____

5. What is the greatest contrast between the characters of Holmes and Watson in "The Red-headed League"? Is it between their powers of observation, their professional abilities, their appreciation of music, or their interest in unusual events? Cite details from the story to support your answer.

   _____

   _____

   _____

   _____

6. In "The Red-headed League," how are the characters Sherlock Holmes and John Clay alike? How are they different?

   _____

   _____

7. In the middle of "The Red-headed League," police agent Jones expresses his confidence in Sherlock Holmes when he remarks that Holmes "has the makings of a detective in him." Do you think Holmes has "the makings of a detective"? Explain your answer.

_____

_____

8. In "The Red-headed League," two characters adopt false names to carry out the clever plan to rob the bank. On the chart below, fill in the false identities of each character. Then explain the job or task that each character adopts to carry out the robbery plan.

	False Identity	**Task**
John Clay		
William Morris		

9. At what point in "The Red-headed League" does Sherlock Holmes show himself to be introspective by nature? Base your response on the meaning of *introspective*.

_____

_____

_____

10. At the end of "The Red-headed League," Holmes says, in French, "l'oeuvre c'est tout"—the work is everything. What does this tell you about Holmes's motivation?

_____

_____

Essay

Write an extended response to the question of your choice or to the question or questions your teacher assigns to you.

11. In "The Red-headed League," Holmes tells Watson, "My life is spent in one long effort to escape from the commonplaces of existence." In an essay, explain how Holmes, as the protagonist of the story, does not lead a "commonplace," or ordinary, life. Also, explain why Holmes has appealed to millions of readers. Use at least two examples from the text to support your main ideas.

12. Fictional detectives often become famous because they have trademarks that stand out in the minds of readers and make them appealing. Such trademarks can be unusual abilities, traits, habits, or interests. Write an essay identifying at least two trademarks that Sir Arthur Conan Doyle gives Sherlock Holmes in "The Red-headed League." Explain how each of these trademarks makes Holmes a vivid and memorable character.

13. What qualities of personality and character make Sherlock Holmes the successful detective he is in "The Red-headed League"? What would it take in an antagonist to defeat him? Write an essay in which you describe Sherlock Holmes and discuss the qualities a criminal would need to get the better of him.

14. **Thinking About the Big Question: Do heroes have responsibilities?** As the protagonist who solves the mystery and thwarts a criminal plot in "The Red-headed League," Sherlock Holmes is portrayed as a hero. Is he also characterized as a person who sees himself as responsible for contributing to society's welfare? In an essay, discuss your view of Holmes as a character within the society of his time and place. Support your main ideas with specific references to the story.

Oral Response

15. Go back to question 2, 5, 7, or to the question that your teacher assigns you. Take a few minutes to expand your answer and prepare an oral response. Find additional details in "The Red-headed League" that support your points. If necessary, make notes to guide your oral response.

Unit 6 Resources: Themes in Literature
124

"The Red-headed League" by Sir Arthur Conan Doyle
Selection Test A

Critical Reading *Identify the letter of the choice that best answers the question.*

_____ 1. Where does "The Red-headed League" take place?
    A. New York City
    B. London
    C. Paris
    D. Pennsylvania

_____ 2. Which of the following correctly describes the *protagonist* in a literary work?
    A. the author's choice of language
    B. the main character
    C. the work's narrator
    D. the most colorful character

_____ 3. In "The Red-headed League," which of these characters turns out to be John Clay?
    A. Jabez Wilson
    B. Dr. Watson
    C. Vincent Spaulding
    D. Sherlock Holmes

_____ 4. In "The Red-headed League," why was the League ended?
    A. Membership declined to very low levels.
    B. The League had financial problems.
    C. William Morris escaped with the League's money.
    D. The bank robbers had completed their tunnel.

_____ 5. To better understand different characters in a story, which of the following is MOST helpful for a reader to do?
    A. restate the things they say to themselves
    B. compare them to characters in real life
    C. imagine what they would be like if they were younger
    D. compare and contrast their actions and personalities

_____ 6. In "The Red-headed League," why does Dr. Watson like working with Sherlock Holmes?
    A. He wants to become a detective.
    B. He is retired and has little else to do.
    C. Holmes's unusual cases interest him.
    D. He shares Holmes's love of music.

_____ 7. In "The Red-headed League," who is the antagonist?

A. Mr. Merryweather

B. Jabez Wilson

C. John Clay

D. Peter Jones

_____ 8. Why does Holmes put special emphasis on the knees of the trousers worn by the pawnbroker's assistant?

A. He wishes to draw attention to the assistant's low wages.

B. He wants to emphasize how ordinary the assistant's clothes are.

C. He suspects that the assistant has been on his knees digging a tunnel.

D. He is afraid to look the assistant directly in the face.

_____ 9. Why is Wilson interested in becoming a member of the League in "The Red-headed League"?

A. Members of the League might become customers of his shop.

B. Membership will bring Wilson prestige and social position.

C. Business is slow, and Wilson can use the extra money.

D. Wilson is lazy and wants an easy job with a high salary.

_____ 10. How does Holmes solve the mystery in "The Red-headed League"?

A. carefully and scientifically

B. playfully

C. cheerlessly

D. eagerly and enthusiastically

_____ 11. Suspense is the reader's feeling of tension or uncertainty about how events in a story will turn out. Which of the following details increases suspense in "The Red-headed League"?

A. The climax of the story occurs on a Saturday.

B. Holmes asks Watson to bring along his army revolver.

C. Mr. Merryweather joins the group traveling to the Square.

D. John Clay is a young man without much experience.

_____ 12. Which identifies the protagonist vs. the antagonist in "The Red-headed League"?

A. Peter Jones against John Clay

B. Sherlock Holmes against John Clay

C. Mr. Merryweather against John Clay

D. Sherlock Holmes against Jabez Wilson

Vocabulary and Grammar

___ 13. If you consider a situation *vexing*, how are you likely to feel?
  A. amused
  B. annoyed
  C. grateful
  D. impressed

___ 14. Which of the following is the best synonym for *formidable*?
  A. interesting
  B. careful
  C. small
  D. awe-inspiring

___ 15. Where in the following sentence should you place a comma?
  After several rejections from publishers Conan Doyle sold *A Study in Scarlet* in 1887.
  A. after *rejections*
  B. after *After*
  C. after *sold*
  D. after *publishers*

Essay

16. In "The Red-headed League," Holmes tells Watson, "My life is spent in one long effort to escape from the commonplace of existence." In an essay, explain how Holmes, as the protagonist of the story, does not lead a "commonplace," or ordinary, life. Also, explain why he has appealed to millions of readers. Use at least two examples from the text to support your main ideas.

17. Because Watson narrates "The Red-headed League," the audience acquires a unique insight into how Watson sees himself. In an essay, describe Watson as he presents himself to the reader. Use at least two examples from the text for support.

18. **Thinking About the Big Question: Do heroes have responsibilities?** As the protagonist who solves the mystery and thwarts a criminal plot in "The Red-headed League," Sherlock Holmes is a hero. Does Sherlock Holmes take on the responsibility of solving the mystery to make society better and safer? Or does Sherlock Holmes take on the responsibility of solving the mystery to make himself more important? In an essay, tell why you think Holmes takes on responsibility. Support your main ideas with specific references to the story.

Unit 6 Resources: Themes in Literature
127

"The Red-headed League" by Sir Arthur Conan Doyle
Selection Test B

Critical Reading *Identify the letter of the choice that best completes the statement or answers the question.*

____ 1. What is the detective's purpose in "The Red-headed League"?
  A. He wants to improve his knowledge of criminal behavior.
  B. He wants to impress friends and colleagues.
  C. He wants to restore a pawnbroker's confidence.
  D. He wants to uncover a plan for a bank robbery.

____ 2. Which is a key detail in Holmes's solution of the case in "The Red-headed League"?
  A. the observation that Jabez Wilson belonged to the Freemasons
  B. the group's walk around the area of Saxe-Coburg Square
  C. the invitation to the police agent from Scotland Yard
  D. the description of the shopkeeper's arrival at the League's offices

____ 3. Why does Watson join Holmes in his work in "The Red-headed League"?
  A. He is learning to be a detective.
  B. He is writing a book about Holmes.
  C. He is fascinated by remarkable events.
  D. He is bored with his free time.

____ 4. Who is the protagonist in "The Red-headed League"?
  A. Sherlock Holmes
  B. Dr. Watson
  C. John Clay
  D. Jabez Wilson

____ 5. What is the greatest contrast between Holmes and Watson in "The Red-headed League"?
  A. their powers of observation
  B. their professional responsibilities
  C. their appreciation of music
  D. their interest in unusual events

____ 6. What is Holmes's attitude toward John Clay in "The Red-headed League"?
  A. He mocks Clay's intelligence.
  B. He is angry about Clay's deceptions.
  C. He respects Clay's abilities.
  D. He is jealous of Clay's royal blood.

____ 7. Which of the following best describes Jabez Wilson?
  A. sneaky
  B. intelligent
  C. unimaginative
  D. clownish

____ 8. How would you classify Holmes and Clay?
A. two antagonists
B. two protagonists
C. antagonist and protagonist
D. protagonist and antagonist

____ 9. In "The Red-headed League," how would you compare the abilities of Scotland Yard agent Jones with those of Sherlock Holmes?
A. Jones and Holmes have similar abilities.
B. Jones is much less able than Holmes.
C. Jones has greater abilities than Holmes.
D. Jones and Holmes are impossible to compare.

____ 10. In "The Red-headed League," what is suspicious about the way Wilson manages to get an interview for the position at the Red-headed League?
A. He is one of the few redheads who answered the advertisement.
B. He almost gives up in despair at not being interviewed.
C. There is nothing in the office but two wooden chairs and a table.
D. Spaulding pushes and pulls Wilson through the crowd.

____ 11. From details both at the beginning and at the end of "The Red-headed League," it seems as if Holmes considers which of the following his chief enemy in life?
A. badly prepared food
B. Scotland Yard
C. feelings of boredom
D. badly played music

Vocabulary and Grammar

____ 12. Which of the following is the best synonym for *introspective*?
A. mild
B. thoughtful
C. honest
D. decent

____ 13. Which of the following is most nearly OPPOSITE in meaning to *formidable*?
A. shapely
B. practical
C. unimpressive
D. reckless

____ 14. In which of the following sentences is the comma usage incorrect?
A. After the case was solved, Holmes and Watson were pleased.
B. To solve a mystery, you need to be patient, observant, and thoughtful.
C. Holmes said, "This gentleman has been my helper in many cases."
D. Wilson, called upon Holmes and told his tale to the two gentlemen.

Essay

15. Fictional detectives often become famous because they have a few trademarks that stand out in the minds of readers and make them appealing. Such trademarks can be unusual abilities, traits, habits, or interests. Write an essay identifying at least two trademarks that Conan Doyle gives Sherlock Holmes in "The Red-headed League." Explain how each of these trademarks makes Holmes a vivid and memorable character.

16. What qualities of personality and character make Sherlock Holmes the successful detective he is in "The Red-headed League"? What would it take in an antagonist to defeat him? Write an essay in which you describe Sherlock Holmes, and discuss the qualities a criminal would need to have to get the better of him.

17. **Thinking About the Big Question: Do heroes have responsibilities?** As the protagonist who solves the mystery and thwarts a criminal plot in "The Red-headed League," Sherlock Holmes is portrayed as a hero. Is he also characterized as a person who sees himself as responsible for society's welfare? In an essay, discuss your view of Holmes as a character within the society of his time and place. Support your main ideas with specific references to the story.

Vocabulary Warm-up Word Lists

Study these words from "There Is a Longing" by Chief Dan George. Then, apply your knowledge to the activities that follow.

Word List A

demanding [di MAN ding] *adj.* requiring great time, skill, and attention
   A United States president has one of the most <u>demanding</u> jobs in the world.

grasp [GRASP] *v.* to take and hold something firmly
   <u>Grasp</u> the wheel and steer carefully when you are driving a car.

longing [LAHNG ing] *n.* strong feeling of wanting something
   After six weeks at camp, many kids had a <u>longing</u> to be home.

purpose [PER puhs] *n.* what a process or an activity is meant to achieve
   The <u>purpose</u> of our raffle is to raise money for the class trip.

segment [SEG muhnt] *n.* section or part of something
   Most of the town wants a new school, but one <u>segment</u> is against it.

separation [sep uh RAY shuhn] *n.* the act of separating or state of being separated
   The <u>separation</u> of white light into different colors creates a rainbow.

survival [suhr VY vuhl] *n.* state of staying alive
   <u>Survival</u> in the desert depends on having enough water to drink.

wrestle [RES uhl] *v.* to try to deal with a difficult problem or emotion
   Many students <u>wrestle</u> with the question of which college to attend.

Word List B

emerge [i MERJ] *v.* to come out of a situation or an experience after a difficult time
   I hope to <u>emerge</u> from this crisis as a stronger person.

endurance [en DOOR uhns] *n.* ability to withstand hardship and continue on
   He had great <u>endurance</u> to weather a blizzard alone on a mountain.

instruments [IN struh muhnts] *n.* key tools, both objects and ideas, in doing something
   For artists, paints and brushes are the <u>instruments</u> of creation.

olden [OLD uhn] *adj.* of a time long ago; very old
   People in <u>olden</u> times wrote letters to communicate with others.

rightly [RYT lee] *adv.* correctly or for a good reason
   She is upset and <u>rightly</u> so because her friend broke a promise.

secure [see KYOOR] *v.* to get or achieve something important
   To <u>secure</u> a spot in the finals, our team must win the next game.

society [suh SY i tee] *n.* a group of people that shares laws and customs
   A diverse <u>society</u> welcomes new members from all over the world.

surroundings [suh ROWN dingz] *n.* a place and all the things around it
   He loves the country's quiet <u>surroundings</u> and will not leave.

"There Is a Longing" by Chief Dan George
Vocabulary Warm-up Exercises

Exercise A *Fill in each blank in the paragraph with an appropriate word from Word List A. Use each word only once.*

Now and then we hear of someone who fights for [1] _____ for days after an accident or a disaster before being rescued. Such a [2] _____ ordeal, requiring so much effort, is the plot of many books and movies. It has the dramatic qualities that appeal to a huge [3] _____ of the population, or at least the part that likes adventure stories. We can understand the characters' feelings and their powerful [4] _____ to survive. Often, they [5] _____ with terrifying problems. If they have companions who are lost, they struggle with the pain of [6] _____. The ending is usually heart-pounding, as they [7] _____ their rescuer's hand. Such stories serve the [8] _____, and if done well, achieve the goal of celebrating the human spirit.

Exercise B *Answer the questions with complete explanations.*

Example: What are some <u>instruments</u> of learning in school?
<u>Instruments</u> of learning are tools that help students learn, such as books, maps, and computers.

1. If you were unhappy with your <u>surroundings</u>, what might you do?
   _____

2. To <u>secure</u> a better grade in a subject, what should you do?
   _____

3. Would a person who lacks <u>endurance</u> do well running a 26-mile marathon?
   _____

4. Would a <u>society</u> from <u>olden</u> days understand computers?
   _____

5. How can friends help you <u>emerge</u> from a difficult situation?
   _____

6. Can a team be <u>rightly</u> judged based only on its number of wins?
   _____

Name _____ Date _____

Read the following passage. Pay special attention to the underlined words. Then, read it again, and complete the activities. Use a separate sheet of paper for your written answers.

In American history, there are familiar Native Americans chiefs like Red Cloud and princesses like Pocahontas. There are also distinguished Native Americans who are not widely known. They had to <u>wrestle</u> with problems like prejudice and often struggled to get an education. Their success stories are proof that in any <u>segment</u> of people, there is always a group of individuals who have the zeal and talents to excel.

Ely Parker, Do-ne-ho-ga-wa in his native Seneca language, is one example. Parker was born in New York State in 1828. His father was a chief of the Seneca tribe. Before Parker was born, his mother had a dream. She saw her son with white men, but she knew that he had not experienced a <u>separation</u> from his Native American roots or a break with his heritage. Her son would have a great <u>purpose</u> in life and achieve many goals.

As a child, Parker struggled to learn. However, he was very determined. With effort, he was able to take hold and <u>grasp</u> both the actual tools and abstract ideas of learning. Later, in his <u>longing</u> for more education, he studied law. However, his strong desire to be a lawyer was not fulfilled because he was not allowed to take the exam to practice law.

That did not stop Parker. He moved on to a <u>demanding</u> course in engineering. Parker's skills and attention to schoolwork led to success. In 1857, he traveled to Galena, Illinois, on a construction project. There, he met Ulysses S. Grant and they became friends. During the Civil War, Parker served on Grant's staff. In 1865, he applied his writing skills and beautiful penmanship to draft the terms of surrender given to Confederate general Robert E. Lee.

When Grant became president in 1869, he made Parker the Commissioner on Indian Affairs. Parker was the first Native American in that position. Although the <u>survival</u> of the great western tribes was already doomed, his efforts to improve relations between the United States government and the tribes undoubtedly saved some lives. The predictions of his mother all came true in Parker's remarkable life.

1. Circle a word that is a clue to the meaning of <u>wrestle</u>. Underline two issues that Parker had to **wrestle** with in his life.

2. Circle a word clue for <u>segment</u>. Underline what one **segment** of people can usually be counted on to demonstrate.

3. Circle the word clue for <u>separation</u>. Give a synonym for **separation**.

4. Underline the phrase that is a clue to <u>purpose</u>. Give a synonym for **purpose**.

5. Circle words that are clues to the meaning of <u>grasp</u>. Explain what Parker was able to **grasp** in school.

6. Circle words that explain the meaning of <u>longing</u>. Underline what got in the way of Parker's **longing** to be a lawyer.

7. Underline two clue words for <u>demanding</u>. Explain how those words relate to the meaning of **demanding**.

8. Circle a word that signals an opposite end to <u>survival</u>. Underline words that are clues to the meaning of **survival**.

"There Is a Longing" by Chief Dan George
Reading Warm-up B

Read the following passage. Pay special attention to the underlined words. Then, read it again, and complete the activities. Use a separate sheet of paper for your written answers.

When Chief Dan George appeared in the movie *Little Big Man* in 1970, he portrayed a Native American. That might seem <u>rightly</u> to be the correct choice. However, for a long time in movies, most Native American roles were taken by white actors. Films also presented Native Americans in a narrow way. They were always placed in their natural <u>surroundings</u> on the Great Plains or in the Southwest. However, what viewers saw was where the people of the proud tribes lived, not how they lived. Each group of Native American peoples, such as the Sioux and the Navajo, had a rich and complex <u>society</u>. Yet, in the movies, family life and cultural traditions were seldom shown.

In the moviemakers' defense, the common view of Native Americans from <u>olden</u> days was short on understanding. In the 1800s, inexpensive "dime novels" were filled with exaggerated tales of life in the West. The frontiersman Buffalo Bill Cody and his Wild West Show toured America and Europe with Native American performers. To <u>secure</u> large audiences, the aim of any show, Cody's extravaganza included a crowd-pleasing highlight. There was always a staged "Indian attack."

However, over time, different images began to <u>emerge</u>. Native American performers came out of the experience of working in entertainment with the determination to improve the portrayal of their people. One example is Jay Silverheels. He played the native character Tonto in the popular 1950s series "The Lone Ranger." Silverheels was a Mohawk from Canada who formed the Indian Actors Workshop. It encouraged Native American performers and pushed for more accurate roles. It was the tools and <u>instruments</u> of the acting craft, such as strong training that created powerful performances, that helped audiences enjoy seeing Native Americans onscreen.

The <u>endurance</u> of actors like Silverheels and George paid off. Their ability to weather the hardships of earlier times produced breakthroughs in film. Today, movies show a deeper view of Native American life and history.

1. Circle the word clue for <u>rightly</u>. Give a synonym for *rightly*.

2. Circle a word that describes a type of <u>surroundings</u> and underline two places with different *surroundings*. Underline a phrase that helps explain the meaning of *surroundings*.

3. Underline features that are part of a <u>society</u>. Circle a word that explains who makes up a *society*.

4. Underline a phrase that is a clue to the meaning of <u>olden</u>. Give an antonym for *olden*.

5. Underline one way Cody managed to <u>secure</u> a large audience. Describe an aim you hope to *secure* in life.

6. Circle the phrase with a clue to the meaning of <u>emerge</u>. Explain what helped a different portrayal of Native Americans to *emerge*.

7. Circle the word clue for <u>instruments</u>. Underline an example of the *instruments* of acting.

8. Underline the phrase with a clue to the meaning of <u>endurance</u>. Give a synonym for *endurance*.

"There Is a Longing" by Chief Dan George
Writing About the Big Question

Do heroes have responsibilities?

Big Question Vocabulary

character	choices	hero	honesty	identify
imitate	intentions	involvement	justice	morality
obligation	responsibility	serve	standard	wisdom

A. *Use one or more words from the list above to complete each sentence.*

1. Our guidance counselor, Mr. Palumbo, helps students make _____ about their college applications.

2. Mayor Selfridge is highly respected for her _____ and her sense of fair play.

3. Because the Internet research returned hundreds of Web sites, it was hard to _____ which sites would be most helpful.

4. We admire the Penningtons because of their _____ in raising money for charitable causes.

5. In a democracy, every citizen has a(n) _____ to vote in elections.

B. *Follow the directions in responding to each of the items below.*

1. List the top two personality traits that a **hero** should have.

   _____

   _____

2. Write two sentences to explain your choice of these two traits. Use at least two of the Big Question vocabulary words.

   _____

   _____

C. *Complete the sentences below. Then, write a short paragraph in which you connect the sentences to the Big Question.*

All heroes do not have to _____. A leader can be a true hero when

_____

_____

_____

_____

_____

Name _____ Date _____

"There Is a Longing" by Chief Dan George
Literary Analysis: Author's Philosophical Assumptions

An author's **purpose,** or goal, is shaped by his or her **philosophical assumptions,** or basic beliefs. These philosophical assumptions may be political, moral, or ethical beliefs. They may be assumptions about human nature. The author may use basic beliefs as support for an argument. The response of the **audience,** or readers, to the author's work will depend on whether the audience shares the author's beliefs.

To read with understanding, find the basic beliefs and assumptions in the author's work. Decide whether you accept them and whether others would be likely to accept them. Then, evaluate whether these assumptions support the author's purpose.

DIRECTIONS: *Consider the philosophical assumption, or basic belief, underlying each of the following passages from "There Is a Longing." Then, write a brief note on the chart to identify and comment on the philosophical assumption.*

Passage	Philosophical Assumption
1. There is a longing in the heart of my people to reach out and grasp that which is needed for our survival.	
2. But they will emerge with their hand held forward, not to receive welfare, but to grasp the place in society that is rightly ours.	
3. Oh, Great Spirit! Give me back the courage of the olden Chiefs. Let me wrestle with my surroundings. Let me once again, live in harmony with my environment.	
4. Like the thunderbird of old, I shall rise again out of the sea; I shall grab the instruments of the white man's success—his education, his skills.	
5. I shall see our young braves and our chiefs sitting in the houses of law and government, ruling and being ruled by the knowledge and freedoms of our great land.	

"There Is a Longing" by Chief Dan George

Reading: Recognize Compare-and-Contrast Organization

Comparing and contrasting means recognizing similarities and differences. In persuasive writing, authors often compare and contrast one point of view with another. As you read, use **self-monitoring** techniques like the ones shown to make sure you understand the comparisons.

- Find the things or ideas being compared.
- Restate the similarities and differences in your own words.
- Explain the significance of the similarities and differences.

If you cannot find, restate, or explain the author's points, reread words or phrases that were unclear, and make sure you understand them.

DIRECTIONS: *Answer the following questions to self-monitor your reading of "There Is a Longing."*

1. According to Chief Dan George, how would the "new warriors" contrast with those of "olden days"?

   _____

   _____

   _____

2. Once the "new warriors" accepted and mastered the challenge, how would Native American society of the future contrast with the conditions that existed in Chief Dan George's time?

   _____

   _____

   _____

3. How does Chief Dan George say that he differed from past chiefs?

   _____

   _____

4. In what ways does the chief hope that he might be like past chiefs?

   _____

   _____

"There Is a Longing" by Chief Dan George
Vocabulary Builder

Word List

determination   emerge   endurance   humbly   longing   segment

A. DIRECTIONS: *In each of the following items, think about the meaning of the underlined word and then answer the question.*

1. Would running 26 miles require <u>endurance</u>? Why or why not?

_____

2. If you faced a challenge or task with <u>determination</u>, would your mind be made up to master or complete it? Explain.

_____

3. If you were accepting an award <u>humbly</u>, would you make a long speech describing your achievement? Why or why not?

_____

4. Would a <u>longing</u> for your homeland be a pleasant feeling? Why or why not?

_____

5. If a <u>segment</u> of the population wanted free college tuition, would everyone be in agreement? Explain.

_____

B. DIRECTIONS: *The Latin root -merg- means "dip" or "plunge." Use the context of each sentence to correct the sentence so that it makes sense. Be careful not to change the word in italics.*

1. Kevin *emerged* from the shower covered in dust and filth.

_____

_____

2. The submarine was easily detectable as it was *submerged* in deep waters.

_____

_____

3. Celia was so *immersed* in her reading that she turned on the television for some distraction.

_____

_____

"There Is a Longing" by Chief Dan George
Enrichment: Communications

Sequoyah

Besides Chief Dan George, another Native American who believed that education and skills were the key to success was Sequoyah (ca. 1760–1843), a Cherokee who grew up in Tennessee. When Sequoyah was young, all Native American languages were spoken rather than written. Believing that the power of white people was closely linked to literacy, Sequoyah decided to invent a writing system for the Cherokee language.

After years of experimentation with pictographs and symbols that had been used in English, ancient Greek, and Hebrew, Sequoyah created a *syllabary,* or a system of characters that stood for syllabic sounds. Because his system was simple and easily learned, within a very short time Cherokees throughout the United States were teaching it and starting to publish books and periodicals in their own language.

DIRECTIONS: *Use Internet or library resources to research additional facts about Sequoyah and his achievements. Record your findings in the space provided. Then, write a sentence or two about the ideas Sequoyah and Chief Dan George might exchange if they had a chance to meet. What would be their likely areas of agreement? Of disagreement?*

_____

_____

_____

_____

_____

_____

_____

_____

Name _____ Date _____

"There Is a Longing" by Chief Dan George
Open-Book Test

Short Answer *Write your responses to the questions in this section on the lines provided.*

1. In the opening lines of "There Is a Longing," why do you think Chief Dan George repeats the words "There is a longing"?

   _____

   _____

2. When Chief Dan George describes the new warriors in "There Is a Longing," what contrast does he draw between their training and the training of warriors in the olden days?

   _____

   _____

3. According to Chief Dan George in "There Is a Longing," why will the "new warriors" of his people require endurance? Base your answer on the meaning of *endurance*.

   _____

   _____

4. What philosophical assumption does Chief Dan George make in "There Is a Longing" about the only weapon left to him?

   _____

   _____

5. When Chief Dan George calls upon the Great Spirit in "There Is a Longing," he makes a comparison of himself and chiefs of the past. What does he say that past chiefs had that he does not have?

   _____

6. Read the following excerpt from "There Is a Longing":

   > Like / the thunderbird of old, I shall rise again / out of the sea . . .

   To what does the speaker compare himself? What point does this comparison make?

   _____

   _____

   _____

7. In "There Is a Longing," Chief Dan George says he will use the tools of the white man's success. What are these tools? Will they be useful?

   _____

   _____

   _____

8. What does Chief Dan George's prayer to the Great Spirit at the midpoint of "There Is a Longing" suggest about the chief's philosophical assumptions?

   _____

   _____

9. The tone, or the author's attitude toward his subject, in "There Is a Longing" could be described as a yearning or desire. Cite details from Chief Dan George's speech that support this statement.

   _____

   _____

   _____

10. What do you think is Chief Dan George's purpose, or goal, for writing the speech "There Is a Longing"? Whom is he trying to inspire?

    _____

    _____

Essay

Write an extended response to the question of your choice or to the question or questions that your teacher assigns you.

11. Chief Dan George's basic message in "There Is a Longing" is the need for training "new warriors." How do his philosophical assumptions tie in with this message? In an essay, discuss the chief's overall message. Also comment on his basic beliefs. Give an example from the selection to support your response. Use the word web to help identify qualities that young Native Americans need for success.

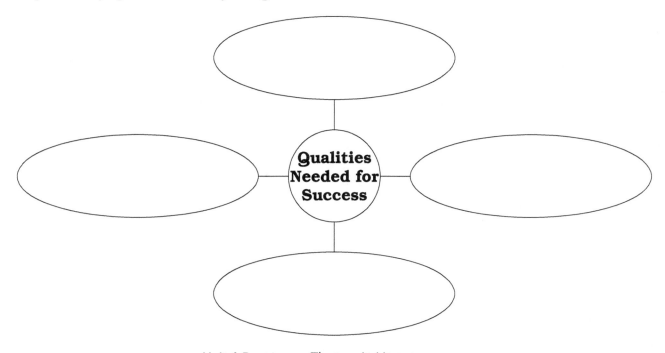

12. How does Chief Dan George compare himself with the younger generation in "There Is a Longing"? In an essay, discuss this topic, using words, phrases, and quotations from the selection to support your opinion.

13. In "There Is a Longing," Chief Dan George addresses both his own people and the people of the majority white culture. What are Chief Dan George's major philosophical assumptions in the speech? In an essay, identify these assumptions, and then comment on how fully you think they are shared by the chief's audience.

14. **Thinking About the Big Question: Do heroes have responsibilities?** In "There Is a Longing," how does Chief Dan George show himself to be a responsible leader? What responsibilities does the chief believe must be undertaken by the youth of his people if they are to succeed in the world? Discuss your views on these topics in a brief essay.

15. Go back to question 4, 5, 6, or to the question your teacher assigns you. Take a few minutes to expand your answer and prepare an oral response. Find additional details in "There Is a Longing" that support your points. If necessary, make notes to guide your oral response.

"There Is a Longing" by Chief Dan George
Selection Test A

Critical Reading *Identify the letter of the choice that best answers the question.*

____ 1. Which of the following best describes the form of "There Is a Longing"?
   A. short story
   B. persuasive speech
   C. myth
   D. rhyming poem

____ 2. What is the basic subject of "There Is a Longing"?
   A. past injustices that were done to young Native Americans
   B. the grip of traditional stories on young Native Americans
   C. the need for young Native Americans to acquire education
   D. the need for new laws that will benefit young Native Americans

____ 3. What are a writer's "philosophical assumptions"?
   A. his or her choice of quotations
   B. his or her use of research tools
   C. his or her basic beliefs
   D. his or her writing style

____ 4. When Chief Dan George compares himself to other chiefs in the past, what point does he make?
   A. Unlike past chiefs, he must make war only with speech.
   B. Like other chiefs, he is a powerful person.
   C. Unlike other chiefs, he has led his nation for a short time.
   D. Like other chiefs, he is concerned for the young.

____ 5. According to Chief Dan George, what qualities will the training of the "new warriors" require?
   A. intelligence and compassion   C. determination and endurance
   B. physical strength and ability   D. generosity and courtesy

____ 6. According to "There Is a Longing," with which of the following assumptions would Chief Dan George be *least* likely to agree?
   A. Education and skills are important for success in life.
   B. Hard work is a worthwhile value for all people.
   C. Traditional ways must be upheld at all costs.
   D. Self-improvement is both possible and necessary.

Unit 6 Resources: Themes in Literature
143

___ 7. At one point in "There Is a Longing," Chief Dan George compares himself to the thunderbird. In this context, which of the following are the most important qualities of the thunderbird?

A. its many-colored feathers

B. the loud noise it produces

C. its struggle and victory

D. its link to the Great Spirit

___ 8. The tone of a piece of writing is the general attitude the writer takes toward the subject, the characters, or the audience. Which of the following best describes the tone of "There Is a Longing"?

A. amusing   C. sad

B. inspiring   D. relaxed

Vocabulary and Grammar

___ 9. If you handle a difficult task with *endurance*, which of the following would best describe your behavior?

A. seeking the cooperation of others

B. giving up on the challenge

C. withstanding necessary hardships

D. gradually giving in to the strain

___ 10. In which of the following sentences is a semicolon correctly used?

A. I have a bicycle; skates; and a snowboard.

B. John said to Sasha; "Let's go on a bicycle trip."

C. John helped Sasha; another rider; put air in her bicycle's tires.

D. I have a bicycle; I'll be riding it later today.

Essay

11. What is Chief Dan George's basic theme in "There Is a Longing"? How do his philosophical assumptions relate to this theme? In an essay, discuss the chief's overall message. Also, comment on his basic beliefs, and explain how these beliefs relate to his message. Use an example from "There Is a Longing" to support your response.

12. **Thinking About the Big Question: Do heroes have responsibilities?** In "There Is a Longing," Chief Dan George shows himself to be a responsible leader. He leads his people with words rather than with weapons of war. What responsibilities does the chief believe the youth of his people must take on if they are to succeed in the world? Answer this question in a brief essay.

"There Is a Longing" by Chief Dan George
Selection Test B

Critical Reading *Identify the letter of the choice that best completes the statement or answers the question.*

____ 1. In the opening lines of "There Is a Longing," why do you think Chief Dan George repeats these words: "There is a longing"?
A. to repeat himself so his audience will be sure to understand him
B. to emphasize the distance between the dream of survival and the reality
C. to emphasize the urgency of the Native American dream
D. to show that Native Americans are just like everyone else in America

____ 2. Based on "There Is a Longing," which is the best description of Chief Dan George's description of new Native American "warriors"?
A. The new warriors will solve the nation's environmental problems.
B. The new warriors will use the weapons of their forefathers.
C. The new warriors will be lawyers and politicians.
D. The new warriors will have skills that give them purpose.

____ 3. Which of the following is an example of an author's philosophical assumptions?
A. his or her choice of a speech's length
B. his or her beliefs about right and wrong
C. his or her style of writing
D. his or her payment for an essay

____ 4. Which of the following best expresses the most important comparison and contrast that Chief Dan George draws in "There Is a Longing"?
A. the differences among past chiefs who were warriors
B. the contrast between the old way and the new way of life
C. the contrast between older warriors and younger ones
D. a comparison between the chief and other elders

____ 5. In "There Is a Longing," how does Chief Dan George say he will fight his people's war?
A. with careful strategy
B. with technology
C. with tongue and speech
D. with traditional weapons

____ 6. Read the following excerpt from "There Is a Longing":
Like / the thunderbird of old, I shall rise again / out of the sea. . . .
Why do you think the speaker compares himself to a thunderbird?
A. He wants to emphasize the power, courage, and strength of his great voice.
B. He wants to show that Native Americans need assistance from powerful people.
C. He wants to compare the struggle of Native Americans to that of a thunderbird.
D. He wants to remind his audience that they must not allow traditions to disappear.

_____ 7. According to Chief Dan George, what are the "instruments of the white man's success"?
   A. education and skills
   B. knowledge of the law
   C. knowledge of medicine
   D. ability to win elections

_____ 8. Which of the following best states Chief Dan George's purpose for writing "There Is a Longing"?
   A. He wants to express the needs and desires of Native Americans.
   B. He tries to complain about the treatment of Native Americans.
   C. He hopes to be elected to a powerful government office.
   D. He needs a grant of money to send Native Americans to school.

Vocabulary and Grammar

_____ 9. Which of the following is the best synonym for *determination*?
   A. regret
   B. argument
   C. will power
   D. evaluation

_____ 10. In which of the following sentences is the colon used incorrectly?
   A. Please bring the following: fruit, vegetables, and cheese.
   B. I have three best friends: Josh, Mike, and Steven.
   C. Find Jenna and Mikaela then look: for Suzanne and Pat.
   D. You will need the following ingredients: flour, butter, and sugar.

Essay

11. According to "There Is a Longing," how does Chief Dan George picture himself and the younger generation? Write an essay in which you summarize and evaluate the chief's portrait of the dreams and needs of Native Americans. Be sure to support your discussion with examples from the text.

12. In "There Is a Longing," Chief Dan George addresses both his own people and the people of the majority white culture. What are Chief Dan George's major philosophical assumptions in the speech? In an essay, identify these assumptions, and then comment on how fully you think they are shared by Chief Dan George's audience.

13. **Thinking About the Big Question: Do heroes have responsibilities?** In "There Is a Longing," how does Chief Dan George show himself to be a responsible leader? What responsibilities does the chief believe must be undertaken by the youth of his people if they are to succeed in the world? Discuss your views on these topics in a brief essay.

Vocabulary Warm-up Word Lists

Study these words from "Glory and Hope." Then, complete the activities that follow.

Word List A

hesitation [hez i TAY shuhn] *n.* a pause before doing something
   His <u>hesitation</u> showed that he was unsure of his opinion.

homeland [HOHM land] *n.* the country where one is born
   He had lived in Egypt for years, but the United States was still his <u>homeland</u>.

international [in ter NASH uh nuhl] *adj.* involving two or more countries
   The United Nations is devoted to <u>international</u> peace.

isolated [EYE suh lay tid] *adj.* being separate from others
   The high fence kept us <u>isolated</u> from our neighbors.

precisely [pree SYS lee] *adv.* exactly
   I will try to explain <u>precisely</u> what I mean.

reign [RAYN] *v.* rule; be the main feature
   When the tyrant is overthrown, the rightful heir to the throne will <u>reign</u>.

tribute [TRIB yoot] *n.* something you do or say that shows respect
   On Veteran's Day, we pay <u>tribute</u> to those who served in the armed forces.

unity [YOO ni tee] *n.* state of being one and working together
   The workers showed their <u>unity</u> by going out on strike together.

Word List B

categories [KAT i gawr eez] *n.* groups of things of the same type
   Animal <u>categories</u> include mammals, birds, fish, and insects.

discrimination [dis kri muh NAY shuhn] *n.* the practice of treating a group of people differently from another in an unfair way
   The law prohibits <u>discrimination</u> against people in wheelchairs.

elevated [EL uh vay tid] *v.* lifted up; raised to a higher level
   Her spirits were <u>elevated</u> when she heard the good news.

exhilaration [eg zil uh RAY shuhn] *n.* feeling of extreme happiness
   Imagine my <u>exhilaration</u> when I received my acceptance letter from college!

fulfilled [fool FILD] *adj.* satisfied with life
   I felt <u>fulfilled</u> when I learned that my essay was going to be published.

gender [JEN der] *n.* the condition of being male or female
   Our club is open to qualified people of either <u>gender</u>.

imprisonment [im PRIZ uhn muhnt] *n.* being locked up in jail
   His <u>imprisonment</u> ended when the governor pardoned him.

triumphed [TRY uhmft] *v.* gained victory or success
   After a tough game, our team finally <u>triumphed</u> over the competition.

"Glory and Hope" by Nelson Mandela
Vocabulary Warm-up Exercises

Exercise A *Fill in each blank in the paragraph with an appropriate word from Word List A. Use each word only once.*

We have gathered here this Memorial Day to honor those who fought bravely to protect our [1] _____. On this day, Americans pay [2] _____ to the men and women who made the ultimate sacrifice for their country. Although we differ on many issues, this is a day of [3] _____ on which we all share the same pride in our fallen heroes. Even in times of [4] _____ peace, we must not forget those who served in times of war. Miles from home and [5] _____ from their families, they served their nation bravely, without questions or [6] _____. It is [7] _____ for that reason that we honor them today. May we someday put an end to war! May peace [8] _____ forever.

Exercise B *Revise each sentence so that the underlined vocabulary word is used in a logical way. Be sure to keep the vocabulary word in your revision.*

Example: Items within each of the <u>categories</u> had no features in common.
Items within each of the <u>categories</u> had several features in common.

1. <u>Discrimination</u> in the workplace based on age is always justified.
   _____

2. The writer was <u>elevated</u> by the announcement that he did not win the book award.
   _____

3. She felt <u>exhilaration</u> when she heard the bad news.
   _____

4. Her proud parents felt <u>fulfilled</u> when Maria dropped out of college.
   _____

5. Before 1920, people of the male <u>gender</u> could not vote in the United States.
   _____

6. His five-year <u>imprisonment</u> was the most enjoyable experience of his life.
   _____

7. They <u>triumphed</u> over the other team by not training as hard or playing as well.
   _____

Name _____ Date _____

"Glory and Hope" by Nelson Mandela
Reading Warm-up A

Read the following passage. Pay special attention to the underlined words. Then, read it again, and complete the activities. Use a separate sheet of paper for your written answers.

Desmond Tutu was born in South Africa in 1931. Like all black people in South Africa at that time, Tutu and his family were harshly treated by the white minority who ruled the country. The government forced blacks and other racial groups to live separately. They were allowed to live and work only in certain restricted and <u>isolated</u> areas, away from the white people. This system of segregation was called *apartheid.*

Tutu wanted to become a doctor, but his family could not afford medical school. Instead, he became a teacher like his father. Tutu wanted people of all races to live together in <u>unity</u>. He wrote to the prime minister to protest apartheid. His letter, however, was ignored. That same year, a law was passed to prevent black children from learning science and math.

Tutu decided that he could serve his people better as a priest than as a teacher. He began studying theology and was eventually ordained as an Anglican priest. In 1975, he was the first black person appointed Dean of St. Mary's Cathedral in Johannesburg. As Secretary-General of the South African Council of Churches, Tutu spoke all over the world. He attracted <u>international</u> attention to the problems in South Africa. As a <u>tribute</u> to his efforts, he was awarded the Nobel Peace Prize in 1984.

The South African government continued to crack down on anyone who opposed its policies. Still, Tutu showed no <u>hesitation</u> in speaking out against apartheid. Finally, after years of struggle, apartheid was abolished in 1991. A free election was held in 1994. The racist National Party would no longer <u>reign</u> in South Africa!

Meanwhile, Archbishop Tutu had gone on to head the Anglican Church in South Africa. He was called upon to help restore social justice to his <u>homeland</u>. As a young man, Tutu had vowed to help make South Africa a place where all people could enjoy equal protection under the law. In the end, that is <u>precisely</u> what he did.

1. Underline the words that help you understand the meaning of <u>isolated</u>. Then, describe an *isolated* area that you know.

2. Circle the word that gives a clue to the meaning of <u>unity</u>. Then, write a sentence using *unity*.

3. Underline the words that tell how Tutu attracted <u>international</u> attention. Why is *international* attention to problems important?

4. Underline the words that tell what the <u>tribute</u> to Tutu was. Explain what a *tribute* is.

5. Underline the words that tell what Tutu showed no <u>hesitation</u> in doing. Tell about a time when you showed *hesitation*.

6. Underline the words that tell who would no longer <u>reign</u> in South Africa. Write a sentence using *reign*.

7. Underline the words that name Tutu's <u>homeland</u>. Can a person have more than one *homeland*? Explain.

8. Underline the words that tell what goal Tutu <u>precisely</u> accomplished. Rewrite the sentence using a synonym for *precisely*.

Name _____ Date _____

"Glory and Hope" by Nelson Mandela
Reading Warm-up B

Read the following passage. Pay special attention to the underlined words. Then, read it again, and complete the activities. Use a separate sheet of paper for your written answers.

South Africa became an independent nation in 1910. At that time, only members of the white minority were allowed to hold positions of power. The openly racist National Party was elected to run the country in 1948. It immediately began a policy of segregation and <u>discrimination</u> called *apartheid,* or "apartness."

The entire population was separated into <u>categories</u> according to race. Each group was assigned a specific area in which its members were allowed to live. All black South Africans were forced to live within those borders. They had no voice in governing their own country. They were sent to inferior schools and were allowed to hold only certain jobs. Although whites made up less than 10 percent of the population, they were given more than 80 percent of the land on which to live.

Even though protests were held around the world, apartheid continued for decades. The African National Congress was a South African organization that spoke out against the injustice of apartheid. Its leader was Nelson Mandela.

In 1962, Mandela was arrested for acts of sabotage and sent to prison for life. His <u>imprisonment</u> helped focus the world's attention on the injustice of apartheid.

After twenty-seven years, Mandela was released. He immediately took up his fight against apartheid once again and felt <u>fulfilled</u> when the system was finally abolished in 1991. In 1993, Mandela and South African president F. W. de Klerk shared the Nobel Peace Prize.

A year later, the first democratic elections were held in South Africa. All adult South Africans, regardless of race or <u>gender</u>, were allowed to participate. Imagine the <u>exhilaration</u> of the native South Africans who voted in a national election for the very first time!

Nelson Mandela easily <u>triumphed</u> over his opponents and was elected president. He was the first black man in the history of South Africa to be <u>elevated</u> to a position of national leadership.

1. Circle the word that identifies one form of <u>discrimination</u>. Explain what **discrimination** means.

2. Circle the word that gives a clue to the meaning of <u>categories</u>. Name some **categories** that you come across each day.

3. Underline the words that describe the length of Mandela's <u>imprisonment</u>. Write a sentence using **imprisonment**.

4. Explain why Mandela felt <u>fulfilled</u> in 1991.

5. Underline the words in the paragraph that tell what all South Africans, regardless of <u>gender</u>, were allowed to do. Tell what **gender** means.

6. Circle the words that tell who felt <u>exhilaration</u>. Tell about something that caused you to feel **exhilaration**.

7. Underline the words that tell what happened to Mandela when he <u>triumphed</u> over his opponents. Describe a time when you **triumphed**.

8. Underline the words that tell what Mandela was <u>elevated</u> to. Explain how Mandela probably felt when he was **elevated** to this.

"**Glory and Hope**" by Nelson Mandela
Writing About the Big Question

 Do heroes have responsibilities?

Big Question Vocabulary

character	choices	hero	honesty	identify
imitate	intentions	involvement	justice	morality
obligation	responsibility	serve	standard	wisdom

A. *Use one or more words from the list above to complete each sentence.*

1. In ancient times, a _____ was often a warrior or a statesman, but today in the United States he or she may just as likely be a sports star or a movie idol.

2. People should not be judged by the color of their skin, said Martin Luther King, Jr., but by the content of their _____.

3. Heroes set a high _____ for all of us, and we would do well to _____ them.

4. If you baby-sit a small child, you have a(n) _____ to look after the child's welfare while you are on duty.

B. *Follow the directions in responding to each of the items below.*

1. List two different times that you read about someone who was admired as a hero and then behaved badly.

_____

_____

2. Write two sentences to explain one of these situations. Use at least two of the Big Question vocabulary words.

_____

_____

C. *Complete the sentences below. Then, write a short paragraph in which you connect the sentences to the Big Question.*

When a leader promises to **serve** his or her nation, he or she must _____.

The leader has an **obligation** to _____.

_____

_____

_____

"Glory and Hope" by Nelson Mandela

Literary Analysis: Author's Philosophical Assumptions

An author's **purpose,** or goal, is shaped by his or her **philosophical assumptions,** or basic beliefs. These philosophical assumptions may be political, moral, or ethical beliefs. They may be assumptions about human nature. The author may use basic beliefs as support for an argument. The response of the **audience,** or readers, to the author's work will depend on whether the audience shares the author's beliefs.

To read with understanding, find the basic beliefs and assumptions in the author's work. Decide whether you accept them and whether others would be likely to accept them. Then, evaluate whether these assumptions support the author's purpose.

DIRECTIONS: *Consider the philosophical assumption, or basic belief, underlying each of the following passages from "Glory and Hope." Then, write a brief note on the chart to identify and comment on the philosophical assumption.*

Passage	Philosophical Assumption
1. Out of an experience of an extraordinary human disaster that lasted too long must be born a society of which all humanity will be proud.	
2. Each time one of us touches the soil of this land, we feel a sense of personal renewal.	

3. The time for the healing of the wounds has come.
   The moment to bridge the chasms that divide us has come.
   The time to build is upon us.	

4. We enter into a covenant that we shall build a society in which all South Africans, both black and white, will be able to walk tall, without any fear in their hearts, assured of their inalienable right to human dignity—a rainbow nation at peace with itself and the world.	
5. Never, never, and never again shall it be that this beautiful land will again experience the oppression of one by another. . . .	

"Glory and Hope" by Nelson Mandela

Reading: Recognize Compare-and-Contrast Organization

Comparing and contrasting means recognizing similarities and differences. In persuasive writing, authors often compare and contrast one point of view with another. As you read, use **self-monitoring** techniques like the ones shown to make sure you understand the comparisons.

- Find the things or ideas being compared.
- Restate the similarities and differences in your own words.
- Explain the significance of the similarities and differences.

If you cannot find, restate, or explain the author's points, reread words or phrases that were unclear and make sure you understand them.

DIRECTIONS: *Answer the following questions to self-monitor your reading of "Glory and Hope."*

1. According to Nelson Mandela, how does the present in South Africa contrast with the past?

   _____

   _____

   _____

2. How does South Africa's international standing now contrast with its position in the past?

   _____

   _____

   _____

3. How does Nelson Mandela's portrait of a future society in South Africa strengthen the contrasts he has drawn between the present and the past?

   _____

   _____

   _____

   _____

Name _____ Date _____

"Glory and Hope" by Nelson Mandela
Vocabulary Builder

Word List

confer   covenant   distinguished   intimately   pernicious   reconciliation

A. DIRECTIONS: *Circle the letter of the best answer to each question.*

1. Which of the following is the best synonym for *confer*?
   A. divide   B. respect   C. give

2. Which of the following most nearly means the OPPOSITE of *pernicious*?
   A. negative   B. harmless   C. courageous

3. If you have made a *covenant* with someone, what did you probably exchange?
   A. information   B. directions   C. solemn promises

B. DIRECTIONS: *For each item, think about the meaning of the underlined word and then answer the question.*

1. Would a <u>covenant</u> typically involve an advertisement or a promise? Explain.
   _____

2. If you regarded a person as <u>pernicious</u>, would you recommend him or her for a job? Explain.
   _____

3. If you <u>confer</u> an award on someone, do you give it or do you take it away?
   _____

4. Would you expect a candidate for mayor to look <u>distinguished</u>? Why or why not?
   _____

5. If you know a novel or a play <u>intimately</u>, have you read it carefully? Explain.
   _____

6. Does <u>reconciliation</u> bring people closer together or drive them apart? Explain.
   _____

C. WORD STUDY: *The Latin root -fer- means to bring or carry. For example, a ferry is a boat that carries passangers. To transfer is to move to another place. Use the context of the sentences and what you know about the Latin root -fer- to explain your answer to each question. Use the italicized vocabulary word in each answer.*

1. If you *defer* your decision on an issue, do you decide now or later?
   _____
   _____

2. When you *refer* to a dictionary, do you use it or ignore it?
   _____
   _____

3. When you make an *inference*, do you draw a conclusion about something?
   _____
   _____

"Glory and Hope" by Nelson Mandela
Enrichment: Using a Map

Africa's 11.7 million square miles account for 20 percent of Earth's land mass, and South Africa, on the southern tip of Africa, with its area of 471,440 square miles, makes up 4 percent of the continent. About 6 percent of Africa's total population resides in South Africa.

Finding Details on a Map

A. DIRECTIONS: *In your school or local library, locate a map of South Africa. Examine the map in order to answer the following questions.*

1. Approximately how wide is South Africa at its widest west-east point?

   _____ miles (_____ kilometers)

2. How far is Cape Town from Johannesburg?

   _____ miles (_____ kilometers)

3. List the countries and physical features (rivers, oceans, and so on) that border South Africa.

   _____

4. Notice South Africa's long coastline. Given its extensive coast, what might you predict about leisure activities and economic activity in South Africa?

   _____

Drawing Conclusions From a Map

B. DIRECTIONS: *In a library, locate an up-to-date atlas. Turn to a physical map of South Africa that shows the elevation levels of different parts of the country. Then, answer these questions and draw conclusions about what you learn from the map.*

Source title: _____

Date of publication: _____ Page number: _____

1. How is the coastline represented on the physical map in your source?

   _____

2. What other significant physical features are shown?

   _____

   _____

3. What three major rivers flow in or on the borders of South Africa?

   _____

4. Think again about South Africa's long coastline. Review the country's inland features. What conclusion can you draw about how goods might be transported from a city in Natal to Cape Town, for example?

   _____

   _____

"There Is a Longing" by Chief Dan George
"Glory and Hope" by Nelson Mandela
Integrated Language Skills: Grammar
Using Colons, Semicolons, and Ellipsis Points Correctly

Use a **colon** in order to introduce a list of items following an independent clause, to introduce a formal quotation, or to follow the salutation in a business letter.

- He bought materials for the salad: lettuce, tomatoes, onions, and radishes.

- Nelson Mandela evokes his fellow South Africans' love for their land in these words: "Each time one of us touches the soil of this land, we feel a sense of personal renewal."

- Dear Sir:

Use a **semicolon** to join independent clauses that are not already joined by a conjunction. Also, use a semicolon to avoid confusion when independent clauses or items in a series already contain commas.

- The government of South Africa finally rejected apartheid; in 1994, the first free elections were held.

- We visited Boston, Philadelphia, and Washington, D.C.; altogether, our tour of the eastern seaboard was a great success.

Ellipsis points (. . .) are punctuation marks that are used to show that something has not been expressed. Usually, ellipsis points indicate one of the following situations:
Words have been left out of a quotation.
A series continues beyond the items mentioned.
Time passes or action occurs in a narrative.

- Nelson Mandela says, "We are moved . . . when the grass turns green and the flowers bloom."

- We thought wistfully about the cats' curiosity, agility, and grace. . . .

- They keep their discontent to themselves . . . but will they do so forever?

A. DIRECTIONS: *Rewrite each sentence on the lines provided, correcting errors in the use of colons, semicolons, and ellipsis points. There is only one error in each sentence.*

1. Julius Caesar described his victory as follows . . . "I came, I saw, I conquered."

   _____

2. Statesmanship is a rare gift, few heads of government in the modern world, in fact, have risen to its challenges.

   _____

   _____

B. WRITING APPLICATION: *On the lines, write a paragraph in which you describe a favorite animal or bird. In your paragraph, use at least one example of each of the following: a colon, a semicolon, and ellipsis points.*

   _____

   _____

   _____

   _____

Name _____ Date _____

"There Is a Longing" by Chief Dan George
"Glory and Hope" by Nelson Mandela

Integrated Language Skills: Support for Writing a Letter

Use the following chart to make prewriting notes for your letter to Nelson Mandela or Chief Dan George about his speech.

Words That Show Your Reactions
_____
_____
Support for Your Reactions
_____
_____
Reason(s) for Writing Your Letter
_____
_____
What People Can Learn From the Message
_____
_____
_____

On a separate page, write a letter using your notes. Make sure that you maintain a respectful tone.

"There Is a Longing" by Chief Dan George
"Glory and Hope" by Nelson Mandela

Integrated Language Skills: Support for Extend Your Learning

Listening and Speaking: "There Is a Longing" by Chief Dan George

Use the following chart to prepare notes for your **panel discussion** on the kind of world you hope future generations will enjoy.

Ideas for Panel Discussion		
Education	**Cultural Identity**	**Equal Rights**

Listening and Speaking: "Glory and Hope" by Nelson Mandela

Use the chart to prepare notes for your panel discussion on the kind of world you hope future generations will enjoy.

Ideas for Panel Discussion		
Equality	**Peace**	**Human Rights**

"Glory and Hope" by Nelson Mandela
Open-Book Test

Short Answer *Write your responses to the questions in this section on the lines provided.*

1. In the beginning of Nelson Mandela's speech "Glory and Hope," he focuses on one of his philosophical assumptions—his love for his country, South Africa. Does Mandela's philosophical assumption refer to his library research, political hopes, basic beliefs, or interpretations of the past?

   _____

   _____

2. Read this excerpt from the beginning of "Glory and Hope."

   Each time one of us touches the soil of this land, we feel a sense of personal renewal.

   What philosophical assumption by the speaker underlies this statement?

   _____

   _____

   _____

3. In the middle of the speech "Glory and Hope," Nelson Mandela pays tribute to South Africa's security forces. What does this suggest about the political and social climate in which the first democratic elections were held?

   _____

   _____

   _____

   _____

4. About two-thirds of the way through "Glory and Hope," Nelson Mandela declares, "We enter into a covenant that we shall build the society in which all South Africans . . ." Reread this sentence, ending with the words "a rainbow nation at peace with itself and the world." What philosophical assumption does the writer use as a basis for his declaration here?

   _____

   _____

5. Why do you think Nelson Mandela uses the word *covenant* in "Glory and Hope" to refer to the kind of society he envisions for South Africa? Base your answer on the meaning of *covenant*.

   _____

   _____

   _____

6. Parallelism is the repetition of grammatical structures in order to express a rhythm and to make words more memorable. Identify one example of parallelism from either the midpoint or the end of "Glory and Hope," and briefly comment on how it contributes to the speech as a whole.

Example of Parallelism

↓

How It Contributes to Speech

7. At the end of "Glory and Hope," Nelson Mandela says South Africa's past oppression made it the "skunk of the world." With what does Nelson Mandela contrast this past?

_____

_____

_____

8. How does Nelson Mandela use comparison and contrast throughout the speech "Glory and Hope"?

_____

_____

_____

9. Consider the title of Nelson Mandela's speech "Glory and Hope." Think about what the speaker is telling his audience. Describe Mandela's purpose in this speech.

_____

_____

_____

10. Imagine that you are in the audience when Nelson Mandela celebrates South Africa's triumph over apartheid in his inaugural speech. What word would you use to describe the speech "Glory and Hope"?

_____

_____

Essay

Write an extended response to the question of your choice or to the question or questions your teacher assigns you.

11. Nelson Mandela combines two strong emotions in the title of his inaugural speech, "Glory and Hope." In an essay, describe ways in which Mandela conveys the meaning of the ideas of glory and hope. Do you believe that this title is an effective reflection of his overall message? Why or why not? Use a few examples from the speech to support your viewpoint.

12. Read the following passage from "Glory and Hope." Then, in an essay, answer the questions that follow.

> We know it well that none of us acting alone can achieve success.
>
> We must therefore act together as a united people, for national reconciliation, for nation building, for the birth of a new world.
>
> Let there be justice for all.
>
> Let there be peace for all.
>
> Let there be work, bread, water and salt for all.

What are Mandela's philosophical assumptions in this passage? How do these assumptions relate to his message of hope? How does Mandela convey his message? Why do you think he closes his speech with this message?

13. In "Glory and Hope," Nelson Mandela uses very different phrases to describe South Africa. He says that in the past, the nation suffered an "extraordinary human disaster" and "the universal base of the pernicious ideology and practice of racism and racial oppression." The new era, however, promises "newborn liberty," "glorious life," and "a common victory for justice, for peace, for human dignity." In an essay, explain the emotions these phrases create for the listener. Describe how you think the audience reacted to the speech.

14. **Thinking About the Big Question: Do heroes have responsibilities?** Nelson Mandela, winner of the Nobel Prize for Peace and first president of a democratic South Africa, has been a hero for his people and the people of the world. In "Glory and Hope," how does Mandela show that political leaders and citizens in a democratic society have responsibilities? What sorts of responsibilities do they share? Discuss these questions in a brief essay.

Oral Response

15. Go back to question 3, 6, 7, or to the question your teacher assigns you. Take a few minutes to expand your answer and prepare an oral response. Find additional details in "Glory and Hope" that support your points. If necessary, make notes to support your oral response.

"Glory and Hope" by Nelson Mandela
Selection Test A

Critical Reading *Identify the letter of the choice that best answers the question.*

_____ 1. Which of the following best describes Nelson Mandela's purpose in "Glory and Hope"?
   A. to compare and contrast glory and hope
   B. to inspire South Africans to make a new beginning
   C. to condemn the supporters of apartheid
   D. to reassure foreign visitors about South Africa

_____ 2. A writer or speaker's "philosophical assumptions" refer to which of the following?
   A. research in a library
   B. political hopes
   C. basic beliefs
   D. interpretations of the past

_____ 3. In "Glory and Hope," why does Nelson Mandela pay tribute to the nation's security forces?
   A. They are exceptionally well-trained.
   B. They helped keep order during the elections.
   C. They protected South Africa's borders from foreigners.
   D. They did not join the supporters of apartheid.

_____ 4. Based on "Glory and Hope," which of the following answers is an example of Nelson Mandela's philosophical assumptions?
   A. the knowledge that people dislike him
   B. the worth of learning about the U.S.
   C. the necessity for revenge in certain cases
   D. the belief in unity and cooperation

_____ 5. Which of the following best expresses the comparison or contrast that Mandela uses in "Glory and Hope"?
   A. It is a comparison between international visitors and South African residents.
   B. It is a contrast between the lives of black and white South Africans.
   C. It is a contrast between the injustices of the past and hopes for the future.
   D. It is a comparison between the South African government and its people.

_____ 6. In "Glory and Hope," to whom does Mandela "dedicate this day"?

    A. to the international visitors listening to his speech

    B. to Second Deputy President F. W. de Clerk

    C. to those who made sacrifices to achieve freedom in South Africa

    D. to supporters who voted for Mandela in the presidential election

_____ 7. Which of the following answers best describes what Nelson Mandela hopes to achieve in "Glory and Hope"?

    A. He hopes to make his audience calm.

    B. He hopes to stir his audience to anger.

    C. He hopes to scold his audience.

    D. He hopes to inspire his audience.

Vocabulary and Grammar

_____ 8. Which of the following results might you expect from someone who is acting in a *pernicious* way?

    A. achievement   **C.** destruction

    B. profit   **D.** gratitude

_____ 9. Which of the following answer choices is the best synonym for *covenant*?

    A. prison   **C.** location

    B. agreement   **D.** speech

_____ 10. Which of the following items contains an error in semicolon usage?

    A. Josh is not here; he left an hour ago.

    B. I have never been to France; it is a dream of mine to go one day.

    C. Note; This letter must be postmarked no later than July 15.

    D. There is a notebook in the drawer; I put it there yesterday.

Essay

11. Nelson Mandela combines two strong emotions in the title of his inaugural speech, "Glory and Hope." In an essay, describe ways in which Mandela conveys the meaning of the ideas of glory and hope. Do you believe that his title is a good reflection of his message? Why or why not? Use a few examples from his speech to support your viewpoint.

12. **Thinking About the Big Question: Do heroes have responsibilities?** Nelson Mandela is a hero for his people and the people of the world. In his speech titled "Glory and Hope," Mandela says that as a political leader he has the responsibility to uphold certain values for his people. In a brief essay, tell what values Mandela says he will emphasize as president of South Africa.

Unit 6 Resources: Themes in Literature
163

"Glory and Hope" by Nelson Mandela
Selection Test B

Critical Reading *Identify the letter of the choice that best completes the statement or answers the question.*

_____ 1. In "Glory and Hope," what does Nelson Mandela refer to as a "pernicious ideology"?
  A. prosperity
  B. elections
  C. racism
  D. business

_____ 2. Read this passage from "Glory and Hope":

   We must therefore act together as a united people, for national reconciliation, for nation building, for the birth of a new world.

   What message does this passage convey?
   A. Success requires united effort on the part of all South Africans.
   B. People will be satisfied with partial success of their goals.
   C. Further revolution may be needed to accomplish success.
   D. My opponents should be warned not to interfere with me.

_____ 3. In "Glory and Hope," what is the "glorious achievement" on which the sun will never set?
  A. Mandela's first election as president
  B. the South African people's move to democracy
  C. the overthrow of Mandela's opponents
  D. the South Africans' triumph over poverty

_____ 4. Which of the following correctly identifies a writer's "philosophical assumptions"?
  A. his or her choice of economic system
  B. his or her basic beliefs
  C. his or her political opinions
  D. his or her similarity to other writers

_____ 5. Which of the following best expresses Nelson Mandela's use of comparison and contrast in "Glory and Hope"?
  A. He compares a national outlook to an international outlook.
  B. He contrasts past oppression with freedom and equality in the future.
  C. He contrasts poverty in the past with the economic strength of today.
  D. He compares past human politeness to the present struggle for respect.

_____ 6. What word best describes the tone of this passage from "Glory and Hope"?

   Let there be justice for all. / Let there be peace for all. / Let there be work, bread, water, and salt for all.

   A. inspirational
   B. repetitive
   C. demanding
   D. relaxed

Vocabulary and Grammar

____ 7. Which of the following is the best synonym for *confer*?
    A. owe   **C.** take away
    B. give   **D.** persuade

____ 8. If two groups or individuals make a *covenant* with each other, what do they agree on?
    A. an opinion   **C.** a contract
    B. a speech   **D.** a surrender

____ 9. Which of the following is an example of incorrect use of a colon?
    A. I have three sisters: Melissa, Erin, and Kristen.
    B. He will be there on the following days: Tuesday, Thursday, and Saturday.
    C. Stuart plays three sports: basketball, soccer, and tennis.
    D. Please buy a basket: and bring some fruit and vegetables.

Essay

10. Read the following passage from "Glory and Hope." Then, in an essay, answer the questions that follow.

> We know it well that none of us acting alone can achieve success.
>
> We must therefore act together as a united people, for national reconciliation, for nation building, for the birth of a new world.
>
> Let there be justice for all.
>
> Let there be peace for all.
>
> Let there be work, bread, water, and salt for all.

What are Mandela's philosophical assumptions in this passage, and how do these assumptions relate to his message of hope? How does Mandela convey his message? Why do you think he closes his speech with this message?

11. In "Glory and Hope," Nelson Mandela uses very different phrases to describe South Africa. He says that in the past, the nation suffered an "extraordinary human disaster" and became "the universal base of the pernicious ideology and practice of racism and racial oppression." The new era, however, promises "newborn liberty," "glorious life," and "a common victory for justice, for peace, for human dignity." In an essay, explain what emotions the phrases create in the listener and what tone the phrases set. Describe how you think the audience most likely reacted to the speech.

12. **Thinking About the Big Question: Do heroes have responsibilities?** Nelson Mandela, winner of the Nobel Prize for Peace and first president of a democratic South Africa, has been a hero for his people and the people of the world. In "Glory and Hope," how does Mandela show that political leaders and citizens in a democratic society have responsibilities? What sorts of responsibilities do they share? Discuss these questions in a brief essay.

Vocabulary Warm-up Word Lists

Study these words from "Pecos Bill" and "Perseus." Then, complete the activities.

Word List A

capable [KAY puh buhl] *adj.* having the power or skill
   Karen is <u>capable</u> of playing "Moonlight Sonata" on the piano.

cyclone [SY klohn] *n.* tornado
   The <u>cyclone</u> did not do as much damage as we had feared.

destruction [di STRUHK shuhn] *n.* the act of ruining or damaging greatly
   Silas viewed the <u>destruction</u> caused by the violent windstorm.

extreme [ek STREEM] *adj.* very great
   Because of the ice, driving put Ted in <u>extreme</u> danger.

fatal [FAYT uhl] *adj.* resulting in death
   The accident caused <u>fatal</u> injuries to two people.

heave [HEEV] *n.* the act of pulling or throwing with great effort
   With a strong <u>heave</u>, Dean got the sack onto the platform.

missile [MIS uhl] *n.* an object that is thrown and intended to cause harm
   The wind tossed the flagpole as if it were a <u>missile</u>.

whirlwind [HWURL wind] *n.* a strong windstorm that moves quickly
   The <u>whirlwind</u> scooped up all the bits of paper in the yard.

Word List B

abode [uh BOHD] *n.* the place where one lives
   "Welcome to my humble <u>abode</u>," said Steven to his guests.

arrogance [AR uh gahns] *n.* snobbery; looking down on others
   Heather's <u>arrogance</u> hurt her friend Ashley very much.

devised [di VYZD] *v.* planned or invented a way of doing something
   Marilyn <u>devised</u> a method of removing stains from the rug.

fearless [FEER lis] *adj.* not being afraid
   Without our <u>fearless</u> leader, we never would have proceeded.

mere [MEER] *adj.* being nothing more or less than; simple
   Ann saw a major obstacle, but Pat saw a <u>mere</u> bump in the road.

pursue [puhr SOO] *v.* to chase or follow someone
   Sharon did not dare to <u>pursue</u> the thief who grabbed her backpack.

radiant [RAY dee uhnt] *adj.* full of happiness and love, showing in one's face
   Sylvia looked at Ray with a <u>radiant</u> smile.

wretched [RECH id] *adj.* extremely bad; miserable
   The prisoner was kept in a <u>wretched</u> cell for days.

"**Pecos Bill: The Cyclone**" by Harold W. Felton
"**Perseus**" by Edith Hamilton
Vocabulary Warm-up Exercises

Exercise A *Fill in each blank in the paragraph with an appropriate word from Word List A. Use each word only once.*

The people of Pleasantville were shocked at the [1] _____ caused by the full-blown [2] _____ that had passed through town earlier that day. When they had first heard that a [3] _____ would be approaching the town, they were not that worried. Who knew it would become a violent storm [4] _____ of such terrible results? It had picked up a large rock from the Andersons' yard and hurled it like a [5] _____ through the plate-glass window of Pinky's Department Store. With a violent [6] _____ , it deposited a car into the municipal pool. Luckily, even though it was the most [7] _____ weather the town had ever known, there were no [8] _____ consequences, only a few minor injuries.

Exercise B *Answer the questions with complete sentences or explanations.*

1. What steps would you take to <u>pursue</u> a runaway dog?
   _____

2. Describe a plan you or someone else has <u>devised</u> for getting chores done.
   _____

3. What would you like to say to someone who displayed too much <u>arrogance</u>?
   _____

4. What kind of feeling would give you a <u>radiant</u> glow?
   _____

5. Describe a task that would be a <u>mere</u> nuisance.
   _____

6. Describe a time you or someone else exhibited <u>fearless</u> behavior.
   _____

7. What kind of weather do you think is the most <u>wretched</u> of all?
   _____

8. What kind of <u>abode</u> would you like to have when you grow up?
   _____

"Pecos Bill: The Cyclone" by Harold W. Felton
"Perseus" by Edith Hamilton

Reading Warm-up A

Read the following passage. Pay special attention to the underlined words. Then, read it again, and complete the activities. Use a separate sheet of paper for your written answers.

Whether you call it a <u>whirlwind</u>, a twister, a tornado, or a <u>cyclone</u>, this phenomenon of nature can cause terrible damage. They can occur at any time of the year, but the greatest number of tornadoes occurs in May and June. However, the tornadoes occurring during April are the deadliest, bringing <u>fatal</u> consequences to an average of nearly thirty people a year.

Tornadoes occur mainly in the central and southern United States. This area is called "tornado alley." It lies between the Rocky Mountains and the Appalachians and runs from Iowa and Nebraska down to the Gulf of Mexico. If you live in this region, you have probably experienced all kinds of <u>extreme</u> weather.

What kind of <u>destruction</u> can a tornado cause? The Fujita Scale (named after T. Theodore Fujita, who invented it) gives us some idea. According to this scale, a level F0 tornado has winds of 40–72 miles per hour. It can cause light damage. Branches might be ripped from trees. Shallowly rooted trees may be lifted from the ground. Damage to signs, traffic signals, and chimneys might occur.

A level F1 tornado, with winds of 73–112 miles per hour, is <u>capable</u> of moderate damage. Mobile homes can be knocked off their foundations. Cars might be flipped over. Roofing materials might be damaged. Almost half of all tornadoes fall into this category.

A level F2 tornado, with winds of 113–157 miles per hour, causes considerable damage. Solid, old trees are uprooted easily. Mobile homes are completely destroyed. Roofs are ripped off buildings. Train cars can be knocked over. A small object can even become a dangerous <u>missile</u>.

The Fujita Scale lists three more levels, F3, F4, and F5, which range from "severe" to "devastating" to "incredible damage." Only about one percent of tornadoes are classified as F5. A strong <u>heave</u> from the winds of one of these tornadoes can toss cars through the air and turn whole houses to piles of sticks and stones.

1. Circle the words that mean the same as <u>whirlwind</u>. Use *whirlwind* in a sentence.

2. Underline the words that tell what a <u>cyclone</u> can do. Describe the aftermath of a *cyclone*.

3. Circle the word that helps to understand <u>fatal</u>. What does *fatal* mean?

4. Underline the word that <u>extreme</u> describes. Describe an *extreme* condition that you once experienced.

5. Circle the word that tells what can cause <u>destruction</u>. Define *destruction*.

6. Underline the words that tell what a level F1 tornado is <u>capable</u> of. Name one positive thing you are *capable* of.

7. Circle the word that describes <u>missile</u>. Use *missile* in a sentence.

8. Underline the word that tells what a <u>heave</u> from an F5 tornado can do. Name an object that would require a *heave* to move it.

"Pecos Bill: The Cyclone" by Harold W. Felton
"Perseus" by Edith Hamilton
Reading Warm-up B

Read the following passage. Pay special attention to the underlined words. Then, read it again, and complete the activities. Use a separate sheet of paper for your written answers.

The ancient Greek legend about Daedalus and his son Icarus is a lesson to everyone about the danger of taking something too far.

Daedalus, a brilliant inventor, was a prisoner of King Minos of Crete. When King Minos asked him to produce clever machines and new ideas, Daedalus had to obey. When he was busy making an invention, he would be <u>radiant</u> with the happiness of creativity, even though he was in prison. Though Daedalus tried to make the best of captivity, bad fortune was going to <u>pursue</u> him.

Minos became angry at Daedalus and banished him to the Labyrinth, a tangled maze. This was no <u>mere</u> game. The Labyrinth had been designed by Daedalus himself, and escaping from it was almost impossible.

Daedalus knew the way out, but he knew that he would be killed if he left the maze. His son, Icarus, because of his great love for his father, chose to live with his father in their new <u>abode</u>.

One day, Icarus told his father that he was bored in the Labyrinth. He wanted them to leave that <u>wretched</u> place. Daedalus said such a plan was impossible, but Icarus convinced his father to make wings for them both. Then, they could fly away from Crete forever.

Daedalus then <u>devised</u> a way for them to fly. He created a pair of wings, using wax to make the feathers stick. He and his son were soon flying above Crete, enjoying the view and the feeling of freedom. In his <u>arrogance</u>, Icarus decided he could fly much higher. As the <u>fearless</u> Icarus soared up toward the heavens, the sun's heat melted the wax on his beautiful wings. Moments later, Daedalus saw his son's body hurtling down to the sea, where it disappeared forever.

1. Underline the words that hint at the meaning of <u>radiant</u>. Use *radiant* in a sentence.

2. Underline the words that tell what would <u>pursue</u> Daedalus. Describe something that would be difficult to *pursue*.

3. Use a synonym for <u>mere</u> to rewrite the sentence in which the word appears. Then, write a sentence of your own using *mere*.

4. Circle the phrase that helps you understand <u>abode</u>. Describe your own *abode*.

5. Underline the name of the place that is described as <u>wretched</u>. Explain what makes the place *wretched*.

6. Circle the words that tell what Daedalus <u>devised</u>. What is another word for *devised*?

7. Underline the words that tell what Icarus, in his <u>arrogance</u>, decided. Describe a person who is displaying *arrogance*.

8. Circle the word that tells who is <u>fearless</u>. Describe an action you saw or read about that was *fearless*.

Name _____ Date _____

Writing About the Big Question

Do heroes have responsibilities?

Big Question Vocabulary

character	choices	hero	honesty	identify
imitate	intentions	involvement	justice	morality
obligation	responsibility	serve	standard	wisdom

A. *Use one or more words from the list above to complete each sentence.*

1. Mayor Jarowski will be sorely missed because he set a high _____
   for _____ and civic _____ in the community.

2. In Shakespeare's play *Julius Caesar*, Brutus is a heroic _____,
   even though his _____ do not turn out the way he planned them.

3. Engraved on the Supreme Court building in Washington, D.C., are the famous
   words, "Equal _____ Under Law."

4. According to a Constitutional Amendment, the President may not
   _____ more than two consecutive four-year terms.

5. Grandfather was a living example of the truth that _____ goes
   deeper than mere knowledge.

B. *Follow the directions in responding to each of the items below.*

1. List two situations in which you think a person's **honesty** might be tested.

   _____

   _____

2. Write two sentences to explain one of these situations. Use at least two of the Big
   Question vocabulary words.

   _____

   _____

C. *Complete the sentence below. Then, write a short paragraph in which you connect the
sentence to the Big Question.*

In some situations, heroes have a responsibility to _____.

_____

_____

_____

_____

Unit 6 Resources: Themes in Literature
170

Name _____ Date _____

"Pecos Bill: The Cyclone" by Harold W. Felton and
"Perseus" by Edith Hamilton
Literary Analysis: Tall Tale and Myth

A **tall tale** is a type of folk tale that contains some or all of the following features:

• a larger-than-life central hero
• far-fetched situations and amazing feats
• humor
• *hyperbole*, or exaggeration

Tall tales are a particularly American form of story. Many tall tales originated during the American frontier period and reflect the challenges and values of that place and time.

A **myth** is an anonymous story that explains the actions of gods or human heroes, the reasons for certain traditions, or the causes of natural features. Every culture has its own *mythology*, or collection of myths, which express the central values of the people who created them. **Mythic heroes** often share three characteristics: they have at least one divine parent, they gain special knowledge or weapons, and they face seemingly impossible tasks. In general, myths tell how gods shape human life while tall tales tell how humans make things happen.

DIRECTIONS: *Write your answers to the following questions on the lines provided.*

1. How would you compare and contrast Pecos Bill and Perseus as **heroes?**

   _____

   _____

2. What elements of **exaggeration** or **fantasy** can you identify in each tale?

   "Pecos Bill: The Cyclone": _____

   _____

   "Perseus": _____

   _____

3. **Mood** is the overall atmosphere or feeling created by a literary work. **Tone** is the author's attitude toward the subject, the characters, or the audience. How would you compare and contrast "Pecos Bill: The Cyclone" with "Perseus" in mood and tone?

   Mood: _____

   _____

   Tone: _____

   _____

4. In their original versions, many tall tales and myths were **oral literature**—or works that were passed down by word of mouth from one generation to the next. What qualities in "The Cyclone" and "Perseus" would lend themselves especially well to oral storytelling?

   _____

   _____

"Pecos Bill: The Cyclone" by Harold W. Felton and
"Perseus" by Edith Hamilton
Vocabulary Builder

Word List

mortified   revelry   skeptics   usurped

A. DIRECTIONS: *Revise each sentence so that the underlined vocabulary word is used logically. Be sure not to change the vocabulary word.*

1. After the tyrant <u>usurped</u> the king's throne, most people acclaimed him as the legitimate ruler.

   _____

2. The professor's arguments were so convincing that many <u>skeptics</u> questioned her conclusions.

   _____

3. When Eugene made such diplomatic comments to our hosts, we felt <u>mortified</u>.

   _____

4. The sounds of <u>revelry</u> from the party next door were low and soothing.

   _____

B. DIRECTIONS: *On the line, write the letter of the choice that is the best synonym for each numbered word.*

___ 1. revelry
   A. slow improvement
   B. agile maneuver
   C. early departure
   D. noisy merrymaking

___ 2. usurped
   A. researched
   B. incorporated
   C. seized power
   D. reorganized

___ 3. skeptics
   A. allies
   B. doubters
   C. forecasters
   D. inventors

___ 4. mortified
   A. buried
   B. embarrassed
   C. disguised
   D. deceived

"Pecos Bill: The Cyclone" by Harold W. Felton and
"Perseus" by Edith Hamilton

Support for Writing to Compare Literary Works

Use a chart like the one shown to make prewriting notes for an essay comparing and contrasting the values that Pecos Bill and Perseus represent.

Values	Pecos Bill	Perseus
Respect		
Fears		
Goals		
Achievements		
Motivations		

Unit 6 Resources: Themes in Literature
173

"Pecos Bill: The Cyclone" by Harold W. Felton
"Perseus" by Edith Hamilton
Open-Book Test

Short Answer *Write your responses to the questions in this section on the lines provided.*

1. Fill out the Venn diagram to show common and different features of tall tales and myths. Then answer the question that follows.

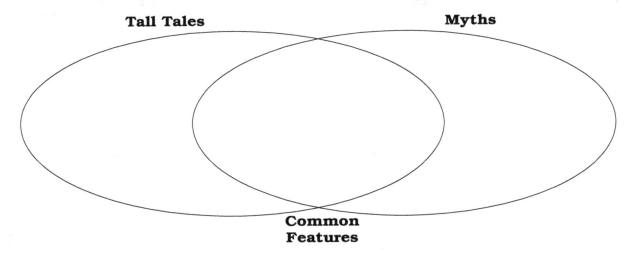

What one feature do both "Pecos Bill: The Cyclone" and "Perseus" have in common?

_____

2. Which selection is a tall tale? Which is a myth? Fill in the chart, and give a feature of tall tale and myth to explain each answer.

	Myth or Tall Tale	**Feature**
"Pecos Bill The Cyclone":		
"Perseus":		

3. Who shapes human life in "Pecos Bill: The Cyclone" and "Perseus"—human figures or gods?

_____

_____

_____

Unit 6 Resources: Themes in Literature
174

4. Consider the character portrayals of Pecos Bill and Perseus in these narratives. What is an important similarity between the two characters?

_____

_____

5. In the beginning of "Pecos Bill: The Cyclone," the reader is told that Bill fenced all of Texas and parts of New Mexico and Arizona with the help of prairie dogs. Is this an example of exotic setting, hyperbole, or historical fact? Explain your answer.

_____

_____

6. How would you describe author Harold Felton's attitude toward his subject in "Pecos Bill: The Cyclone"?

_____

_____

7. Tall tales and myths might be humorous, serious, or suspenseful. How would you describe "Pecos Bill: The Cyclone" and "Perseus"?

_____

_____

_____

8. In this excerpt from the middle of "Pecos Bill: The Cyclone," the cyclone is given characteristics of a human being. How is the cyclone like a human character?

> This year it did not come to watch. It deliberately came to spoil the celebration. Jealous of Bill and of his success, it resolved to do away with the whole institution of the Fourth of July once and for all.

_____

_____

_____

9. As Perseus grows up, why does Danaë allow him to become a fisherman on a little island?

_____

_____

_____

10. In the middle of "Perseus," Perseus and Hermes come upon the people who are holding revelry. What actions are these people engaging in? Use the meaning of *revelry* in your answer.

_____

_____

Essay

Write an extended response to the question of your choice or to the question or questions your teacher assigns you.

11. In an essay, compare and contrast the personalities of Pecos Bill in "Pecos Bill: The Cyclone" and of Perseus in the Greek myth. How are the two characters alike? How are they different? Be sure to support your main ideas with specific references to the text of the selections.

12. In "Perseus," the central character seems to get a lot of help when he needs it most. For example, Hermes and Athena show up just when Perseus has taken on an impossible task. Is Perseus still heroic? In an essay, explain why you think Perseus is or is not heroic. Use examples and details from the selection to support your view.

13. In "Perseus," the Gray Women, the Gorgons, and the sea serpent are all supernatural challenges for Perseus to overcome. In "The Cyclone," Pecos Bill does battle with an overwhelming natural force. In an essay, explain why you think that fantastic creatures or awesome natural forces have a powerful hold on human imagination and why they appear so often in tales of adventure. In an essay, give examples from the selections or from other stories, ancient or modern, to support your ideas.

14. **Thinking About the Big Question: Do heroes have responsibilities?** In an essay, discuss how these two narrative stories—"Pecos Bill: The Cyclone" and "Perseus"— imply that heroes have responsibilities. What are the responsibilities of the heroes in these stories?

Oral Response

15. Go back to question 1, 4, 8, or to the question your teacher assigns you. Take a few minutes to expand your answer and prepare an oral response. Find additional details in "Pecos Bill: The Cyclone" and/or "Perseus" that support your points. If necessary, make notes to guide your oral response.

"Pecos Bill: The Cyclone" by Harold W. Felton
"Perseus" by Edith Hamilton
Selection Test A

Critical Reading *Identify the letter of the choice that best answers the question.*

____ 1. "Pecos Bill: The Cyclone" is an example of what type of literature?
  A. epic narrative
  B. tall tale
  C. mythic narrative
  D. personal narrative

____ 2. According to "The Cyclone," who invented the Fourth of July?
  A. George Washington
  B. Alexander Hamilton
  C. Sam Houston
  D. Pecos Bill

____ 3. Why did the cyclone decide to ruin the cowpunchers' Fourth of July celebration?
  A. The cowpunchers had called the cyclone a coward.
  B. Pecos Bill had promised the weather would be fine on the Fourth of July.
  C. The cyclone was jealous of Pecos Bill's success.
  D. The cyclone wanted to destroy the prairie dogs and the badgers.

____ 4. In "Pecos Bill: The Cyclone," Widow Maker is which of the following?
  A. Pecos Bill's favorite prairie dog
  B. a hard-nosed cowpuncher
  C. Pecos Bill's horse
  D. the cyclone's brother

____ 5. Which of the following is a typical element of tall tales?
  A. exaggeration
  B. heroes from ancient myth
  C. a story that teaches a moral lesson
  D. a tragic ending

____ 6. Tone is the author's attitude toward the subject matter, the characters, or the audience. Which of the following best describes Felton's tone in "Pecos Bill: The Cyclone"?
  A. solemn and persuasive
  B. tongue-in-cheek and amusing
  C. bitter and ironic
  D. factual and objective

____ 7. Which of the following statements most accurately describes Perseus?
   A. He is loyal and brave.
   B. He tries to fulfill the prophecy.
   C. He seeks to serve Zeus.
   D. He is a warrior seeking revenge.

____ 8. Which of the following is the true father of Perseus?
   A. King Acrisius of Argos
   B. the god Zeus
   C. Dictys the fisherman
   D. Polydectes of the island

____ 9. In myths, what is a sure way for a mortal to make the gods angry?
   A. attacking a monster who is superior to mortals
   B. acting impulsively on emotion
   C. proclaiming that a mortal is superior to a god
   D. refusing to obey the orders of a king

____ 10. When Perseus enters Polydectes' banquet hall, he knows that everyone will stare. Perseus lifts Medusa's head, turning the king and his courtiers to stone. What quality of the hero does this incident demonstrate?
   A. endurance in bad times
   B. devotion to the gods
   C. loyalty to family
   D. intelligent use of opportunities

____ 11. Which of the following states an important difference between "Pecos Bill: The Cyclone" and "Perseus"?
   A. Pecos Bill is a more believable character than Perseus.
   B. In "The Cyclone," the mood is humorous; in "Perseus," the mood is serious and suspenseful.
   C. The details in "The Cyclone" are more realistic than the details in "Perseus."
   D. "The Cyclone" is full of suspense; "Perseus" is predictable.

____ 12. Which of the following identifies a similarity between "Pecos Bill: The Cyclone" and "Perseus"?
   A. They both feature a larger-than-life hero.
   B. They are both composed in a serious, formal style.
   C. The settings in both selections are strange and exotic.
   D. The selections both emphasize the ideals of patience and serenity.

_____ 13. Based on this pair of selections, which of the following states an important difference between tall tales and myths?

    A. Tall tales are harder to understand than myths.

    B. The hero in a tall tale must struggle harder for success than the hero in a myth.

    C. Myths are always longer than tall tales.

    D. The tone in tall tales is often humorous, whereas the tone in myths is usually serious.

Vocabulary

_____ 14. Which of the following best describes the attitude of *skeptics*?

    A. doubt

    B. curiosity

    C. admiration

    D. anger

_____ 15. Which of the following would most likely be the setting for *revelry*?

    A. a joyful celebration of a victory by the hometown football team

    B. a physics lecture at a university

    C. a high-level conference at the White House

    D. a conversation between shoppers at a department store

Essay

16. In an essay, compare and contrast the personalities and adventures of Pecos Bill in "The Cyclone" and of Perseus in the Greek myth. How are the two alike and how are they different? Be sure to support your main ideas with specific references to the selections.

17. Conflict and suspense are two elements that tall tales and myths often have in common. In an essay, define each of these elements. Then, discuss conflict and suspense in *either* "Pecos Bill: The Cyclone" *or* in "Perseus." Support your main ideas with specific references to the selection that you choose.

18. **Thinking About the Big Question: Do heroes have responsibilities?** The main characters in "Pecos Bill: The Cyclone" and "Perseus" each take on a responsibility. Each hero character does something fantastic to improve life for ordinary people. In an essay, tell what responsible action each hero takes on. Then, tell how the action improves the lives of the people.

"Pecos Bill: The Cyclone" by Harold W. Felton
"Perseus" by Edith Hamilton

Selection Test B

Critical Reading *Identify the letter of the choice that best completes the statement or answers the question.*

____ 1. Tall tales and myths share all the following elements *except*
   A. exaggeration.
   B. a larger-than-life central hero.
   C. a humorous tone.
   D. seemingly impossible tasks.

____ 2. Which of the following is the setting for "Pecos Bill: The Cyclone"?
   A. the Fourth of July
   B. Thanksgiving Day
   C. New Year's Day
   D. Christmas

____ 3. Which of the following most prominently signals Pecos Bill's status as a folk hero?
   A. his knowledge of prairie dogs
   B. his refusal to say the word *afraid*
   C. the name of his horse
   D. his ownership of a twenty-dollar gold piece

____ 4. Which literary device is illustrated in the following excerpt from "Pecos Bill: The Cyclone"?
   This year it did not come to watch. It deliberately came to spoil the celebration. Jealous of Bill and of his success, it resolved to do away with the whole institution of the Fourth of July once and for all.
   A. simile
   B. metaphor
   C. symbol
   D. personification

____ 5. For which of the following was Widow Maker's show especially remarkable?
   A. the appearance of Scat and Rat
   B. the race of the mustangs
   C. the twenty-seven gaits Bill had taught the horse
   D. the contest between the horse and the cyclone

____ 6. Where and when did many tall tales originate?
   A. in ancient Greece
   B. during the American frontier period
   C. in twentieth-century Britain
   D. among the ancient Aztecs

_____ 7. From the portrait of Pecos Bill in "Pecos Bill: The Cyclone," which of the following most likely motivates him to do battle with the cyclone?
  A. his concern for the cowpunchers
  B. his jealousy of the cyclone's power
  C. his anxiety about his own reputation
  D. his eagerness and zest for a challenge

_____ 8. According to the narrator, what explains the origin of the "Staked Plains" region?
  A. the Spanish name that the Mexicans gave the area
  B. the fact that the cyclone rolled on the ground, destroying the mountains and trees
  C. the fact that Pecos Bill told the prairie dogs to dig holes in the region
  D. the fact that Pecos Bill and the cyclone were fighting for high stakes

_____ 9. The tone of a literary work is the attitude the author displays toward the characters, the subject matter, or the audience. On the whole, which of the following best describes the tone of "Pecos Bill: The Cyclone"?
  A. solemn
  B. awed
  C. tongue-in-cheek
  D. ironic

_____ 10. In "Perseus," why does King Acrisius confine his daughter to an underground house?
  A. He wants to make certain she has no children.
  B. He is angry about her relationship with Polydectes.
  C. He wants to shield her from the Furies.
  D. The priestess at Delphi has ordered him to do so.

_____ 11. When Danaë and the infant Perseus are adrift in the great chest, it seems reasonable to assume that they will escape because
  A. Danaë has shown herself to be clever.
  B. Perseus, though still a child, is supernaturally strong.
  C. the infant hero of a myth is bound to survive.
  D. mortals usually succeed in contests with gods.

_____ 12. As Perseus grows up, Danaë allows him to become a fisherman on the little island because
  A. Acrisius cannot know where he is.
  B. Dictys has two sons to help him.
  C. Zeus has offered no assistance.
  D. Perseus must prepare for his destiny.

_____ 13. Hermes and Athena come to Perseus' aid because
  A. a hero in myth often receives supernatural assistance.
  B. Zeus is angry with Polydectes for his tyranny over the islanders.
  C. Athena has long been jealous of Medusa and sees her chance for revenge.
  D. mythological gods hate injustice.

_____ 14. Which of the following best states an important similarity between Pecos Bill and Perseus?
  A. They both struggle against natural forces.
  B. They are both larger-than-life characters.
  C. They both die tragically.
  D. They both come to other people's aid.

_____ 15. Which of the following literary elements is most often common to tall tales and myths?
  A. exotic settings
  B. hyperbole
  C. irony
  D. simile

_____ 16. Which of the following best expresses the contrast in tone between "Pecos Bill: The Cyclone" and "Perseus"?
  A. tongue-in-cheek vs. serious
  B. nostalgic vs. pessimistic
  C. subjective vs. objective
  D. ominous vs. enthusiastic

Vocabulary

_____ 17. Which of the following is the best synonym for *usurped*?
  A. fell down suddenly
  B. struggled courageously
  C. took power or authority without right
  D. certified as genuine

_____ 18. Which of the following would most likely make you feel *mortified*?
  A. an embarrassing mistake
  B. a New Year's Eve celebration
  C. an agreeable birthday party
  D. the news of an approaching hurricane

Essay

19. In the myth of Perseus, the central character seems to get a lot of help when he needs it most. Hermes and Athena show up just as he has taken on an impossible task. Is Perseus still heroic? Explain why you think Perseus is heroic or not heroic. Use examples from the myth to support your ideas.

20. In "Perseus," the Gray Women, the Gorgons, and the sea serpent are all supernatural challenges for Perseus to overcome. In "The Cyclone," Pecos Bill does battle with an overwhelming natural force. Stories from many times and cultures feature monsters and immensely powerful forces of nature, such as volcanoes, earthquakes, tidal waves, and tornadoes. In an essay, explain why you think fantastic creatures or awesome natural forces have such a powerful hold on the imagination and why they appear so often in tales of adventure. Give examples from the selections or from other stories—ancient or modern—to support your ideas.

21. **Thinking About the Big Question: Do heroes have responsibilities?** In an essay, discuss how these two narrative stories, "Pecos Bill: The Cyclone" and "Perseus," imply that heroes have responsibilities. What are the responsibilities of the heroes in these stories?

Unit 6 Resources: Themes in Literature
182

Writing Workshop
Exposition: Comparison-and-Contrast Essay

Prewriting: Gathering Details

Use the following Venn diagram to gather and organize details for your essay. Record similarities in the space where the circles overlap, and note differences in the outer sections of the circles.

Topic: _____   Topic: _____

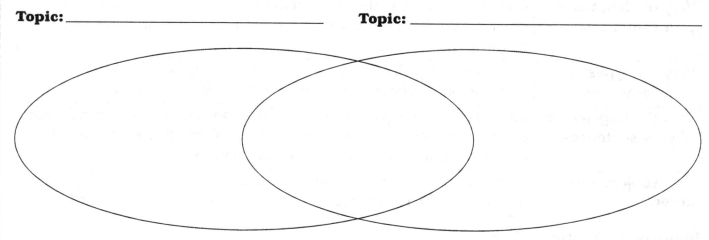

Drafting: Choosing an Organization

Use the two graphic organizers to select an organization that suits your topic.

Point-by-Point Organization

1st Point

Subject 1:	Subject 2:

2nd Point

Subject 1:	Subject 2:

3rd Point

Subject 1:	Subject 2:

Subject-by-Subject Organization

Points on Subject 1

Points on Subject 2

Writing Workshop
Comparison-and-Contrast Essay: Integrating Grammar Skills

Revising to Vary Sentence Structure and Length

A series of similar sentences can be very boring to read. By varying sentence lengths and structures, you can make your writing livelier and more memorable. Follow these rules:

Vary the lengths of your sentences.	Combine, extend, and/or chop sentences to achieve a mix of short, medium, and long sentences. Avoid too many sentences of similar length in a row.
Vary the types of your sentences.	Instead of using all statements, consider an occasional question, exclamation, or command, especially in less formal writing.
Vary the beginnings of your sentences.	Instead of beginning all sentences with a modified or unmodified noun or pronoun, start some sentences with set-off modifiers, prepositional phrases, verbal phrases, or subordinate clauses.
Vary subject-verb order.	Instead of having the verb follow the subject in all of your sentences, use an occasional sentence in which the subject follows the verb.

Identifying Sentence Variety

A. DIRECTIONS: *For both items, circle the letter of the passage that is better written.*

1. A. The Black Plague was spread by infected rats. It was a highly contagious disease. It spread rapidly in the dirty, crowded medieval cities.

   B. The Black Plague was spread by infected rats. A highly contagious disease, it spread rapidly in the dirty, crowded medieval cities.

2. A. A flu epidemic struck soon after World War I. The epidemic was a truly devastating one in America. Far more people died than in any subsequent flu outbreak.

   B. A flu epidemic struck soon after World War I. How truly devastating it was in America! Far more people died than in any subsequent flu outbreak.

Fixing Sentences to Vary Structures and Lengths

B. DIRECTIONS: *On the lines provided, rewrite the following paragraph to vary sentence structures and sentence lengths.*

More Americans died in the Civil War than in any other war. Several diseases that swept the military camps caused many of these deaths. People back then did not really understand the relationship between dirt and disease. Scientists like Lister and Pasteur had not yet conducted their important experiments. These experiments were important because they showed how vital it was to keep things clean to stop the spread of infection.

_____

_____

_____

_____

Name _____ Date _____

Unit 6 Vocabulary Workshop—1
Idioms

If English is your first language, you probably know more idioms than you realize. Idioms are very commonly used in speech and writing.

DIRECTIONS: *After each definition, write an idiom that fits into the blanks. Then, write a short dialogue between two people who are angry at each other using at least three of the idioms.*

HINT: *Three of the idioms contain the word "chip"; two contain the word "fit."*

1. a person much like his or her parent _____
2. let the consequences be what they may be _____
3. an inclination to fight _____
4. something suspicious is going on _____
5. to become very angry or upset _____
6. frustrated and angry _____
7. start over again _____

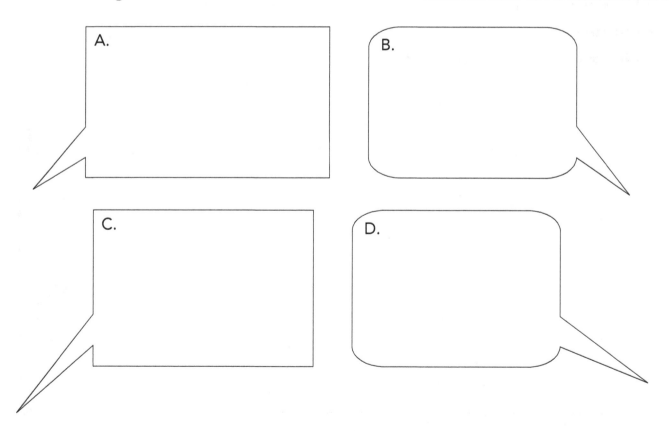

Unit 6 Vocabulary Workshop—2
Idioms

A well-chosen idiom now and then is just fine, but overusing idioms can take away from the credibility of your speech and writing.

DIRECTIONS: *Write an advertisement for a product of your choice. In the ad, use at least five of the following idioms. You may use a dictionary if you do not know the meaning of an idiom. Have fun with this!*

- **put two and two together**
- **a dime a dozen**
- **dressed to the nines**
- **look out for number one**
- **five o'clock shadow**
- **dressed to kill**
- **if looks could kill**
- **kill time**
- **kill two birds with one stone**

Name _____ Date _____

Communications Workshop
Comparing Media Coverage

After choosing your news broadcasts, fill out the following chart. Use your notes to compare and contrast the two news stories, and present your findings to the class.

What is the "headline" or main point of each story?
What are the important details in each story?
Does each reporter use language that is factual, emotional, objective, or involved? Explain.
What are the photos or video clips that add information or emotion to the news story?
What questions might you ask each reporter about his or her story?

Unit 6: Themes in Literature: Heroism
Benchmark Test 12

Literary Analysis: Protagonist and Antagonist *Answer the following questions.*

1. Which of these characters does an author usually develop most fully in a literary work?
   A. a secondary character
   B. a protagonist
   C. an antagonist
   D. a flat character

2. Which character generally opposes the main character in a literary work?
   A. a secondary character
   B. a protagonist
   C. an antagonist
   D. a tragic character

Read the selection. Then, answer the questions that follow.

From the huge waves that splashed the sides of the boat, the crew knew that the storm was approaching. Although the captain had listened to the weather report before setting out, the crew members were not prepared for this type of problem. Their rain gear was insufficient, and the boat seemed dwarfed by the water that was rising around them. The captain was an accomplished sailor, but it would take all of his expertise to get the crew and boat safely back to port.

3. In the selection, why would the captain be considered the protagonist?
   A. He is a minor character who is acted upon by the storm.
   B. He is a minor character who makes poor decisions.
   C. He is a major character who plays the role of the villain.
   D. He is a major character who plays the role of the hero.

4. In the selection, what or who is the antagonist?
   A. the crew
   B. the captain
   C. the boat
   D. the storm

5. Which of these universal conflicts does the struggle in the passage represent?
   A. human being vs. nature
   B. human being vs. society
   C. good vs. evil
   D. younger generation vs. older generation

Unit 6 Resources: Themes in Literature
188

Literary Analysis: Philosophical Assumptions

Read this passage. Then, answer the questions that follow.

Graham Penfield is an American oddity. The 46-year-old bookstore owner has never set foot inside a shopping mall. Not once. Ever. Why? "Never wanted to," Penfield says unapologetically. When coaxed a little, he elaborates: "From what I hear and read about them, malls sound like noisy, crowded, artificial environments. Why would I want to visit one?" According to some mall regulars, that's precisely why they flock to shopping malls—to immerse themselves in the noise and crowds and faux-village-square atmosphere. For these folks, bigger is better, and it doesn't get any bigger than the new mall in Islington. It covers 78 acres and is seven times as large as Yankee Stadium. When I described this mall to Penfield, he blinked and looked at me as though I had lobsters crawling out of my ears. "Madness!" he declared. I confess that I nodded eagerly in agreement.

6. Which of these statements best expresses a philosophical assumption made by the author of the selection?
   A. People who avoid malls are strange.
   B. The new mall in Islington is absurdly large.
   C. Mall noises and crowds are exciting.
   D. The larger the mall, the better it is.

7. Which of these details helps point to the author's philosophical assumption about malls?
   A. Graham Penfield is described as 46 years old.
   B. Graham Penfield is identified as a bookstore owner.
   C. People who flock to malls are called "mall regulars."
   D. Malls are described as having a "faux-village-square atmosphere."

8. Which of these audiences would most likely share the author's philosophical assumption about malls?
   A. Mall Builders of America, Inc.
   B. fans who attend Yankee Stadium
   C. bookstore owners
   D. the Preserve Small-Town America Society

9. Ally's favorite pastime is shopping at a large local mall. How is she likely to respond to the author's philosophical assumption about malls?
   A. She is likely to disagree with it.
   B. She is likely to support it.
   C. She is likely to express it even more forcefully.
   D. She is likely to want more information.

Literary Analysis: Tall Tale and Myth

Read this passage. Then, answer the questions that follow.

I'm that same David Crockett, fresh from the backwoods, half-horse, half-alligator, a little touched with the snapping turtle; can wade the Mississippi, leap the Ohio, ride a streak of lightning, slip without a scratch down a honey locust, can whip my weight in wildcats.

10. What feature or element suggests that the passage comes from a tall tale?
    A. It uses first-person point of view.
    B. It is about a legendary hero.
    C. It uses exaggeration to describe far-fetched feats.
    D. It suggests that the hero is aided by supernatural forces.

11. Which of these literary elements is illustrated by the phrase "slip without a scratch down a honey locust"?
    A. simile
    B. hyperbole
    C. metaphor
    D. allusion

12. Which characteristic best qualifies Crockett as a legendary hero?
    A. his humility
    B. his larger-than-life personality and achievements
    C. the rural setting in which he lives
    D. his truthfulness

Choose the letter of the response that best answers the question.

13. What is a myth?
    A. a story told in dialect
    B. a fanciful story that explains a natural phenomenon or event
    C. an accurate explanation of why something occurred
    D. a fictional adventure story

Reading Skill: Compare and Contrast

Read this passage from Jane Austen's novel Pride and Prejudice. *Then, answer the questions that follow.*

Mr. Bennet was so odd a mixture of quick parts, sarcastic humor, reserve, and caprice, that the experience of three-and-twenty years had been insufficient to make his wife understand his character. *Her* mind was less difficult to develop. She was a woman of mean understanding, little information, and uncertain temper. When she was discontented, she fancied herself nervous. The business of her life was to get her daughters married: its solace was visiting and news.

14. Which of these aspects of character is being compared or contrasted in this passage?
    A. the characters' similar values
    B. the characters' similar backgrounds
    C. the characters' different personalities
    D. the characters' different beliefs

15. Based on the description in the passage, which of these actions would be most characteristic of Mrs. Bennet?
    A. giving a lecture at a local college
    B. replying calmly to a verbal challenge
    C. greeting bad news lightly
    D. wondering what her daughters should wear to a social outing

16. Based on the information in the passage, which of the following words best describes Mr. Bennett?
    A. sad
    B. nervous
    C. many-faceted
    D. outgoing

Reading Skill: Analyze Primary Sources

17. Which statement is true of primary sources?
    A. All primary source documents are reliable.
    B. Some primary sources are more reliable than others.
    C. All primary sources are unreliable.
    D. All primary sources are published material.

18. Which type of writing would qualify as a primary source?
    A. an encyclopedia entry
    B. a history textbook
    C. a review of someone's biography
    D. a ship captain's log

19. Which of the following is least likely to be a primary source?
    A. a short story
    B. an autobiography
    C. a news article
    D. a diary

Vocabulary: Word Roots

20. The words *spectator, spectacles,* and *perspective* all share the root *-spect-*. Using this knowledge, what can you conclude the root *-spect-* means?
    A. look; see
    B. opinion; angle
    C. thought; idea
    D. glass

21. The word root *-fer-* means "carry" or "produce." Using this knowledge, what can you conclude about *fertile* soil?
    A. It is dry.
    B. It is thin and poor.
    C. Plants do not grow in it.
    D. Plants grow fairly easily in it.

22. The words *minimum, minority,* and *minute* all share the root *-min-*. Using this knowledge, what can you conclude the root *-min-* means?
    A. divide
    B. small
    C. increase
    D. time

23. The word root *-merg-* means "dip" or "plunge." Using this knowledge, what can you conclude submarines do when they *submerge*?
   A. go below the surface of the water
   B. go above the surface of the water
   C. steer away from another ship
   D. steer toward shore

Grammar

24. Which of these statements is a rule for using a comma correctly?
   A. Use it at the end of a sentence.
   B. Use it to separate more than two items in a list.
   C. Use it to separate hours from minutes.
   D. Use it to introduce a list of items.

25. Which of the following sentences uses a comma *incorrectly*?
   A. He yelled, "Look out for grizzlies!"
   B. Rita laughed, and then she turned the key in the ignition.
   C. He brought along apples, and pears.
   D. Finally, we began the descent.

26. Which of the following sentences is punctuated correctly?
   A. Her face lit up by a candle, was radiant.
   B. Her face, lit up by a candle, was radiant.
   C. Her face, lit up by a candle was radiant.
   D. Her face, lit up, by a candle, was radiant.

27. What do ellipsis points usually indicate to a reader?
   A. A conversation will follow.
   B. The action is over.
   C. Words have been left out.
   D. The characters are not speaking.

28. Which of the following sentences uses a colon correctly?
   A. Please bring the following items: a toothbrush, a sleeping bag, and soap.
   B. Do not stand up; you could: get hurt.
   C. A dandelion passed: gently floating.
   D. The pool was very crowded: I had trouble finding you.

29. Where should a semicolon be placed in the following sentence?

   He tried to talk to her she refused.

   A. between *tried* and *to*
   B. between *she* and *refused*
   C. between *her* and *she*
   D. between *he* and *tried*

WRITING

30. Write a brief comparison-and-contrast essay about two literary works. Your essay should include the following characteristics:

    - an analysis and discussion of similarities and differences
    - accurate, factual details about each literary work
    - a balanced presentation of each work using either subject-by-subject or point-by-point organization
    - varied sentence structure and length

31. Write two journal entries from the perspective of a famous character in literature, history, or cinema. Be sure to include thoughts and feelings about noteworthy events as that particular person would view them.

32. Write a friendly letter, using the appropriate formatting and tone, to a former teacher or coach expressing gratitude for something valuable you have learned.

Name _____ Date _____

Diagnostic Tests and Vocabulary in Context Use and Interpretation

The Diagnostic Tests and Vocabulary in Context were developed to assist teachers in making the most appropriate assignment of *Prentice Hall Literature* program selections to students. The purpose of these assessments is to indicate the degree of difficulty that students are likely to have in reading/comprehending the selections presented in the *following* unit of instruction. Tests are provided at six separate times in each grade level—a *Diagnostic Test* (to be used prior to beginning the year's instruction) and a *Vocabulary in Context*, the final segment of the Benchmark Test appearing at the end of each of the first five units of instruction. Note that the tests are intended for use not as summative assessments for the prior unit, but as guidance for assigning literature selections in the upcoming unit of instruction.

The structure of all Diagnostic Tests and Vocabulary in Context in this series is the same. All test items are four-option, multiple-choice items. The format is established to assess a student's ability to construct sufficient meaning from the context sentence to choose the only provided word that fits both the semantics (meaning) and syntax (structure) of the context sentence. All words in the context sentences are chosen to be "below-level" words that students reading at this grade level should know. All answer choices fit *either* the meaning or structure of the context sentence, but only the correct choice fits *both* semantics and syntax. All answer choices—both correct answers and incorrect options—are key words chosen from specifically taught words that will occur in the subsequent unit of program instruction. This careful restriction of the assessed words permits a sound diagnosis of students' current reading achievement and prediction of the most appropriate level of readings to assign in the upcoming unit of instruction.

The assessment of vocabulary in context skill has consistently been shown in reading research studies to correlate very highly with "reading comprehension." This is not surprising as the format essentially assesses comprehension, albeit in sentence-length "chunks." Decades of research demonstrate that vocabulary assessment provides a strong, reliable prediction of comprehension achievement— the purpose of these tests. Further, because this format demands very little testing time, these diagnoses can be made efficiently, permitting teachers to move forward with critical instructional tasks rather than devoting excessive time to assessment.

It is important to stress that while the Diagnostic Tests and Vocabulary in Context were carefully developed and will yield sound assignment decisions, they were designed to *reinforce*, not supplant, teacher judgment as to the most appropriate instructional placement for individual students. Teacher judgment should always prevail in making placement—or indeed other important instructional—decisions concerning students.

Name _____ Date _____

Diagnostic Tests and Vocabulary in Context
Branching Suggestions

These tests are designed to provide maximum flexibility for teachers. Your *Unit Resources* books contain the 40-question **Diagnostic Test** and 20-question **Vocabulary in Context** tests. At *PHLitOnline,* you can access the Diagnostic Test and complete 40-question Vocabulary in Context tests. Procedures for administering the tests are described below. Choose the procedure based on the time you wish to devote to the activity and your comfort with the assignment decisions relative to the individual students. Remember that your judgment of a student's reading level should always take precedence over the results of a single written test.

Feel free to use different procedures at different times of the year. For example, for early units, you may wish to be more confident in the assignments you make—thus, using the "two-stage" process below. Later, you may choose the quicker diagnosis, confirming the results with your observations of the students' performance built up throughout the year.

The **Diagnostic Test** is composed of a single 40-item assessment. Based on the results of this assessment, make the following assignment of students to the reading selections in Unit 1:

Diagnostic Test Score	Selection to Use
If the student's score is 0–25	more accessible
If the student's score is 26–40	more challenging

Outlined below are the three basic options for administering **Vocabulary in Context** and basing selection assignments on the results of these assessments.

1. For a one-stage, quicker diagnosis using the *20-item* test in the *Unit Resources:*

Vocabulary in Context Test Score	Selection to Use
If the student's score is 0–13	more accessible
If the student's score is 14–20	more challenging

2. If you wish to confirm your assignment decisions with a *two-stage* diagnosis:

Stage 1: Administer the 20-item test in the *Unit Resources*	
Vocabulary in Context Test Score	Selection to Use
If the student's score is 0–9	more accessible
If the student's score is 10–15	(Go to Stage 2.)
If the student's score is 16–20	more challenging

Stage 2: Administer items 21–40 from *PHLitOnline*	
Vocabulary in Context Test Score	Selection to Use
If the student's score is 0–12	more accessible
If the student's score is 13–20	more challenging

3. If you base your assignment decisions on the full 40-item **Vocabulary in Context** from *PHLitOnline:*

Vocabulary in Context Test Score	Selection to Use
If the student's score is 0–25	more accessible
If the student's score is 26–40	more challenging

Grade 9—Benchmark Test 11
Interpretation Guide

For remediation of specific skills, you may assign students the relevant Reading Kit Practice and Assess pages indicated in the far-right column of this chart. You will find rubrics for evaluating writing samples in the last section of your Professional Development Guidebook.

Skill Objective	Test Items	Number Correct	Reading Kit
Literary Analysis			
Epic and Epic Hero	1, 2, 4, 5, 6, 7		pp. 258, 259
Epic Simile	3		pp. 260, 261
Contemporary Interpretations of Classical Works	8, 9, 10, 11		pp. 262, 263
Reading Skill			
Analyze Cultural and Historical Context	12, 13, 14, 15, 16, 17, 18		pp. 264, 265
Identify Characteristics of Various Types of Texts	19, 20, 21		pp. 266, 267
Vocabulary			
Prefixes *be-*, *dis-*	22, 23		pp. 268, 269
Grammar			
Simple and Compound Sentences	24, 25, 27		pp. 270, 271
Complex and Compound-Complex Sentences	26		pp. 272, 273
Fragments and Run-Ons	28, 29		pp. 274, 275
Writing			
Everyday Epic	30	Use rubric	pp. 276, 277
Biography	31	Use rubric	pp. 278, 279
Technical Directions	32	Use rubric	pp. 280, 281

Name _____ Date _____

Grade 9—Benchmark Test 12
Interpretation Guide

For remediation of specific skills, you may assign students the relevant Reading Kit Practice and Assess pages indicated in the far-right column of this chart. You will find rubrics for evaluating writing samples in the last section of your Professional Development Guidebook.

Skill Objective	Test Items	Number Correct	Reading Kit
Literary Analysis			
Protagonist and Antagonist	1, 2, 3, 4, 5		pp. 282, 283
Philosophical Assumptions	6, 7, 8, 9		pp. 284, 285
Tall Tale and Myth	10, 11, 12, 13		pp. 286, 287
Reading Skill			
Compare and Contrast	14, 15, 16		pp. 288, 289
Analyze Primary Sources	17, 18, 19		pp. 290, 291
Vocabulary			
Roots: *-min-, -spect-, -merg-, -fer-*	20, 21, 22, 23		pp. 292, 293
Grammar			
Commas	24, 25, 26		pp. 294, 295
Colons, Semicolons, and Ellipsis Points	27, 28, 29		pp. 296, 297
Writing			
Compare-and-Contrast Essay	30	Use rubric	pp. 306, 307
Journal Entry	31	Use rubric	pp. 302, 303
Friendly Letter	32	Use rubric	pp. 304, 305

ANSWERS

Big Question Vocabulary—1, p. 1

Sample Answers

Honesty: My hero is always honest. If he breaks something accidentally, he makes sure to tell the owner and replace it.

Justice: My hero wants to make sure that justice is done. He catches thieves so that property is returned to its rightful owner.

Morality: My hero always acts in a way that is moral. He tells the truth, and never lies, steals, or cheats.

Responsibility: My hero is always responsible. If he says he is going to do something, he does it.

Wisdom: My hero is wise. He learns from his experiences and uses that wisdom to guide the children.

Big Question Vocabulary—2, p. 2

1. My **hero** is Al Gore.
2. Gore has shown good **character** by dedicating his life to stopping global warming.
3. He **serves** the world at large by spreading information about global warming and what we can do to stop it.
4. His **intention** is to have people change their habits to minimize burning fuels that damage our environment.
5. I can **imitate** his mission and spread the word about ending global warming to all my friends and relatives.

Big Question Vocabulary—3, p. 3

This unsung hero award goes to Martin Becker for outstanding work with the campaign to clean up and rebuild the children's playground in our neighborhood. Becker was quiet about his actions but it is important to **identify** him and thank him for all he has done. He took on the **obligation** of making all of the **choices** for the playground equipment and held the contractors to a very high **standard**. His **involvement** with this project made it a success!

"Play Hard; Play Together; Play Smart" *from* The Carolina Way
by Dean Smith with John Kilgo

Vocabulary Warm-up Exercises, p. 8

A.
1. competitive
2. championship
3. stray
4. previous
5. enjoyable
6. strategic
7. execution
8. professional

B. Sample Answers
1. One of the *fundamentals* of any game is having rules to follow.
2. If I *duplicate* the photo of my dog and me, you will see my dog's unusual markings.

3. It is a wise *philosophy* to concentrate on the positive things in life.
4. If you made the *maximum* effort, you tried as hard as you could.
5. If your *ultimate* goal is college, it is the most important reason to do well now.
6. Kate's *determination* to succeed showed when she continued to work after everyone else was done.
7. I will *refresh* my iced tea from the pitcher that is in the fridge.

Reading Warm-up A, p. 9

Sample Answers

1. (deliberately); to give athletes a good workout
2. (before); by doing gymnastics
3. (wandered away); *Stray into mischief* means to get into trouble.
4. (like); I find swimming *enjoyable* because I like the water, and swimming is an all-around good exercise.
5. play hard to win; (challenging) or (enjoyable)
6. throwing a ball into a basket; When the *execution* of a play is successful, a player scores a point for his or her team.
7. *Amateur* is an antonym for *professional*. A college player is a student and an amateur who plays on a college team. A *professional* player plays basketball for a living and is paid for doing so.
8. (best); honored with trophies

Reading Warm-up B, p. 10

Sample Answers

1. a winning team; *Maximum results* means the most to be achieved.
2. (essential); *Significance* is a synonym for *importance*.
3. (largest); When completed, the granite rendering of the famous Native American chief will be the largest monument in the world.
4. (basic); One of the *fundamentals* of carving stone might be knowing what tools to use.
5. (energize); World War II began and he served in the U.S. Army and was wounded.
6. keep working on it year after year; *Determination* is sticking with something and not giving up.
7. exact statue he had in mind; *Copy* is a synonym for *duplicate*.
8. (belief); This *philosophy* means to take your time so you do not make mistakes.

Dean Smith

Listening and Viewing, p. 11

Sample Answers

Segment 1. The phrase "the Carolina way" means the right way of doing something. Students may suggest that Smith's philosophy can also apply to working hard in academics and careers and can be seen as a way of living life in general.

Segment 2. Sports writing is an important part of our culture because it documents great achievements and good examples of people who have worked hard for their success, like Coach Smith. Students may answer that readers of *The Carolina Way* can learn from the leadership lessons Coach Smith has taught his players over the years and from his anecdotes of teaching players and students how to enable success by working hard.

Segment 3. Kilgo writes out each chapter, and Smith revises each one so that Kilgo's words sound natural. Students may suggest that working with a co-author can be beneficial because the work gets done more efficiently; it can also be challenging to match one writer's style and voice with the other's.

Segment 4. Writing has been rewarding for John Kilgo because it is satisfying to him to record famous and historical events and present sports figures more in-depth. Dean Smith enjoys helping people through his books and likes getting letters from his readers. Students may suggest a certain article or book about a sports event or figure that was inspirational to them and explain why it was captivating.

Unit 6: Learning About Themes in Literature, p. 12

1. B; 2. A; 3. B; 4. C; 5. A; 6. A; 7. B

"Play Hard; Play Together; Play Smart" *from* The Carolina Way
by Dean Smith with John Kilgo

Model Selection: Themes in Literature, p. 13

Sample Answers

1. The values Smith stresses include effort, determination, courage, dedication, unselfishness, trust, mastery of fundamentals, poise, and precision.

2. Opinions will vary. Students may state that the values that Smith emphasizes are found in different cultures in different times because they are practical, realistic ideals that may lead to success in a variety of fields. Other students may state that the values are culturally distinct because not all societies, for example, would agree with Smith's outlook on such topics as winning and unselfishness.

3. Evaluate students' paragraphs for adequate support (reasons and examples) for their opinions.

Open-Book Test, p. 14

Short Answer

1. The power of love is a universal theme.
   Difficulty: *Average* **Objective:** *Literary Analysis*

2. Three symbolic meanings of the circle are completion, protection, and loyalty.
   Difficulty: *Easy* **Objective:** *Literary Analysis*

3. Such transmission is oral tradition.
   Difficulty: *Average* **Objective:** *Literary Analysis*

4. This narrative would be classified as a legend.
   Difficulty: *Easy* **Objective:** *Literary Analysis*

5. A philosophy is less rigid and more open to change than a system is.
   Difficulty: *Challenging* **Objective:** *Interpretation*

6. Smith believes that winning is the byproduct of his philosophy. He cites Tom Osborne, the former football coach at the University of Nebraska, who had a similar belief.
   Difficulty: *Average* **Objective:** *Interpretation*

7. The anecdote strengthens by example the theme of playing unselfishly, because the player alone on the court got the point that he needed his teammates.
   Difficulty: *Challenging* **Objective:** *Literature Analysis*

8. Students should complete the diagram with: loyalty, mastery of fundamentals, and dedicated effort.
   Difficulty: *Average* **Objective:** *Literary Analysis*

9. Students may note Smith's emphasis on the graduation rate of his players and his choice of words: "We taught and drilled," "we practiced well and learned."
   Difficulty: *Easy* **Objective:** *Interpretation*

Essay

10. Students should include one specific example for each of the philosophy's three elements. For instance, for "playing together" they might cite Smith's anecdote about the player at the Air Force Academy. For "playing hard," students might refer to Smith's mention of having the whole team run sprints if a player slacked off at practice. For "playing smart," students might cite Smith's emphasis on mastering fundamentals at practice and executing them with poise. In their essays, students should include evaluations of Smith's examples and anecdotes.
    Difficulty: *Easy* **Objective:** *Essay*

11. Students should point out that by "playing hard," Smith means putting forth maximum effort and dedication. By "playing together," he means bringing an unselfish team approach to the game. By "playing smart," he means poise, precise execution, and mastery of fundamentals. In their essays, students should use specific examples and reasons to support their ideas about how the elements work together and about applications of Smith's philosophy to other areas of life.
    Difficulty: *Average* **Objective:** *Essay*

12. Students may point out that Smith's emphasis on effort, loyalty, and leadership ties in with shared values held by people in many cultures. In their essays, students might refer to other works in which loyalty and

dedicated effort emerge as important values. Use criteria such as clarity, coherence, and specific support to evaluate students' essays.

Difficulty: *Challenging* **Objective:** *Essay*

13. Students should cite details from the selection—such as the anecdote about making the whole team run sprints if a single player slacks off or the story about the player at the Air Force Academy—that underline Smith's belief that teammates should develop a keen sense of responsibility toward each other.

Difficulty: *Average* **Objective:** *Essay*

Oral Response

14. Oral responses should be clear, well organized, and well supported by appropriate examples from the selection.

Difficulty: *Average* **Objective:** *Oral Interpretation*

Selection Test A, p. 17

Learning About Themes in Literature

1. ANS: D	DIF: Easy	OBJ: Literary Analysis
2. ANS: A	DIF: Easy	OBJ: Literary Analysis
3. ANS: B	DIF: Easy	OBJ: Literary Analysis
4. ANS: D	DIF: Easy	OBJ: Literary Analysis
5. ANS: D	DIF: Easy	OBJ: Literary Analysis

Critical Reading

6. ANS: D	DIF: Easy	OBJ: Comprehension
7. ANS: A	DIF: Easy	OBJ: Interpretation
8. ANS: D	DIF: Easy	OBJ: Comprehension
9. ANS: B	DIF: Easy	OBJ: Interpretation
10. ANS: A	DIF: Easy	OBJ: Comprehension
11. ANS: C	DIF: Easy	OBJ: Interpretation
12. ANS: B	DIF: Easy	OBJ: Interpretation
13. ANS: B	DIF: Easy	OBJ: Interpretation
14. ANS: C	DIF: Easy	OBJ: Interpretation
15. ANS: C	DIF: Easy	OBJ: Interpretation

Essay

16. Students should include one specific example for each of the philosophy's three elements. For instance, for "playing together" they might cite Smith's anecdote about the player at the Air Force Academy. For "playing hard," students might quote Smith's mention of having the whole team run sprints if a player slacked off at practice. For "playing together," students might refer to Smith's comments about top scorers. In their essays, students should include evaluations of Smith's examples and anecdotes.

Difficulty: *Easy* **Objective:** *Essay*

17. Students' essays will vary, but they should include a specific application of each of the three elements in Smith's philosophy to academic course work. Evaluate students' essays for clarity, coherence, and specific support.

Difficulty: *Easy* **Objective:** *Essay*

18. Students should cite details from the selection that illustrate Smith's belief that teammates should develop a keen sense of responsibility toward each other. Examples might include the anecdote about making the whole team run sprints if a single player slacks off, or the story about the player at the Air Force Academy who liked to shoot every time he got the ball.

Difficulty: *Average* **Objective:** *Essay*

Selection Test B, p. 20

Learning About Themes in Literature

1. ANS: D	DIF: Average	OBJ: Literary Analysis
2. ANS: C	DIF: Average	OBJ: Literary Analysis
3. ANS: C	DIF: Challenging	OBJ: Literary Analysis
4. ANS: B	DIF: Average	OBJ: Literary Analysis
5. ANS: A	DIF: Average	OBJ: Literary Analysis
6. ANS: C	DIF: Average	OBJ: Literary Analysis

Critical Reading

7. ANS: B	DIF: Average	OBJ: Interpretation
8. ANS: C	DIF: Average	OBJ: Interpretation
9. ANS: C	DIF: Average	OBJ: Comprehension
10. ANS: B	DIF: Challenging	OBJ: Interpretation
11. ANS: C	DIF: Average	OBJ: Comprehension
12. ANS: B	DIF: Average	OBJ: Interpretation
13. ANS: D	DIF: Average	OBJ: Comprehension
14. ANS: C	DIF: Average	OBJ: Comprehension
15. ANS: B	DIF: Average	OBJ: Comprehension
16. ANS: C	DIF: Challenging	OBJ: Interpretation
17. ANS: C	DIF: Average	OBJ: Interpretation
18. ANS: D	DIF: Average	OBJ: Interpretation
19. ANS: C	DIF: Average	OBJ: Literary Analysis

Essay

20. Students should point out that by playing hard, Smith means putting forth maximum effort and dedication; by playing together, he means bringing an unselfish, team approach to the game; and by playing smart, he means poise, precise execution, and mastery of fundamentals. In their essays, students should use specific examples and reasons to support their ideas about how the elements work together and about applications of Smith's philosophy to other areas of life.

Difficulty: *Average* **Objective:** *Essay*

21. In their essays, students should point out that Smith sees himself, first and foremost, as a teacher committed to the education process. As a coach, he asked realistic things from his players. He stresses the importance of adapting to change and of practice as a learning experience. He relates, with obvious pride, that a very high percentage of his players attained their college degrees, and he explicitly refers to his own career as that of a teacher.

Difficulty: *Average*   **Objective:** *Essay*

22. Students may point out that Smith's emphasis on effort, loyalty, and leadership ties in to shared values held by people in many cultures. In their essays, students might refer to such works as Homer's *Odyssey,* in which loyalty and dedicated effort emerge as important values. Use criteria such as clarity, coherence, and specific support to evaluate students' essays.

Difficulty: *Challenging*   **Objective:** *Essay*

23. Students should cite details from the selection–such as the anecdote about making the whole team run sprints if a single player slacks off, or the story about the player at the Air Force Academy–that underline Smith's belief that teammates should develop a keen sense of responsibility toward each other.

Difficulty: *Average*   **Objective:** *Essay*

from the Odyssey, Part I by Homer

Vocabulary Warm-up Exercises, p. 24

A. 1. plucked
2. compelled
3. shepherd
4. companions
5. urged
6. entreat
7. penalty
8. immortal

B. Sample Answers
1. agony
   The team had suffered the *agony* of defeat too many times already.
2. cave
   The bears hibernated in the *cave* for the winter.
3. dreaded
   The sumo wrestler tried to beat his *dreaded* opponent.
4. uncaring
   In *A Christmas Carol*, Scrooge was *uncaring* about the sufferings of his employee, Bob Cratchit.
5. kingdom
   The shipwrecked sailors ended up in the *kingdom* of the Cyclops.

6. declined
   Nilda *declined* a second helping of fettuccine.
7. calm
   In a *calm* moment, we enjoyed the sunset.

Reading Warm-up A, p. 25

Sample Answers
1. A desire to do well; I felt *compelled* to stay home and study.
2. (their help); *Entreat* means "to ask in a very serious way."
3. tended a flock of sheep; I think the most important aspect of a *shepherd's* job is keeping the sheep safe.
4. (they could never die); Some people would like to believe that they are *immortal*.
5. (three Charities); A few of my favorite *companions* are Alice, Rosa, Charlie, and Dominic.
6. to compete in a singing contest with the Muses; Yesterday, my mother *urged* me to practice my clarinet.
7. the Sirens; A *penalty* I once had to pay was an overdue fine at the library.
8. (all of the Sirens' feathers); Eyebrows can be *plucked* out.

Reading Warm-up B, p. 26

Sample Answers
1. (awe-inspiring); A *formidable* character about whom I have read is Superman.
2. large cave; The bats slept in a *cavern* by the sea.
3. (peaceful); A *tranquil* spot that I like to visit is a meadow overlooking the ocean.
4. island; a spacious cavern covered in luxurious green vines; four fountains; meadows of soft green vegetation covered with violets; A *realm* I would like to reign over would be a warm, beautiful place where everyone got along and no one ever got sick.
5. wishing to return to his wife, Penelope, and their son, Telemachus; The last time I *refused* a generous offer was when my friend asked if she could drive me home, which would have been quite a bit out of her way.
6. (Calypso held him captive for seven years); Someone who is *indifferent* shows no emotion and acts uncaringly.
7. (Zeus' anger); *Tempt* means "to say or do something that might cause a problem."
8. grief, pain; Another situation that would cause *anguish* is the death of a loved one.

Writing About the Big Question, p. 27

A. 1. choices, character/hero
2. hero
3. honesty/justice/morality/responsibility, hero
4. standard
5. identify

B. Sample Answers

1. I realized that I had a responsibility to feed and care for Buster, our pet dog; after a talk with Mom, I realized I should study harder to get better grades in social studies.

2. Owning a family pet means that you have an **obligation** to care for that animal. Your **involvement** with the pet often results in lots of emotional satisfaction.

C. Sample Answer

A hero has an obligation to set a high standard. The choices he or she makes must be consistent with the ideals and values of society. Heroic status is a high honor, but it also carries with it obligations and responsibilities. That is why the recent scandals involving prominent baseball players and drugs are so disturbing. Sports heroes should set a model, especially for the young people who are among their best fans.

Literary Analysis: Epic Hero, p. 28

Sample Answers

1. **Mental:** He resolves to resist the temptations of the Lotus-Eaters.
   Physical: He rounds up some of his men and ties them on board to keep them from the Lotus-Eaters.

2. **Mental:** He devises the plan to fool the Cyclops and escape, using the name "Nohbdy" as the key.
   Physical: He leads his men in attacking the Cyclops at just the right time—after he has gotten the Cyclops drunk.

3. **Mental:** He works out a plan to escape the lure of the Sirens: stopping the ears of his crew with beeswax.
   Physical: He endures being tied to the mast and steels himself to hear the song that all others find irresistible.

4. **Mental:** His strategy enables the crew to avoid panic, minimize their losses, and at last escape.
   Physical: Never yielding, he leads his men in attempting to overcome the hazards of the monster and of the whirlpool.

Reading: Analyze the Influence of Historical and Cultural Context, p. 29

Sample Answers

1. An *odyssey* is a long, adventurous journey. The word was coined from the title of Homer's epic, the *Odyssey*, which recounts the numerous wanderings of the hero Odysseus.

2. The word *Homeric* means "large-scaled; massive; epic in scope." This word developed because of the impressive length and scope of Homer's epic poems and from their magnificent imagery and style.

3. around 800 B.C.

4. The passage implies that the ancient Greeks prized the values of a civilized social life, agricultural production, and knowledge. The Cyclopes, by contrast, lived a chaotic, ignorant, asocial life, and they were each indifferent to what others do.

Vocabulary Builder, p. 30

Sample Answers

A. 1. You would dislike the person because you would perceive him or her as crafty and treacherous.
   2. People tend to plunder, or loot, during wartime.
   3. It took Maria a short time to finish.
   4. You would use gentle words.
   5. You would feel fatigued.

B. 1. B; 2. D; 3. A; 4. C; 5. E

Enrichment: Geography, p. 31

Sample Answers

1. Ithaca is an island off the western coast of Greece.

2. The land of the Cyclops might have been located off the southern coast of Sicily.

3. The narrow body of water between two land masses might be difficult to pass through.

4. He sailed south to the Strait of Messina.

5. Students should plot locations in the following order: Troy, northern Africa, Aeolia, waters near Ithaca, Aeolia, Capri, and Strait of Messina.

Integrated Language Skills: Grammar, p. 32

A. 1. simple
   2. compound
   3. compound
   4. simple
   5. simple

B. Examine students' paragraphs for correct usage of the two types of sentences. You might ask students to work in small groups to identify examples of simple and compound sentences.

Open-Book Test, p. 35

Short Answer

1. The phrase is "skilled in all ways of contending." As the hero in an epic, Odysseus faces many challenges. He needs to possess the strength and intelligence to overcome unusual and difficult problems.
   Difficulty: *Easy* **Objective:** *Literary Analysis*

2. The cause of the doom was disobedience and mutiny. Instead of obeying Odysseus' orders and returning to the ships after the skirmish, the men drank wine and feasted on cattle. The main army of Cicones attacked them, killing many of the Greeks.
   Difficulty: *Challenging* **Objective:** *Interpretation*

3. Odysseus is heroic in that he drives three men to the ships, who had wanted to stay with the Lotus Eaters, and ties them to their rowing benches.
   Difficulty: *Challenging* **Objective:** *Literary Analysis*

4. The description paints a picture of a race of giants who live without laws and who do not tend their fields or crops. The Greeks regarded a legal system and organized agriculture as important foundations of a civilized society.

   Difficulty: *Average* **Objective:** *Reading*

5. Odysseus is curious and boastful. Because of these two traits, he puts the men in danger by insisting on staying in the cave to see what the Cyclops is like and by taunting the Cyclops after tricking and defeating him.

   Difficulty: *Challenging* **Objective:** *Literary Analysis*

6. Tiresias is a blind prophet whom Odysseus must consult in order to reach home.

   Difficulty: *Easy* **Objective:** *Interpretation*

7. He means that the wind is moving the ship, since the men do not have to row, and the steersman is guiding the ship.

   Difficulty: *Challenging* **Objective:** *Reading*

8. The story may have developed because of the dangerous and turbulent waters seafarers faced in order to take a ship through the strait.

   Difficulty: *Average* **Objective:** *Interpretation*

9. In the *Odyssey*, Part 1, a very skilled man *plunders* Troy, or takes goods and money from the city.

   Difficulty: *Average* **Objective:** *Vocabulary*

10. Strengths: crafty, cunning, able to contend with enemies and difficult situations, prays to the gods, tries to obey the laws and prophecies Weaknesses: desire for adventure and curiosity despite danger, pride, wanting to boast of his success in cunning, inability to make men obey crucial warnings

    Difficulty: *Average* **Objective:** *Literary Analysis*

Essay

11. Students may choose one of many adventures from the *Odyssey*, Part 1. If they choose the Lotus Eaters episode, they should mention landing on the coast of the Lotus Eaters, the three crewmen being seduced by the honeyed Lotus plant and not wanting to return to the ship, and Odysseus' forcefulness in persuading them to return to the ship.

    Difficulty: *Easy* **Objective:** *Essay*

12. Students should explain that Odysseus and his men sailed on the "salt immortal sea." Upon reaching shore, they sacrificed animals to attract the dead, who wanted to taste blood. Odysseus could learn about the future from the dead prophet Tiresias.

    Difficulty: *Average* **Objective:** *Essay*

13. Students should explain that Homer called on the Muse for inspiration. He asks her to "Sing in me." He may also have called on the Muse because the story involves many actions by the gods, some of whom help Odysseus but many of whom conspire against him. Students may also explain that Homer may have asked for help since the epic was long and full of many adventures; he wanted assistance in his mammoth task.

    Difficulty: *Challenging* **Objective:** *Essay*

14. Students may mention the way in which Odysseus rescued the men from various troubles, such as the Cyclops and Scylla and Charybdis as an example of his craftiness, cunning, and ability to contend with enemies. His actions in the Land of the Dead and in the episode of the Cattle of the Sun God show he tried to obey the gods and laws. His desire for dangerous adventure in his visit to the Cyclops is negative, however, as is his pride in wanting to boast of his accomplishments. Curiosity and pride lead Odysseus to behave irresponsibly in this episode.

    Difficulty: *Average* **Objective:** *Essay*

Oral Response

15. Oral responses should be clear, well organized, and well supported by appropriate examples from the selection.

    Difficulty: *Average* **Objective:** *Oral Interpretation*

Selection Test A, p. 38

Critical Reading

1. **ANS:** D	**DIF:** Easy	**OBJ:** Comprehension
2. **ANS:** B	**DIF:** Easy	**OBJ:** Literary Analysis
3. **ANS:** A	**DIF:** Easy	**OBJ:** Interpretation
4. **ANS:** C	**DIF:** Easy	**OBJ:** Reading
5. **ANS:** D	**DIF:** Easy	**OBJ:** Comprehension
6. **ANS:** C	**DIF:** Easy	**OBJ:** Comprehension
7. **ANS:** C	**DIF:** Easy	**OBJ:** Comprehension
8. **ANS:** A	**DIF:** Easy	**OBJ:** Literary Analysis
9. **ANS:** B	**DIF:** Easy	**OBJ:** Literary Analysis
10. **ANS:** C	**DIF:** Easy	**OBJ:** Interpretation
11. **ANS:** C	**DIF:** Easy	**OBJ:** Interpretation

Vocabulary and Grammar

12. **ANS:** B	**DIF:** Easy	**OBJ:** Vocabulary
13. **ANS:** C	**DIF:** Easy	**OBJ:** Vocabulary
14. **ANS:** D	**DIF:** Easy	**OBJ:** Grammar

Essay

15. Students should point out that Odysseus' strengths include craftiness, cunning, the ability to contend with enemies and difficult situations, pious respect for the gods, and dutiful attention to laws and prophecies. Odysseus' weaknesses include his curiosity and appetite for adventure despite the dangers involved, his pride and boastfulness about his own ingenuity, and his inability to make his crew obey crucial warnings, as in the episode of the oxen of the sun god.

    Difficulty: *Easy* **Objective:** *Essay*

16. Students should focus entirely on one of the adventures from Part 1 of the *Odyssey*. Check to see that they address all of the points: the location, the challenge, and the solution. If they choose the Lotus-Eaters

episode, for example, they should mention landing on the coast of the Lotus-Eaters, the three crewmen being seduced by the honeyed Lotus plant and not wanting to return to the ship, and Odysseus' forcefulness in persuading them to return to the ship. Evaluate the essays for clarity, conciseness, and accuracy.

Difficulty: *Easy*   **Objective:** *Essay*

17. Students may mention the way in which Odysseus rescued the men from various troubles, such as the Cyclops and Scylla and Charybdis, as an example of his craftiness, cunning, and ability to contend with enemies. His actions in the Land of the Dead and in the episode of the Cattle of the Sun God show he tried to obey the gods and laws.

Difficulty: *Average*   **Objective:** *Essay*

Selection Test B, p. 41

Critical Reading

1.	ANS: C	DIF: Average	OBJ: Comprehension
2.	ANS: A	DIF: Challenging	OBJ: Literary Analysis
3.	ANS: D	DIF: Average	OBJ: Interpretation
4.	ANS: B	DIF: Average	OBJ: Comprehension
5.	ANS: C	DIF: Average	OBJ: Reading
6.	ANS: A	DIF: Average	OBJ: Interpretation
7.	ANS: B	DIF: Average	OBJ: Interpretation
8.	ANS: C	DIF: Challenging	OBJ: Interpretation
9.	ANS: C	DIF: Challenging	OBJ: Interpretation
10.	ANS: C	DIF: Average	OBJ: Literary Analysis
11.	ANS: D	DIF: Average	OBJ: Literary Analysis
12.	ANS: C	DIF: Average	OBJ: Literary Analysis
13.	ANS: C	DIF: Challenging	OBJ: Comprehension
14.	ANS: C	DIF: Average	OBJ: Reading

Vocabulary and Grammar

15.	ANS: A	DIF: Average	OBJ: Vocabulary
16.	ANS: C	DIF: Average	OBJ: Vocabulary
17.	ANS: D	DIF: Average	OBJ: Grammar
18.	ANS: B	DIF: Average	OBJ: Grammar

Essay

19. Students who believe that Odysseus is admired by his crew might cite the series of situations in which the hero saves his men from harm or death. Students might point out that the crew obeys Odysseus' orders almost without exception. However, the crew's mutinous acts in the land of the Cicones and in Helios' land might serve as evidence of their lack of respect for Odysseus.

Difficulty: *Average*   **Objective:** *Essay*

20. Students should recognize that Odysseus, as an epic hero, is a model of the characteristics most admired in ancient Greece. They may mention the following characteristics: physical strength, mental quickness, bravery,

respect for the gods, leadership abilities, perseverance, fairness, honesty, and self-control. Events that demonstrate some of these qualities include Odysseus' outwitting the Cyclops, his bravery in battling Scylla, and his resistance to the temptations of Calypso, the Lotus-Eaters, and the cattle of the sun god.

Difficulty: *Average*   **Objective:** *Essay*

21. Students who believe that Odysseus controls his own destiny might cite his heroic deeds and ability to escape from life-threatening situations. They might point out that Odysseus must make choices all during his journey, as when he decides whether to stay with Calypso and whether to easily escape the Cyclops' cave or to remain to meet his challenge. Students who argue that the gods largely determine Odysseus' fate might cite Zeus' control of the winds, Poseidon's grudge against Odysseus for maiming Polyphemus, and the prophet Teiresias' predictions of the fate that eventually befalls Odysseus.

Difficulty: *Challenging*   **Objective:** *Essay*

22. Students may mention the way in which Odysseus rescued the men from various troubles, such as the Cyclops and Scylla and Charybdis, as an example of his craftiness, cunning, and ability to contend with enemies. His actions in the Land of the Dead and in the episode of the Cattle of the Sun God show he tried to obey the gods and laws. His desire for dangerous adventure in his visit to the Cyclops is negative, however, as is his pride in wanting to boast of his accomplishments. Curiosity and pride lead Odysseus to behave irresponsibly in this episode.

Difficulty: *Average*   **Objective:** *Essay*

from the Odyssey, Part II by Homer

Vocabulary Warm-up Exercises, p. 45

A. 1. intend
2. serene
3. vessel
4. faithful
5. presence
6. throngs
7. fame
8. marvel

B. Sample Answers

1. Darryl's *pride* made him seem stuck-up and difficult to be with.
2. Because she was using a *shield*, Diana deflected several arrows.
3. During *combat*, Nathan fought well.
4. In the *guise* of an old woman, young Ashton fooled many of his friends.
5. In great *outrage*, Helen urged everyone to revolt.
6. Jon's *wrath* led him to criticize Janet for her hurtful comments.

7. Brett's wonderful *handiwork* could not have been accomplished without great patience and skill.

Reading Warm-up A, p. 46

Sample Answers

1. (as the home of Odysseus); I might bring *fame* to myself by singing and dancing.
2. waited patiently for her husband's return from the Trojan War; The *faithful* dog waited patiently for his master to return.
3. the entire island would always have enough water; *Presence* means "being in a particular place."
4. (people); I have seen *throngs* of people gather for my city's annual Fourth of July parade and celebration.
5. (plan); This weekend, I *intend* to do some homework and then go to a movie.
6. ferry; The kind of *vessel* on which I would most like to travel or spend an afternoon is a sailboat.
7. (the many enchanting coves with crystal-clear waters); The people who can surf those gigantic waves in Hawaii made me *marvel*.
8. peaceful; The out-of-the-way path in the park where I walk my dog is *serene*.

Reading Warm-up B, p. 47

Sample Answers

1. holding; A *shield* is a broad piece of armor carried by warriors to protect themselves.
2. (only in defense of the state and home); Zachary believed that diplomacy was always preferable to *combat*.
3. did not like; Someone with too much *pride* would talk about how well he or she does something and would not act humbly at all.
4. (not worthy of any respect); One type of behavior that I find *contemptible* is lying.
5. (the finest cloth); The patchwork quilt that my aunt made me is the most amazing *handiwork* that I have ever seen.
6. an old beggar; If I could assume the *guise* of an animal, I would be an eagle because I think it would be fun to fly.
7. anger and outrage; If I ever felt *wrath*, I would take a deep breath and count to ten to control it.
8. (destroyed Arachne's loom); I would not want to be around someone who is full of *outrage* because that person would probably be yelling and screaming angrily and could even become dangerous.

Writing About the Big Question, p. 48

A. 1. hero, imitate
   2. involvement
   3. intentions
   4. wisdom
   5. obligation, responsibility

B. Sample Answers

1. I had to decide whether to go to the movies last weekend or study for Monday's math test; I had to choose between trying out for a role in the school play or joining the soccer team.
2. Last month, my **involvement** in dramatics made me eager to try out for a role in the school play. However, Karen made me change my mind when she pointed out that I had an **obligation** to help out the soccer team.

C. Sample Answer

The true character of a hero can be seen in his or her behavior during times of crisis. In the adventure with the Cyclops, for example, Odysseus is clever and resourceful. However, his curiosity and boastfulness are also evident. Odysseus lives up to a heroic standard, but he is also somewhat flawed.

Literary Analysis: Epic Simile, p. 49

A. 1. C; 2. B
B. 1. D; 2. B

Reading: Analyze the Influence of Historical and Cultural Context, p. 50

Sample Answers

1. The deep emotion of father and son at their reunion does not seem specifically rooted in ancient Greek culture; instead, it seems universal.
2. This episode seems universal, considering the well-known loyalty of dogs as "man's best friend."
3. The suitors' insolence and arrogance and their conduct in Odysseus' palace are specific aspects of an ancient Greek cultural context. The ambitious, unruly suitors might perceive an undefended woman (even one of high status) as "fair game." On the other hand, the young men's desire for luxury and power might be regarded as universal.
4. Some aspects of these episodes seem specific to the context: for example, the details of the weaving trick and the olive tree trunk. However, the desire of both husband and wife to know where they stand with each other after a separation of twenty years is easily understandable in universal, human terms.
5. Although Odysseus' desire to protect his wife, his son, and himself is understandable, his wholesale slaughter seems specifically rooted in the ancient Greek context, where violence and murder were accepted means of revenge.

Vocabulary Builder, p. 51

Sample Answers

A. 1. One would expect equity, which means "fairness" or "justice," from a judge.
   2. No, you would not treat someone whom you admire with contempt because *contempt* implies a lack of respect.

3. The word *maudlin* involves your emotions because it means "foolishly sentimental."

4. Their intentions are likely to be bad.

5. A fantastic story would inspire *incredulity* because you would find the story hard to believe.

6. You would probably react with annoyance.

B. 1. The first team overtakes the second one in the rankings.

2. You have solved it, because *disentangle* means to "straighten out."

3. They are more notable for their differences, since *dissimilar* means "not alike" or "different."

Enrichment: Greek Divinities, p. 52

Sample Answers

1. Zeus controls the sky, including the powerful thunder and lightning. This implies that he has a vantage point from which to see all that goes on. In addition, he stands for what is right and just, and he therefore brings order to the world.

2. Odysseus blinds Poseidon's son, the Cyclops Polyphemus. Though Poseidon was on the Greeks' side during the Trojan War, this act turns him against Odysseus.

3. It is Athena's role as goddess of wisdom that causes her to act as peacekeeper. She leads Odysseus and the suitors' families to understand that shedding more blood would be senseless and destructive.

Integrated Language Skills: Grammar, p. 53

A. 1. complex

2. compound-complex

3. complex

4. compound-complex

B. Examine students' paragraphs for correct usage of the four types of sentences. You might ask students to work in small groups to identify examples of all four types of sentences.

Open-Book Test, p. 56

Short Answer

1. Homer compares the crying to the cries of a hawk that has lost its nestlings to a farmer.

   Difficulty: *Easy* **Objective:** *Literary Analysis*

2. Students should explain that Telemachus believes that Athena and Zeus are powerful, but thinks they are far away and may be concerned with other affairs besides the events on Ithaca.

   Difficulty: *Average* **Objective:** *Interpretation*

3. The dog Argus recognizes Odysseus. After he wags his tail, Argus dies. Homer may have included the scene to underline the dog's loyalty to his master and, by implication, to contrast this loyalty ironically with the suitors' disloyalty.

   Difficulty: *Challenging* **Objective:** *Interpretation*

4. The suitor says that the beggar could be a god in disguise, visiting Earth to see how people are behaving. The passage seems to display an awareness that what Antinous has done directly flouts the social norms of a culture in which hospitality was greatly valued.

   Difficulty: *Average* **Objective:** *Reading*

5. Students should explain that Penelope grieves and longs for Odysseus; the suitors court her against her wishes and consume the goods of the household; she tricks the suitors into a delay by weaving and unweaving on her loom, but her trick is discovered; her parents urge her to remarry, and she feels her son cannot stand by while his property is consumed.

   She has waited for years and believed in the return of Odysseus.

   Difficulty: *Average* **Objective:** *Interpretation*

6. Odysseus handles his bow like a musician with a harp.

   Difficulty: *Average* **Objective:** *Literary Analysis*

7. Odysseus is ready to reveal himself and take revenge on the suitors.

   Difficulty: *Easy* **Objective:** *Reading*

8. Telemachus throws a spear, killing the suitor. The action reveals that Telemachus is quick-witted and resourceful.

   Difficulty: *Easy* **Objective:** *Interpretation*

9. Homer compares Odysseus to a swimmer who longs to reach the shore. Students should explain that the details in the comparison, such as the rough waters and Poseidon's blows, aptly fit Odysseus' situation during his wanderings and also portray the desperation of his longing for Penelope.

   Difficulty: *Challenging* **Objective:** *Literary Analysis*

10. Odysseus shows his *contempt*, or disdain or scorn, for the suitors.

    Difficulty: *Average* **Objective:** *Vocabulary*

Essay

11. Odysseus reveals himself to Telemachus and makes plans; Odysseus goes to his own hall and encounters the suitors in a disguise as a beggar; still disguised, Odysseus talks with Penelope; Odysseus wins the contest by shooting the arrow through the twelve axhandle sockets; Odysseus kills all the suitors; Odysseus reunites with Penelope.

    Difficulty: *Easy* **Objective:** *Essay*

12. Students should explain the comparison in the simile and then evaluate the appropriateness of the simile for the context.

    Difficulty: *Average* **Objective:** *Essay*

13. Students should identify three problems, solutions, and consequences. For example: Problem 1: Odysseus needs to travel unrecognized on Ithaca; Solution 1: Athena disguises him as a beggar; Consequence 1: Odysseus is able to get information about the current situation, and

he is able to enter the palace without arousing the suit-ors' suspicion. Evaluate students' essays for clarity, coherence, and accuracy.

Difficulty: *Challenging* **Objective:** *Essay*

14. Students may choose almost any of the plot strands of Part 2 to support the central idea that Odysseus feels responsibility for his family and their welfare. The suit-ors threaten not only the hero's life, but also his mar-riage and the inheritance he has accumulated for his son. These dangers, in turn, mean that the hero must struggle to overcome the heavy odds against him and destroy the suitors.

Difficulty: *Average* **Objective:** *Essay*

Oral Response

15. Oral responses should be clear, well organized, and well supported by appropriate examples from the selection.

Difficulty: *Average* **Objective:** *Oral Interpretation*

Selection Test A, p. 59

Critical Reading

1. ANS: C	DIF: Easy	OBJ: Comprehension
2. ANS: A	DIF: Easy	OBJ: Comprehension
3. ANS: C	DIF: Easy	OBJ: Comprehension
4. ANS: C	DIF: Easy	OBJ: Reading
5. ANS: B	DIF: Easy	OBJ: Comprehension
6. ANS: B	DIF: Easy	OBJ: Literary Analysis
7. ANS: D	DIF: Easy	OBJ: Interpretation
8. ANS: A	DIF: Easy	OBJ: Literary Analysis
9. ANS: D	DIF: Easy	OBJ: Interpretation
10. ANS: C	DIF: Easy	OBJ: Interpretation

Vocabulary and Grammar

11. ANS: A	DIF: Easy	OBJ: Vocabulary
12. ANS: B	DIF: Easy	OBJ: Vocabulary
13. ANS: C	DIF: Easy	OBJ: Grammar
14. ANS: B	DIF: Easy	OBJ: Grammar

Essay

15. Students should mention the obstacles facing Odysseus, Telemachus, and their small group of faithful household members. In the conflict with the suitors, Odysseus faces long odds but triumphs. The situation with Penelope is also suspenseful, as each partner tests the other. Evalu-ate students' essays for clarity, coherence, and specific references to the text.

Difficulty: *Easy* **Objective:** *Essay*

16. Students should include the plot line that the suitors threaten not only the hero's life, but also his marriage and the inheritance he has accumulated for his son.

These dangers, in turn, mean that the hero must strug-gle to overcome the heavy odds against him and destroy the suitors.

Difficulty: *Average* **Objective:** *Essay*

Selection Test B, p. 62

Critical Reading

1. ANS: D	DIF: Challenging	OBJ: Reading
2. ANS: A	DIF: Average	OBJ: Literary Analysis
3. ANS: C	DIF: Average	OBJ: Comprehension
4. ANS: A	DIF: Average	OBJ: Interpretation
5. ANS: D	DIF: Average	OBJ: Interpretation
6. ANS: B	DIF: Average	OBJ: Comprehension
7. ANS: A	DIF: Average	OBJ: Interpretation
8. ANS: C	DIF: Challenging	OBJ: Interpretation
9. ANS: C	DIF: Average	OBJ: Interpretation
10. ANS: D	DIF: Average	OBJ: Literary Analysis
11. ANS: A	DIF: Average	OBJ: Interpretation
12. ANS: C	DIF: Average	OBJ: Comprehension
13. ANS: D	DIF: Challenging	OBJ: Reading

Vocabulary and Grammar

14. ANS: D	DIF: Challenging	OBJ: Vocabulary
15. ANS: C	DIF: Average	OBJ: Vocabulary
16. ANS: C	DIF: Average	OBJ: Vocabulary
17. ANS: B	DIF: Average	OBJ: Grammar

Essay

18. Students should identify three problems, solutions, and consequences. The following is an example: Problem 1: Odysseus needs to travel unrecognized on Ithaca. Solution 1: Athena disguises him. Consequence 1: Odysseus is able to get information on the situation and also to enter the palace. Evaluate students' essays for clarity, coherence, and accuracy.

Difficulty: *Average* **Objective:** *Essay*

19. Students should focus on a single event or action and speculate on how the epic would change if that event or action had not occurred in the same way that it does in the text. Students may, for example, select the instance in which Athena appears to Odysseus and disguises him as a beggar. If Athena had not done this, it is likely that Odysseus' return home would have been very dif-ferent. He might have been jailed or even slain immedi-ately. Students should support their speculation about an alternative outcome with specific details.

Difficulty: *Average* **Objective:** *Essay*

20. Students may choose almost any of the plot strands of Part 2 to support the central idea that Odysseus feels

responsibility for his family and their welfare. The suitors threaten not only the hero's life, but also his marriage and the inheritance he has accumulated for his son. These dangers, in turn, mean that the hero must struggle to overcome the heavy odds against him and destroy the suitors.

Difficulty: *Average*   **Objective:** *Essay*

Poetry by Edna St. Vincent Millay, Margaret Atwood, Derek Walcott, and Constantine Cavafy

Vocabulary Warm-up Exercises, p. 66

A. 1. valuable
2. ancient
3. weaving
4. design
5. boring
6. shuttle
7. merchandise
8. purchase

B. Sample Answers

1. Yes, I would be scared of a *fierce* dog because I know it could be violent and attack at any time.
2. To a person to whom I had just been introduced, I might make the *gesture* of extending my hand for a handshake.
3. If a temptation were *irresistible*, I would not be able to walk away from it because I would not be able to say no.
4. I would not be afraid of a *mythical* creature such as a fire-breathing dragon because I know that such a creature does not exist.
5. No, I would not want to be inside a walled city during a *siege* because the city would be surrounded by enemies who would not allow food and water to get inside.
6. Yes, if several *squadrons* of armed soldiers were protecting my city, I would feel safe because I would know that many individuals stood between danger and me.
7. If someone ran a circus in the *tradition* of old-time circuses, that person would probably not use new technology.

Reading Warm-up A, p. 67

Sample Answers

1. thread into cloth; I could make a blanket by *weaving*.
2. (in Mesopotamia and Turkey as long as 10,000 years ago); I would like to learn more about the *ancient* civilization of China.
3. It could be used to catch fish and trap game; One possession I have that is *valuable* is an antique dresser that belonged to my grandmother.

4. (patterns); I like the *design* of my new bedspread, which is a simple one of dots and lines.
5. By hand, a person had to lift each warp thread to pass the weft under and over it. One activity that I find *boring* is peeling potatoes.
6. (This tapered device holds the weft thread. It passes between warp threads, pushing, or beating, the threads into place.); Without the *shuttle*, weaving is a very difficult process.
7. woven items; The *merchandise* I would make to sell is watercolor drawings.
8. (shops); Three things that I want to *purchase* are sweaters, CDs, and a new bike.

Reading Warm-up B, p. 68

Sample Answers

1. (Greeks); *Tradition* means "with some of the same features as something done in the past."
2. According to Greek legend; A *mythical* creature I have read about and seen pictures of is a unicorn.
3. She was so beautiful; I find hot fudge sundaes *irresistible*.
4. (difficult [possibly win]); My cousin had many *trials*, one of which was breaking his leg and another was his dad losing his job.
5. she dipped the baby Achilles into the magic waters of the River Styx; One friendly *gesture* I use often is waving good-bye to my mother in the morning.
6. (fighters); The lions I saw on a TV documentary about Africa were *fierce*.
7. (Troy); When a city is under *siege*, it is surrounded by an enemy, and the people in the city cannot come and go at will and they cannot get the supplies they need.
8. his supporters in Greece; Skills that soldiers in *squadrons* need are discipline and a good aim.

Writing About the Big Question, p. 69

A. 1. morality, choices
2. justice
3. imitate
4. wisdom

B. Sample Answers

1. My older brother got a traffic ticket for running a red light, but the ticket was unfair. My friend Ned was falsely accused by our science teacher of cheating on a test.
2. My older brother's **intentions** were good when he sped up at an intersection as the light was turning yellow. He felt he had an **obligation** to avoid an accident with a pedestrian who was crossing the street against the light right at that moment.

C. Sample Answer

In my own life, I know I am responsible for Rasmus, our pet Labrador. If I do not live up to this obligation, one consequence might be that our dog would get sick or become badly behaved. When I make responsible choices, one positive result is that I feel fulfilled and happy.

Literary Analysis: Contemporary Interpretations, p. 70

1. C; 2. A; 3. B; 4. B; 5. A

Vocabulary Builder, p. 71

A. Sample Answers

1. They are eager to purchase the old silver coin because they believe it is authentic.
2. Because the landscape was so picturesque, we took dozens of photographs.
3. The siege of the city was unsuccessful, so the soldiers outside the walls retreated.
4. Because he is a person of lofty ideals, we admire him greatly.
5. As a merchant with great integrity, he never defrauds his customers.

B. 1. C; 2. D; 3. A; 4. B; 5. D

Open-Book Test, p. 73

Short Answer

1. The gesture is crying or wiping away tears.
   Difficulty: *Easy*   **Objective:** *Interpretation*
2. The theme consists of differences in the experience and emotions of men and women.
   Difficulty: *Challenging*   **Objective:** *Literary Analysis*
3. If it were not authentic, the gesture would be false or deceptive.
   Difficulty: *Average*   **Objective:** *Vocabulary*
4. The speaker is one of Homer's sirens, whose objective is to trick the reader to come near.
   Difficulty: *Average*   **Objective:** *Literary Analysis*
5. Sample answers: A bird costume is a disguise, hiding the true self. A bird suit expresses fun or merriment, which deceives and disarms the listener into a false sense of security.
   Difficulty: *Easy*   **Objective:** *Literary Analysis*
6. Billy Blue alludes to Odysseus in the *Odyssey.*
   Difficulty: *Easy*   **Objective:** *Literary Analysis*
7. In "Ithaca," the journey and its adventures and experience gained are more important than Odysseus' objective of reaching the end of the journey.
   Difficulty: *Average*   **Objective:** *Literary Analysis*
8. The language in Walcott's poem is less solemn and dignified than Homer's language. It contains contemporary phrases like "main man" and "things sure fell apart," which readers today will understand.
   Difficulty: *Challenging*   **Objective:** *Interpretation*

9. Allusions to the *Odyssey:* journey to Ithaca (plot); Lestrygonians (character); Cyclopes (character); Poseidon (character); Phoenician markets (setting); let it [voyage] last for long years (plot); anchor at the isle (setting).
   Difficulty: *Average*   **Objective:** *Literary Analysis*
10. The journey provides people with wisdom and experience.
    Difficulty: *Average*   **Objective:** *Interpretation*

Essay

11. In "An Ancient Gesture," Millay presents the story of the *Odyssey* from Penelope's point of view. The poem may imply that staying home was harder than traveling. In "Ithaca," Cavafy underlines that the importance of development and growth during the journey is more important than arrival at the final destination. Evaluate students' essays for clarity and coherence, and make sure that students have supported their statements with references to the text.
    Difficulty: *Easy*   **Objective:** *Essay*
12. Students should note that Cavafy is comparing the journey to Ithaca to the journey of life. For the speaker, Ithaca is more than just a physical location that motivates a journey; it is a profound learning experience. Making the most of the actual journey of life is more important than reaching specific goals.
    Difficulty: *Average*   **Objective:** *Essay*
13. Students should note that while Atwood's Sirens share many features of Homer's Sirens, Atwood's work actually presents the Sirens' point of view. Millay, like Atwood, presents many details from Homer's text but describes Penelope's feelings in greater depth. Walcott includes the original details of Odysseus' journey but uses contemporary language and interpretations. Cavafy mentions some details of Odysseus' journey to Ithaca that appear in Homer's epic, but he wants people to think of this journey as the journey of life and that the journey is what is important, not the destination.
    Difficulty: *Challenging*   **Objective:** *Essay*
14. Responses will vary. Evaluate students' writing on clarity, coherence, and specific support.
    Difficulty: *Average*   **Objective:** *Essay*

Oral Response

15. Oral responses should be clear, well organized, and well supported by details from the selections.
    Difficulty: *Average*   **Objective:** *Oral Interpretation*

Selection Test A, p. 76

Critical Reading

1. **ANS:** B	**DIF:** Easy	**OBJ:** Comprehension
2. **ANS:** B	**DIF:** Easy	**OBJ:** Interpretation
3. **ANS:** B	**DIF:** Easy	**OBJ:** Literary Analysis

4. **ANS:** C	**DIF:** Easy	**OBJ:** Comprehension
5. **ANS:** D	**DIF:** Easy	**OBJ:** Interpretation
6. **ANS:** A	**DIF:** Easy	**OBJ:** Interpretation
7. **ANS:** B	**DIF:** Easy	**OBJ:** Comprehension
8. **ANS:** C	**DIF:** Easy	**OBJ:** Literary Analysis
9. **ANS:** C	**DIF:** Easy	**OBJ:** Literary Analysis
10. **ANS:** A	**DIF:** Easy	**OBJ:** Interpretation
11. **ANS:** A	**DIF:** Easy	**OBJ:** Literary Analysis

Vocabulary

12. **ANS:** A	**DIF:** Easy	**OBJ:** Vocabulary
13. **ANS:** C	**DIF:** Easy	**OBJ:** Vocabulary

Essay

14. Students should choose one poem and identify what they think the writer's purpose is. For example, in "An Ancient Gesture," Millay's purpose is to present the story from Penelope's point of view. The poem may also imply that staying home was harder than traveling. Evaluate students' essays for clarity and coherence, and check to see that students have supported their statements with references to the text.

Difficulty: *Easy* Objective: *Essay*

15. Evaluate students' essays for clarity and coherence and for specific references to the text. If students choose "An Ancient Gesture," for example, they may say that both works show Penelope's loneliness and sorrow. In Homer, the reader learns more details about Penelope's life, such as her feeling that she cannot resist the pressures to marry again. Millay's poem focuses more on Penelope's pain and shows her overwhelmed and crying. Some students may feel that Millay's poem helps them understand Penelope better. Others may feel that Homer gives more information and lets Penelope speak more.

Difficulty: *Easy* Objective: *Essay*

16. Penelope is the heroine. Her heroic action was her patient waiting for the return of Ulysses, or Odysseus. According to the poet, Penelope made the authentic, ancient, and heroic gesture of crying because of her loneliness and the uncertainty of his return.

Difficulty: *Average* Objective: *Essay*

Selection Test B, p. 79

Critical Reading

1. **ANS:** C	**DIF:** Average	**OBJ:** Comprehension
2. **ANS:** D	**DIF:** Average	**OBJ:** Interpretation
3. **ANS:** C	**DIF:** Challenging	**OBJ:** Literary Analysis
4. **ANS:** B	**DIF:** Average	**OBJ:** Comprehension
5. **ANS:** C	**DIF:** Average	**OBJ:** Interpretation
6. **ANS:** D	**DIF:** Challenging	**OBJ:** Interpretation

7. **ANS:** D	**DIF:** Average	**OBJ:** Literary Analysis
8. **ANS:** A	**DIF:** Average	**OBJ:** Interpretation
9. **ANS:** D	**DIF:** Average	**OBJ:** Literary Analysis
10. **ANS:** C	**DIF:** Average	**OBJ:** Interpretation
11. **ANS:** A	**DIF:** Average	**OBJ:** Comprehension
12. **ANS:** D	**DIF:** Average	**OBJ:** Comprehension
13. **ANS:** B	**DIF:** Average	**OBJ:** Interpretation
14. **ANS:** A	**DIF:** Average	**OBJ:** Interpretation
15. **ANS:** C	**DIF:** Challenging	**OBJ:** Interpretation

Vocabulary

16. **ANS:** A	**DIF:** Average	**OBJ:** Vocabulary
17. **ANS:** B	**DIF:** Average	**OBJ:** Vocabulary
18. **ANS:** C	**DIF:** Average	**OBJ:** Vocabulary
19. **ANS:** C	**DIF:** Challenging	**OBJ:** Vocabulary

Essay

20. Students should note that Cavafy is comparing the journey to Ithaca to the journey of life. To the speaker, Ithaca is more than just a physical location that motivates a journey; it is a profound learning experience. Making the most of the actual journey of life is more important than reaching specific goals.

Difficulty: *Average* Objective: *Essay*

21. Students should note that while Atwood's Sirens share many details with Homer's Sirens, Atwood's work actually presents the Sirens' point of view. Millay, like Atwood, presents many details from Homer's epic but describes Penelope's feelings in greater depth. Walcott includes the original details of Odysseus' journey but uses contemporary language and interpretations. Cavafy mentions details of Odysseus' journey to Ithaca that appear in Homer's epic, but he wants people to think of this journey as the journey of life.

Difficulty: *Average* Objective: *Essay*

22. Responses will vary. Evaluate students' writing on clarity, coherence, and specific support.

Difficulty: *Average* Objective: *Essay*

Writing Workshop

Timed Essay: Integrating Grammar Skills, p. 83

A. 1. S; 2. F; 3. R; 4. S

B. Sample Answers

1. I am taking a class in summer school, and so is Joanna.
2. We are learning some recent advances in computers.
3. I would rather be outside when the warm weather is so inviting.
4. correct

Benchmark Test 11, p. 84

MULTIPLE CHOICE

1. ANS: C
2. ANS: C
3. ANS: A
4. ANS: A
5. ANS: D
6. ANS: C
7. ANS: B
8. ANS: B
9. ANS: C
10. ANS: A
11. ANS: D
12. ANS: A
13. ANS: C
14. ANS: D
15. ANS: C
16. ANS: A
17. ANS: B
18. ANS: D
19. ANS: A
20. ANS: D
21. ANS: D
22. ANS: B
23. ANS: D
24. ANS: A
25. ANS: D
26. ANS: C
27. ANS: C
28. ANS: A
29. ANS: D

WRITING

30. Students should identify heroic traits of the individual they describe and then provide actions or other details that illustrate those traits.
31. Students should provide accurate details of the person's life in chronological order. Citing concrete examples, they should make clear for what reasons or achievements the person is famous.
32. Students should write technical directions that are clear, well-organized, and easy to follow. Instructions should include multiple steps.

"Three Skeleton Key" by George G. Toudouze

Vocabulary Warm-up Exercises, p. 93

A.
1. vivid
2. occupied
3. reeking
4. devoured
5. exception
6. descriptions
7. emerged
8. superior

B. Sample Answers
1. We were disgusted by the *nauseating* smell of his cigar.
2. Our mother warned us to stay inside during the *treacherous* weather.
3. He began *regaining* weight when he started snacking all the time.
4. As *guardians* of the secret information, we revealed it to nobody.
5. The story was set in a *fantastic* world that was nothing like the real world we live in.
6. The mountain range was a *barrier* that slowed down the progress of the wagon train.
7. The principal's voice was a *distraction* when we were trying to listen to our teacher's lesson.

Reading Warm-up A, p. 94

Sample Answers
1. the entire lower deck of the ship; Rats may have *occupied* a house that had been standing vacant for a long time.
2. (garbage and rotting fish); Spoiled food in the refrigerator would cause a *reeking* kitchen.
3. with great enthusiasm; Still, they *came out* from that ship with great enthusiasm.
4. (houseguests); I think that a cat is far *superior* to a dog.
5. less than flattering; *Descriptions* are "statements telling what something is like."
6. (filthy vermin); Other *vivid* words include "disgusting beasts" and "vile pests."
7. my fair share of farm products; *Devoured* means "ate very quickly and greedily" while *ate* makes no reference to how hungry someone is or how quickly or slowly the person has eaten.
8. a few overly curious individuals who showed insufficient respect for my privacy; An *exception* to the rule of not to use *ain't* would be if you were writing dialogue in a story and wanted to use dialect.

7. my fair share of farm products; *Devoured* means "ate very quickly and greedily" while *ate* makes no reference to how hungry someone is or how quickly or slowly the person has eaten.

8. a few overly curious individuals who showed insufficient respect for my privacy; An *exception* to the rule of not to use *ain't* would be if you were writing dialogue in a story and wanted to use dialect.

Reading Warm-up B, p. 95

Sample Answers

1. (the ship); *Framework* means "a structure supporting something."

2. the water on the outside and the people and cargo within; A wall and a fence can each serve as a *barrier*.

3. (dangers); A person who pretends to be your friend and then spreads false rumors about you is *treacherous*.

4. (Seasickness); Spinning around in circles on an amusement park ride was a *nauseating* experience for me.

5. Gazing at the beautiful starry sky; Knowing that my parents were in the audience at the school play was a *distraction* for me.

6. (safety); Good *guardians* would have a strong sense of responsibility and would be able to make good decisions.

7. their [passengers'] confidence; I had trouble *regaining* strength in my leg after I broke it.

8. (mermaids, sea serpents); *Fantastic* creatures from books include Tolkien's hobbits and the dragons in Anne McCaffrey's Pern series.

Writing About the Big Question, p. 96

A. 1. morality/responsibility/justice/honesty/obligation
   2. responsibility
   3. serve
   4. intentions
   5. wisdom/justice/honesty

B. Sample Answers

1. Answers will vary.

2. Sentences should explain students' choices and should use at least two of the Big Question vocabulary words.

C. Sample Answer

A hero may not choose wisely all the time, but he or she must make choices that are consistent with society's values. For example, Odysseus would not be behaving consistently with ancient Greek values if he spared the suitors. The Greek heroic code required that Odysseus slay the men who had dishonored his household and threatened his son.

Literary Analysis: Protagonist and Antagonist, p. 97

1. The protagonist is the story's narrator, who serves along with two other workers as a lighthouse keeper on a lonely island off the coast of South America.

2. His unusual qualities include his enjoyment of his lonely occupation and his refusal to allow the terrifying events he recalls to interfere with his enjoyment of life at Three Skeleton Key.

3. The ships' rats are the antagonist in the story.

4. The author uses personification when he describes the rats as "wise," "intelligent," "clannish," "brave," and "vengeful" and when he uses sentences such as "From the several tussles that broke out, they resented being ridiculed for their failure to capture the ship."

5. They are involved in a struggle for survival.

Reading: Compare and Contrast Characters, p. 98

Sample Answers

1. Itchoua is older and therefore more experienced. It is he, for example, who first recognizes that the *Cornelius de Witt* is an empty ship.

2. Le Gleo, unlike the others, cracks under the strain of the rats' attack and begins to suffer from nightmares and then madness. His reaction shows that people react in very different ways to pressure and crises.

3. Toudouze succeeds in personifying the rats very effectively, suggesting that they are intelligent, tough creatures capable of planning their own actions and of experiencing emotions such as revenge and resentment.

4. At both the beginning and the end of the story, the narrator seems to love his profession and to have affectionate feelings for Three Skeleton Key. He says, for example, that he practically wept when his assignment on the island came to an end. The comparison suggests that the narrator may not be bothered by strange and dangerous happenings.

Vocabulary Builder, p. 99

A. 1. A; 2. C; 3. B

B. Sample Answers

1. The review would be critical.

2. They would feel concerned about the decline in sales.

3. I would not feel comfortable because the bus would be moving jerkily.

4. No, because *provisions* means "supplies for the future."

5. No, because a *monotonous* lecture would probably be boring.

6. No, because *incessantly* means "constantly" or "without interruption."

C. 1. It has not affected you greatly, because *minimal* means "very small."

2. They are probably not significant, since *minuscule* means "tiny."

Enrichment: Lighthouses, p. 100

Students' notes will vary depending on the advances that they identify, but the following are milestones that might be mentioned: the 1584 lighthouse built by Louis de Foix in the Gironde estuary in southwestern France—the first lighthouse built in the open sea; the tower design developed by John Smeaton in the eighteenth century for wind and wave resistance; the Argand Lamp invented in 1782; the first revolving light installed in a Swedish lighthouse in 1781; and the incandescent lamp that came into use in the 1920s and is still standard today.

Open-Book Test, p. 101

Short Answer

1. The narrator wants to earn and save a certain amount of money before he gets married.

   Difficulty: *Easy*   **Objective:** *Literary Analysis*

2. the rats

   Difficulty: *Easy*   **Objective:** *Literary Analysis*

3. The writer uses "intelligent," "clannish," "seawise," "knowledge of the sea," and "uncanny ability to foretell the weather" to describe the rats as a powerful force.

   Difficulty: *Average*   **Objective:** *Literary Analysis*

4. Hear the rats' teeth grate on the glass; see their beady eyes, sharp claws, and teeth; poisoned the lungs with their "pestilential, nauseating smell."

   Difficulty: *Easy*   **Objective:** *Interpretation*

5. Le Gleo cracks under the strain, while Itchoua and the narrator remain calm.

   Difficulty: *Average*   **Objective:** *Reading*

6. Not lighting the lantern is the only way the men, the protagonists, can think of to signal to the mainland about their desperate situation. This causes a conflict because this decision goes against the men's training. The lantern is the only source of aid for seafarers who might otherwise suffer a shipwreck.

   Difficulty: *Challenging*   **Objective:** *Literary Analysis*

7. First, the narrator recalls a terrifying experience and describes the island in ominous terms. At the end, however, he says he regrets having to leave the island.

   Difficulty: *Challenging*   **Objective:** *Reading*

8. The conflict is best described as a clash between life and death.

   Difficulty: *Average*   **Objective:** *Literary Analysis*

9. The sharks help the men by eating some of the rats.

   Difficulty: *Average*   **Objective:** *Interpretation*

10. (1) Tug maneuvered the barge which was full of meat. This served as a lure for the rats to swim out and board the barge as it lurched in the water. (2) Incendiary shell from patrol boat set the barge on fire, causing the rats to plunge into the water. (3) Shrapnel caused a diminution of their numbers, and then sharks ate the survivors.

    Difficulty: *Average*   **Objective:** *Vocabulary*

Essay

11. Students should identify the narrator as the protagonist and the rats as the antagonists in the story. Students

should comment on such stages in the plot as the men's realization that the rats have attacked the derelict's crew, the wreck of the ship, the rats' attack on the lighthouse, and the episode with the barge of meat and the fire, which is the climax of the story. Finally, students should point out that the reader is interested in the protagonist's struggle because it represents the universal human instinct for survival.

    Difficulty: *Easy*   **Objective:** *Essay*

12. Students should point out that a third-person point of view might have reduced the story's immediacy. In particular, the men's realization of the true causes for the strange behavior of the abandoned ship might have been less suspenseful. Our firsthand impressions of the protagonist might also have been less vivid. Students should support their ideas with examples.

    Difficulty: *Average*   **Objective:** *Essay*

13. Students should mention the description of the ship's purposeful approach to the island and its wreck, or the narrator's use of words like "wise," "intelligent," "brace," and "vengeful" to describe the rats. Students' responses should be supported by examples from the story.

    Difficulty: *Challenging*   **Objective:** *Essay*

14. Students may point out that the narrator goes out of his way to emphasize the way in which the decision not to light the lantern weighed on the conscience of the men, since their action might result in peril or even death for seafarers. The narrator's decision to shock Le Gleo by striking him across the mouth also shows a certain responsibility, since Le Gleo's panic might otherwise have had the effect of unhinging all three men.

    Difficulty: *Average*   **Objective:** *Essay*

Oral Response

15. Oral responses should be clear, well organized, and well supported by appropriate examples from the selection.

    Difficulty: *Average*   **Objective:** *Oral Interpretation*

Selection Test A, p. 104

Critical Reading

1. ANS: C	DIF: Easy	OBJ: Comprehension
2. ANS: A	DIF: Easy	OBJ: Interpretation
3. ANS: B	DIF: Easy	OBJ: Comprehension
4. ANS: A	DIF: Easy	OBJ: Literary Analysis
5. ANS: B	DIF: Easy	OBJ: Interpretation
6. ANS: D	DIF: Easy	OBJ: Literary Analysis
7. ANS: C	DIF: Easy	OBJ: Interpretation
8. ANS: A	DIF: Easy	OBJ: Reading
9. ANS: C	DIF: Easy	OBJ: Interpretation
10. ANS: C	DIF: Easy	OBJ: Reading
11. ANS: C	DIF: Easy	OBJ: Interpretation

Vocabulary and Grammar

12. ANS: B	DIF: Easy	OBJ: Vocabulary
13. ANS: B	DIF: Easy	OBJ: Vocabulary
14. ANS: B	DIF: Easy	OBJ: Grammar
15. ANS: D	DIF: Easy	OBJ: Grammar

Essay

16. Students should identify the narrator as the protagonist and the rats as the antagonist in the story. Students should comment on such stages in the plot as the men's realization that the rats have attacked the derelict's crew, the wreck of the ship, the rats' attack on the lighthouse, and the episode with the barge of meat and the fire, which is the climax of the story. Finally, students should point out that the reader is interested in the protagonist's struggle because it represents the instinct for survival.

    Difficulty: *Easy* **Objective:** *Essay*

17. Students should point out that a third-person point of view might have reduced the story's immediacy. In particular, the men's realization of the true causes for the strange behavior of the abandoned ship might have been less suspenseful. Our firsthand impressions of the protagonist might have also been less vivid. Students should support their ideas with examples.

    Difficulty: *Easy* **Objective:** *Essay*

18. Students may point out that the narrator emphasizes the way in which the decision not to light the lantern weighed on the conscience of the men, since their action might result in peril or even death for seafarers. The narrator's decision to shock Le Gleo by striking him across the mouth also shows a certain responsibility, since Le Gleo's panic might otherwise have had the effect of unhinging all three men.

    Difficulty: *Average* **Objective:** *Essay*

Selection Test B, p. 107

Critical Reading

1. ANS: D	DIF: Average	OBJ: Literary Analysis
2. ANS: B	DIF: Average	OBJ: Comprehension
3. ANS: A	DIF: Average	OBJ: Interpretation
4. ANS: B	DIF: Average	OBJ: Comprehension
5. ANS: C	DIF: Average	OBJ: Literary Analysis
6. ANS: B	DIF: Average	OBJ: Reading
7. ANS: D	DIF: Average	OBJ: Comprehension
8. ANS: B	DIF: Average	OBJ: Comprehension
9. ANS: C	DIF: Average	OBJ: Comprehension
10. ANS: A	DIF: Challenging	OBJ: Reading
11. ANS: B	DIF: Average	OBJ: Interpretation
12. ANS: C	DIF: Average	OBJ: Literary Analysis

Vocabulary and Grammar

13. ANS: A	DIF: Average	OBJ: Vocabulary
14. ANS: B	DIF: Average	OBJ: Vocabulary
15. ANS: B	DIF: Average	OBJ: Grammar

Essay

16. Students should point out that the narrator seems well-versed in his job and adjusted to the lonely, demanding life that a career like his involves. In the crisis of the attack, he behaves calmly and does not become unhinged, as Le Gleo does. Students may also point out that the narrator's coolness at the end of the story seems confusing after the terrifying account of the rats' attack.

    Difficulty: *Average* **Objective:** *Essay*

17. Students should mention the description of the ship's purposeful approach to the island and its wreck or the narrator's use of words like "wise," "intelligent," "brave," and "vengeful" to describe the rats. Students' responses should be supported by examples from the story.

    Difficulty: *Challenging* **Objective:** *Essay*

18. Students may point out that the narrator goes out of his way to emphasize the way in which the decision not to light the lantern weighed on the conscience of the men, since their action might result in peril or even death for seafarers. The narrator's decision to shock Le Gleo by striking him across the mouth also shows a certain responsibility, since Le Gleo's panic might otherwise have had the effect of unhinging all three men.

    Difficulty: *Average* **Objective:** *Essay*

"The Red-headed League"
by Sir Arthur Conan Doyle

Vocabulary Warm-up Exercises, p. 111

A. 1. occupation
2. exceedingly
3. interfere
4. advertisement
5. obvious
6. bizarre
7. vulnerable
8. despair

B. Sample Answers
1. In my town, *commerce* takes place in the big mall and downtown.
2. You should show *deference* to older people because it is polite to respect people who are older than you.
3. An *effective* way to prepare for an exam would be to study and get enough sleep the night before.
4. Sometimes, *intuition* can be mistaken and you must use your reasoning powers.

5. If I had *misgivings*, I probably would not go along with my friend's plans.

6. If my close friend were telling me a boring and long *narrative*, I might politely tell her I did not have the time to listen to the whole thing right then.

7. It might be a bad idea to be *relentless* when trying to reach a goal that is not very important.

8. I would probably feel complimented if someone said I am *unique* because being one of a kind is very special and something to be proud of.

Reading Warm-up A, p. 112

Sample Answers

1. his practice was not attracting very many patients; It is *obvious* to me that I am going to have to study hard to pass my French midterm.

2. (profession); I think that nursing is an *occupation* I would be good at.

3. (Detective stories); A synonym for *exceedingly* is "extremely."

4. (newspaper); Holmes was a very popular character, so the people who took out the *advertisement* would use him to get people's attention and to sell their product.

5. his ambition to be recognized as a writer of serious fiction; *Interfere* means "getting involved when you are not wanted."

6. (decision); Killing off his popular character would be *bizarre* because the Holmes character made Doyle very successful and it could ruin his career to no longer be writing about Sherlock Holmes.

7. (cries); If the school decided to close and there was nothing anyone could do about it, students might feel *despair*.

8. (survived); After my friend's boyfriend broke up with her, she felt very *vulnerable*.

Reading Warm-up B, p. 113

Sample Answers

1. (natural instincts); No, I think reasoning is more useful. Even if a detective has excellent *intuition*, he or she still needs to analyze the facts in a logical way to reach valid conclusions.

2. (story); I generally prefer a written *narrative* because I can go back and reread parts that I do not understand or that I especially enjoy.

3. (doubts); I had *misgivings* at first about signing up for dance lessons, but I have been enjoying them very much.

4. When someone is shown *deference*, or respect, he or she is more likely to be cooperative and speak freely and confidentially.

5. (distinctive); I write poetry that I think is *unique*.

6. (business); Criminals would be interested in *commerce* because that is where the money and products are that they would try to steal.

7. (quickly gather information); I am *effective* when I study because I use study skills such as note-taking.

8. their search for the truth; My little brother is *relentless* in his nagging me to play with him.

Writing About the Big Question, p. 114

A. 1. morality
2. obligation, responsibility
3. identify
4. honesty
5. serve

B. Sample Answers

1. I have often thought I would like to read to the blind. I would also like to help people in my neighborhood learn more about recycling.

2. **Involvement** in a program of volunteers who read to the blind would appeal to me. I believe we all have a **responsibility** to help those who are less fortunate.

C. Sample Answer

When a crime is being committed, a hero will step in to uphold honesty, justice, and morality. The hero's involvement may take the form of risking his or her own life. This is probably the reason why crime shows such as *Law* and *Order* are so popular on television. Viewers like to see good triumph over evil.

Literary Analysis: Protagonist and Antagonist, p. 115

1. The protagonist is Sherlock Holmes. He is a detective.

2. Holmes is brilliant but also different. He wants to escape the boredom of routine in his everyday life, and the cases he works on offer him an escape.

3. The antagonist is John Clay (Vincent Spaulding), who poses as an assistant in Jabez Wilson's shop in order to stage a bank robbery.

4. The conflict includes a desire to win and a struggle between good and evil.

Reading: Compare and Contrast Characters, p. 116

Sample Answers

1. Holmes is intense, while Watson is easy-going.

2. Holmes is a superb detective, while Jones is a routine official with limited intelligence but admirable courage.

3. Both Holmes and Clay are brilliant masterminds, but Holmes pursues justice, while Clay pursues a criminal career.

4. His outlooks at the beginning and the end of the story seem very similar. He is interested in only one thing: escaping boredom and routine.

Vocabulary Builder, p. 117

A. 1. B; 2. A; 3. C; 4. C; 5. A; 6. D
B. Sample Answers
1. You would face a difficult challenge.

2. You would be annoyed.
3. The person would be feeling thoughtful.

C. 1. C; 2. D; 3. B; 4. A

Enrichment: Investigative Careers, p. 118

Students' questions might include the following: Why do you wish to work for the FBI? What experience do you have in detective work? Who will provide references for your work? Where are you willing to travel? How do you respond to dangerous situations? And so on.

"Three Skeleton Key" by George Toudouze
"The Red-headed League"
by Sir Arthur Conan Doyle

Integrated Language Skills: Grammar, p. 119

A. 1. Sir Arthur Conan Doyle, the creator of Sherlock Holmes, first studied to be an eye doctor.
2. When Doyle was in medical school, he became aware of a certain professor.
3. This doctor, who could diagnose illnesses that puzzled his colleagues, may have been the model for the great Sherlock Holmes.

B. Examine students' paragraphs for correct comma usage.

"The Red-headed League"
by Sir Arthur Conan Doyle

Open-Book Test, p. 122

Short Answer

1. Sherlock Holmes is the protagonist. John Clay is the antagonist.
   Difficulty: *Easy* **Objective:** *Literary Analysis*

2. Holmes's unusual cases interest Watson.
   Difficulty: *Easy* **Objective:** *Interpretation*

3. Significant details include Holmes's tapping the pavement with his stick and his observation of the knees of the trousers worn by the pawnbroker's assistant.
   Difficulty: *Average* **Objective:** *Interpretation*

4. The League was ended because the bank robbers had no further use for it, since they had completed their tunnel. Holmes reveals this deduction at the end of the short story.
   Difficulty: *Easy* **Objective:** *Interpretation*

5. The greatest contrast is between their powers of observation. Watson admits that he had seen and heard exactly the same evidence about the case as Holmes had, but that Holmes's interpretation of these data was more insightful and penetrating than his own.
   Difficulty: *Average* **Objective:** *Reading*

6. The characters are both clever and offbeat; they differ in that Clay is on the side of evil, while Holmes defends justice and order.
   Difficulty: *Challenging* **Objective:** *Reading*

7. Yes, because Holmes is clever, efficient, observant, logical, and motivated to solve a crime.
   Difficulty: *Challenging* **Objective:** *Interpretation*

8. John Clay = Vincent Spaulding, pawnbroker's assistant
   William Morris = Duncan Ross, "interviewer" for the League
   Difficulty: *Average* **Objective:** *Literary Analysis*

9. Holmes shows himself to be introspective, that is, looking into his own thoughts, when he smokes his pipe for a "three-pipe problem" and also when he suggests to Watson that they attend a concert of German music.
   Difficulty: *Average* **Objective:** *Vocabulary*

10. Holmes's motivation is his self-appointed work, the thing he lives to do—solve mysteries.
    Difficulty: *Challenging* **Objective:** *Literary Analysis*

Essay

11. Students may cite evidence from the text to focus on Holmes's upper-class lifestyle, refined tastes, and detective career. Students should explain Holmes's appeal by pointing out that he represents a number of character traits that are universally aspired to, including intelligence, wit, decisiveness, and courage.
    Difficulty: *Easy* **Objective:** *Essay*

12. In their essays, students might include the following trademarks: Holmes smokes a pipe when deep in thought; enjoys listening to classical music; asks rapid questions; makes keen observations; is sometimes sharp-tongued; and has a nature that oscillates between laziness and enthusiasm.
    Difficulty: *Average* **Objective:** *Essay*

13. Students may list some or all of the following qualities for Holmes: keen intelligence, sharp powers of observation, great ability at deductive reasoning, critical thinking, excellent problem-solving skills, a precisely honed sense of timing and anticipation, and the ability to juggle many thoughts at once. Students may respond that the criminal who would have a chance of defeating Holmes would have to be better than Holmes in these areas.
    Difficulty: *Challenging* **Objective:** *Essay*

14. Some students may regard Holmes as a responsible citizen, citing details such as his eagerness to thwart the plot and to arrest the dangerous criminal John Clay. Other students, however, may regard Holmes as more self-involved than self-sacrificing. They may cite passages such as Holmes's eagerness to escape from boredom and "the commonplaces of existence."
    Difficulty: *Average* **Objective:** *Essay*

Oral Response

15. Oral responses should be clear, well organized, and well supported by appropriate examples from the selection.
    Difficulty: *Average* **Objective:** *Oral Interpretation*

Selection Test A, p. 125

Critical Reading

1. ANS: B	DIF: Easy	OBJ: Comprehension
2. ANS: B	DIF: Easy	OBJ: Literary Analysis
3. ANS: C	DIF: Easy	OBJ: Comprehension
4. ANS: D	DIF: Easy	OBJ: Interpretation
5. ANS: D	DIF: Easy	OBJ: Reading
6. ANS: C	DIF: Easy	OBJ: Interpretation
7. ANS: C	DIF: Easy	OBJ: Literary Analysis
8. ANS: C	DIF: Easy	OBJ: Interpretation
9. ANS: C	DIF: Easy	OBJ: Comprehension
10. ANS: A	DIF: Easy	OBJ: Interpretation
11. ANS: B	DIF: Easy	OBJ: Interpretation
12. ANS: B	DIF: Easy	OBJ: Literary Analysis

Vocabulary and Grammar

13. ANS: B	DIF: Easy	OBJ: Vocabulary
14. ANS: D	DIF: Easy	OBJ: Vocabulary
15. ANS: D	DIF: Easy	OBJ: Grammar

Essay

16. Students may use evidence from the text to focus on Holmes's upper-class lifestyle, refined tastes, and detective career. Students should explain Holmes's appeal by pointing out that he represents a number of character traits that are universally aspired to, including intelligence, wit, decisiveness, and courage.

    Difficulty: *Easy*   **Objective:** *Essay*

17. Students may focus on Watson's admitted confusion when faced with clues to a crime and his agitation and frustration under stress. Students' responses should be supported by examples from the story.

    Difficulty: *Easy*   **Objective:** *Essay*

18. Some students may regard Holmes as a responsible citizen, citing details such as his eagerness to thwart the plot and to arrest the dangerous criminal, John Clay. Other students may regard Holmes as more egocentric and self-involved than self-sacrificing. They may cite passages such as Holmes's eagerness to escape from boredom and "the commonplaces of existence."

    Difficulty: *Average*   **Objective:** *Essay*

Selection Test B, p. 128

Critical Reading

1. ANS: D	DIF: Average	OBJ: Comprehension
2. ANS: B	DIF: Average	OBJ: Interpretation
3. ANS: C	DIF: Average	OBJ: Interpretation
4. ANS: A	DIF: Average	OBJ: Literary Analysis
5. ANS: A	DIF: Average	OBJ: Reading
6. ANS: C	DIF: Challenging	OBJ: Literary Analysis
7. ANS: C	DIF: Average	OBJ: Interpretation
8. ANS: D	DIF: Average	OBJ: Literary Analysis
9. ANS: B	DIF: Average	OBJ: Reading
10. ANS: D	DIF: Average	OBJ: Interpretation
11. ANS: C	DIF: Average	OBJ: Reading

Vocabulary and Grammar

12. ANS: B	DIF: Average	OBJ: Vocabulary
13. ANS: C	DIF: Challenging	OBJ: Vocabulary
14. ANS: D	DIF: Average	OBJ: Grammar

Essay

15. In their essays, students might include the following trademarks: Holmes smokes a pipe when deep in thought, he enjoys listening to concert music, he asks rapid questions, he makes keen observations, he is sometimes sharp-tongued, and he has a nature that shifts from laziness to enthusiasm.

    Difficulty: *Average*   **Objective:** *Essay*

16. Students may list some or all of the following qualities for Holmes: keen intelligence, sharp powers of observation, great ability at deductive reasoning, critical thinking, excellent problem-solving skills, a precisely honed sense of timing and anticipation, and the ability to juggle many thoughts at once. Students may respond that the criminal who would have a chance of defeating Holmes would have to be at least as good in these areas as the detective.

    Difficulty: *Challenging*   **Objective:** *Essay*

17. Some students may regard Holmes as a responsible citizen, citing details such as his eagerness to thwart the plot and to arrest the dangerous criminal John Clay. Other students, however, may regard Holmes as more self-involved than self-sacrificing. They may cite passages such as Holmes's eagerness to escape from boredom and "the commonplaces of existence."

    Difficulty: *Average*   **Objective:** *Essay*

"There Is a Longing" by Chief Dan George

Vocabulary Warm-up Exercises, p. 132

A. 1. survival
2. demanding
3. segment
4. longing
5. wrestle
6. separation
7. grasp
8. purpose

B. Sample Answers
1. If you were unhappy with your *surroundings*, you might move to a different place or try to change the place you are in to make it more to your liking.

2. To *secure* a better grade in a subject, you should pay attention in class, do all homework, and ask for extra help when you need it.

3. No, a person who lacks *endurance* would not do well running a marathon because that takes the ability to overcome the hardships of a long course, and someone with little endurance would not have that.

4. No, a *society*, or group of people, who lived in *olden* days would not understand computers because computers are a recent invention.

5. Friends can help you *emerge*, or come out of, a difficult situation by providing lots of support.

6. No, a team cannot be *rightly*, or correctly, judged based only on its wins because good sportsmanship is also important in being a great team.

Reading Warm-up A, p. 133

Sample Answers

1. (struggled); <u>prejudice</u>, <u>education</u>
2. (group); <u>the zeal and talents to excel</u>
3. (break); *Parting* is a synonym for *separation*.
4. <u>achieve many goals</u>; *Intention* is a synonym for *purpose*.
5. (take hold); Parker was able to *grasp* the tools of learning, such as being able to write well and to understand ideas.
6. (strong desire); <u>he was not allowed to take the exam to practice law</u>
7. <u>skills and attention</u>; Anything that is *demanding*, such as schoolwork or a job, requires skills and attention to be successful.
8. (doomed); <u>saved lives</u>

Reading Warm-up B, p. 134

Sample Answers

1. (correct); *Accurately* is a synonym for *rightly*.
2. (natural); <u>Great Plains</u>; <u>the Southwest</u>; <u>where the people of the proud tribes lived</u>
3. <u>family life and cultural traditions and beliefs</u>; (people)
4. <u>In the 1800s</u>; *Modern* is an antonym for *olden*.
5. <u>Cody's extravaganza included a crowd-pleasing highlight. There was always a staged "Indian attack."</u> It is my aim to *secure* a good job, and I hope to accomplish that by graduating from high school and going to college.
6. (came out of the experience); Native American performers such as Jay Silverheels, who formed the Indian Actors Workshop, were determined to change the depiction of native peoples and to help a more positive portrayal to *emerge*.
7. (tools); <u>strong training</u>
8. <u>Their ability to weather the hardships</u>; *Stamina* is a synonym for *endurance*.

Writing About the Big Question, p. 135

A. 1. choices
   2. honesty/responsibility
   3. identify
   4. involvement
   5. obligation/responsibility

B. Sample Answers

   1. Answers will vary. Possible answers include courage, intelligence, responsibility, strength, determination, honesty, and morality.
   2. Sentences will vary but should include at least two of the Big Question vocabulary words.

C. Sample Answer

All heroes do not have to be physically strong or imposing. A leader can be a true hero when he or she displays moral strength and courage, even at the risk of harm or injury. Dr, Martin Luther King, Jr., was this kind of hero. He risked jail and physical injury many times in the course of his struggles during the civil rights movement.

Literary Analysis: Author's Philosophical Assumptions, p. 136

Sample Answers

1. The human instinct for survival is very strong.
2. Earning self-respect and a worthy place in society is a better goal than having to receive the handouts of welfare.
3. Living in harmony with one's surroundings is an important goal.
4. Education and skills are necessary for success in today's society.
5. Knowledge, freedom, the rule of law, and just government are important values for everyone in today's society.

Reading: Recognize Compare-and-Contrast Organization, p. 137

Sample Answers

1. The "new warriors" would have training that would last much longer and be more demanding. It would involve years of study and separation from home and family.
2. Native Americans would master skills that afford them a sense of worth and purpose. There would be no further need to accept welfare.
3. He differs from past chiefs in that his weapons are "speech and tongue."
4. He hopes that he will be like past chiefs in his courage and his ability to live in harmony with his environment.

Vocabulary Builder, p. 138

A. Sample Answers

   1. Yes, because you would have to have strength to run that far.
   2. Yes, because you would want to succeed.

3. If you were accepting an award <u>humbly</u>, you be too modest to make a long speech about yourself and your achievement.

4. A <u>longing</u> for your homeland would not be a pleasant feeling, because you would miss your country and wish to return.

5. If a <u>segment</u> of the population wanted free college tuition, not everyone would be in agreement, because this view represents only a part of the population.

B. 1. Kevin *emerged* from the shower clean and refreshed.

2. The submarine was undetectable as it was *submerged*, or hidden, in deep waters.

3. Celia was so *immersed* in her reading that she didn't hear her mother call her for dinner.

Enrichment: Communications, p. 139

Students may record that Sequoyah was a person of many gifts and talents: He was a skilled painter and silversmith, and he served in the U.S. Army in the Creek War in 1813–14. Apparently, he never learned to speak, read, or write English. If Sequoyah and Chief Dan George had met, they would probably have agreed on the values of education and skills. They might have disagreed about whether Native Americans should be independent or try to be more like the majority (white) society.

Open-Book Test, p. 140

Short Answer

1. The repetition emphasizes the urgency and need for the Native American dream.

Difficulty: *Easy*   **Objective:** *Interpretation*

2. The training of the new warriors will be much longer and more demanding, since it will involve the acquisition of education and skills.

Difficulty: *Average*   **Objective:** *Reading*

3. The new warriors will need the ability to withstand hardship, because their training will involve separation from home and family.

Difficulty: *Average*   **Objective:** *Vocabulary*

4. Speech is the only weapon left to him to fight his people's war.

Difficulty: *Average*   **Objective:** *Literary Analysis*

5. Courage and harmony with the environment

Difficulty: *Easy*   **Objective:** *Reading*

6. The thunderbird. The point of the comparison is to set a goal for the struggle of Native Americans, so that they will rise up and be victorious like the thunderbird.

Difficulty: *Challenging*   **Objective:** *Reading*

7. Chief Dan George will use the tools of education and skills. He has seen these bring success to the white man, so they are likely to be useful to Native Americans as well.

Difficulty: *Average*   **Objective:** *Interpretation*

8. The prayer suggests that Chief Dan George respects traditional values and beliefs, and that he puts a special premium on courage and endurance.

Difficulty: *Challenging*   **Objective:** *Literary Analysis*

9. Chief Dan George creates a tone of yearning when he repeats the word "longing" and when he speaks about his people's survival and their need for "a sense of worth and purpose."

Difficulty: *Challenging*   **Objective:** *Interpretation*

10. The author's purpose is to express the needs and desires of Native Americans. He tries to inspire the youth among his people.

Difficulty: *Easy*   **Objective:** *Literary Analysis*

Essay

11. To succeed in life, young Native Americans must acquire education and skills. This message is related to the chief's philosophical assumptions about the value of education and the necessity for determination and endurance.

Difficulty: *Easy*   **Objective:** *Essay*

12. Students may say that Chief Dan George believes that young Native Americans are the "new warriors," and he is an aging chief who now makes war through his words. He says his power is gone, yet he expects to see young braves in places of power in houses of law and government.

Difficulty: *Average*   **Objective:** *Essay*

13. Students may point out such philosophical assumptions as the following: education and skills are the keys to improving and securing the lives of Native Americans; traditional ways of life must adjust to the realities of competition and survival in modern-day society; courage, determination, and endurance will be required for the "new warriors" to succeed and achieve their goal. Most students will comment that most of Chief Dan George's listeners, both white and Native American, will share these basic beliefs.

Difficulty: *Challenging*   **Objective:** *Essay*

14. Chief Dan George shows himself to be responsible in that he feels he must continue to lead his people, this time with words rather than with weapons of war. According to the chief, the youth of his people must undertake the responsibility of acquiring education and skills.

Difficulty: *Average*   **Objective:** *Essay*

Oral Response

15. Oral responses should be clear, well organized, and well supported by appropriate examples from the selection.

Difficulty: *Average*   **Objective:** *Oral Interpretation*

Selection Test A, p. 143

Critical Reading

1. ANS: B	DIF: Easy	OBJ: Interpretation
2. ANS: C	DIF: Easy	OBJ: Comprehension
3. ANS: C	DIF: Easy	OBJ: Literary Analysis
4. ANS: A	DIF: Easy	OBJ: Reading
5. ANS: C	DIF: Easy	OBJ: Comprehension
6. ANS: C	DIF: Easy	OBJ: Interpretation

| 7. ANS: C | DIF: Easy | OBJ: Interpretation |
| 8. ANS: B | DIF: Easy | OBJ: Interpretation |

Vocabulary and Grammar

| 9. ANS: C | DIF: Easy | OBJ: Vocabulary |
| 10. ANS: D | DIF: Easy | OBJ: Grammar |

Essay

11. Students should single out the training of "new warriors" as Chief Dan George's basic message or theme. In order to succeed in life, young Native Americans must acquire education and skills. This theme is related to the chief's philosophical assumptions about the value of education and the necessity for determination and endurance.

Difficulty: *Easy* **Objective:** *Essay*

12. According to the chief, the youth of his people must undertake the responsibility of acquiring education and skills in order to succeed in the world.

Difficulty: *Average* **Objective:** *Essay*

Selection Test B, p. 145

Critical Reading

1. ANS: C	DIF: Average	OBJ: Interpretation
2. ANS: D	DIF: Average	OBJ: Interpretation
3. ANS: B	DIF: Average	OBJ: Literary Analysis
4. ANS: B	DIF: Challenging	OBJ: Reading
5. ANS: C	DIF: Average	OBJ: Comprehension
6. ANS: C	DIF: Average	OBJ: Interpretation
7. ANS: A	DIF: Average	OBJ: Comprehension
8. ANS: A	DIF: Average	OBJ: Interpretation

Vocabulary and Grammar

| 9. ANS: C | DIF: Average | OBJ: Vocabulary |
| 10. ANS: C | DIF: Average | OBJ: Grammar |

Essay

11. Students may say that Chief Dan George believes that young Native Americans are the "new warriors" and that he is an aging chief who now makes war through his words. He uses words and phrases like "my people's war" and the young people's "training." For Native Americans as a people, Chief Dan George holds out a future marked by achievement, self-esteem, and respect.

Difficulty: *Average* **Objective:** *Essay*

12. Students may point out such philosophical assumptions as the following: education and skills are the keys to improving the lot of Native Americans; traditional ways of life must adjust to the realities of competition and survival in modern-day society; or courage, determination, and endurance will be required for the "new warriors" to succeed and achieve their goal. Most students will comment that most of Chief Dan George's listeners, both white and Native American, will share these basic beliefs.

Difficulty: *Challenging* **Objective:** *Essay*

13. Chief Dan George shows himself to be responsible in that he feels he must continue to lead his people, this time with words rather than with weapons of war. According to the chief, the youth of his people must undertake the responsibility of acquiring education and skills.

Difficulty: *Average* **Objective:** *Essay*

"Glory and Hope" by Nelson Mandela

Vocabulary Warm-up Exercises, p. 148

A. 1. homeland
2. tribute
3. unity
4. international
5. isolated
6. hesitation
7. precisely
8. reign

B. Sample Answers

1. *Discrimination* in the workplace based on age is wrong.
2. The writer was *elevated* by the announcement that he had won the book award.
3. She felt *exhilaration* when she heard the good news.
4. Her proud parents felt *fulfilled* when Maria graduated college.
5. Before 1920, people of the female *gender* could not vote in the United States.
6. His five-year *imprisonment* was the most horrible experience of his life.
7. They *triumphed* over the other team by training hard and playing better.

Reading Warm-up A, p. 149

Sample Answers

1. away from the white people; There is an *isolated* area just outside of my town where an old, empty house stands.
2. (together); I always hope for *unity* within my family.
3. spoke all over the world; *International* attention would be important because other nations would know what was happening and pressure the South African government into ending apartheid.
4. he was awarded the Nobel Peace Prize in 1984; A *tribute* is something you do or say that shows admiration or respect.
5. speaking out against apartheid; I showed *hesitation* in agreeing to join the drama club because I did not think I was a very good actor.
6. The racist National Party; The new ruler will *reign* for 4 years only.
7. South Africa; I think a person can have only one actual *homeland*, because "homeland" means "the country of one's birth," and that can be only one country.

8. help make South Africa a place where all people could enjoy equal protection under the law; In the end, that is *exactly* what he did.

Reading Warm-up B, p. 150

Sample Answers

1. (segregation); *Discrimination* is treating one group of people differently from another in an unfair way.

2. (separated); Some *categories* I come across each day are types of foods, like fruits and vegetables, and types of books, like fiction and nonfiction.

3. for life; People in the neighborhood felt safer when they heard about the *imprisonment* of the burglar who had robbed five houses.

4. He felt *fulfilled* because his dream of bringing an end to apartheid had finally come true.

5. participate; voted in a national election for the very first time! *Gender* means "the condition of being male or female."

6. (native South Africans); I felt *exhilaration* when my swim team won the division championship.

7. was elected president; I *triumphed* over my fear of flying.

8. a position of national leadership; When Mandela was *elevated* to a position of leadership, he probably felt excited and honored.

Writing About the Big Question, p. 151

A. 1. hero
2. character
3. standard, imitate
4. responsibility/obligation

B. Sample Answers

1. I looked up to our soccer team captain, but then he disappointed me when he cheated on a math test; our whole family was shocked when a local judge was charged with tax evasion.

2. I had admired Sean, our soccer team captain, for his **honesty** and **responsibility**. I couldn't believe it when an investigation revealed Sean's **involvement** in a plan for several students to cheat on last week's math test.

C. Sample Answer

When a leader promises to serve his or her nation, he or she must persevere, even during hard or challenging times. The leader has an obligation to remain calm and confident under pressure. President Franklin D. Roosevelt displayed these qualities when he led our country through the challenges of the Great Depression and World War II.

Literary Analysis: Author's Philosophical Assumptions, p. 152

Sample Answers

1. The tragedy of the past must create a future society that will serve as a model for all humanity.

2. The people (of South Africa) have a deep attachment to their homeland and to nature.

3. Healing and progress are important values.

4. All people have a right to human dignity and freedom from fear.

5. Oppression of one individual or group by another individual or group is unacceptable.

Reading: Recognize Compare-and-Contrast Organization, p. 153

Sample Answers

1. The past structure of apartheid has been abolished, and in the present, all South Africans enjoy freedom and democracy.

2. The nations of the world have now accepted South Africa, whereas in the past, South Africa was an outcast because of the policy of apartheid.

3. Nelson Mandela offers a vision of a glorious society, in which unity, peace, justice, and human dignity will prevail. Toward the end of his speech, he vows that "never again" will one group be oppressed by another.

Vocabulary Builder, p. 154

A. 1. C; 2. B; 3. C

B. Sample Answers

1. It would involve a promise.

2. No, because the person would not be helpful.

3. You give it to the person.

4. Yes, because a candidate for public office will likely attract votes if he or she looks impressive.

5. Yes, because you would know it very well.

6. It brings them closer together, because *reconciliation* means "agreement" or "compromise."

C. 1. You decide later, since you postpone your choice.

2. You use it by "bringing back" your attention to it.

3. Yes, because you "take or bring" an insight or conclusion into an action, an event, or a statement.

Enrichment: Using a Map, p. 155

Sample Answers

A. 1. approximately 1,100 miles or 1,500 kilometers, measured across South Africa at the southern tip of Namibia

2. approximately 800 miles or 1,300 kilometers

3. Indian Ocean, Atlantic Ocean, Namibia, Botswana, Zimbabwe, Mozambique, and Swaziland

4. The long coastline may provide many places for tourists to spend time swimming or taking in the view. The coastline may also provide numerous ports or harbors from which people can fish or travel by boat.

B. 1. The coastline is shown in green, meaning that it is at sea level.

2. Some mountains run from Mozambique down along the eastern coast all the way to Cape Town. Much of

the interior of South Africa is fairly flat, with the elevation shown in the range of 2,000 to 5,000 feet above sea level. The western coast shows some rise in the land, but it is not as mountainous or as elevated as the eastern coast.

3. Limpopo, Vaal, and Orange

4. Given the mountainous nature of the trip from Natal to Cape Town, goods would likely be transported by boat or ship around the coast rather than over land.

"There Is a Longing" by Chief Dan George
"Glory and Hope" by Nelson Mandela

Integrated Language Skills: Grammar, p. 156

A. 1. Julius Caesar described his victory as follows: "I came, I saw, I conquered."

2. Statesmanship is a rare gift; few heads of government in the modern world, in fact, have risen to its challenges.

B. Examine students' paragraphs for correct usage of colons, semicolons, and ellipsis points.

"Glory and Hope" by Nelson Mandela

Open-Book Test, p. 159

Short Answer

1. Mandela's philosophical assumptions refer to basic beliefs.
   Difficulty: *Easy* **Objective:** *Literary Analysis*

2. The people of South Africa have a deep attachment to their homeland and to nature.
   Difficulty: *Average* **Objective:** *Literary Analysis*

3. Mandela's words suggest that the first democratic elections were an experiment that involved considerable risks of conflict and disorder. The security forces, however, managed to maintain law and order.
   Difficulty: *Average* **Objective:** *Interpretation*

4. All people have a right to human dignity and freedom from fear.
   Difficulty: *Challenging* **Objective:** *Literary Analysis*

5. *Covenant* means "agreement or contract." Mandela probably uses this word because it has sacred connotations and therefore reflects the gravity and importance of his idea.
   Difficulty: *Average* **Objective:** *Vocabulary*

6. Students may point out the three sentences beginning with "The time for the healing of the wounds has come" at the midpoint of the speech, or they may cite the sentences beginning with "Let there be justice for all" toward the end of the speech. Students should point out that parallelism contributes to the memorable, rhetorical quality of Mandela's inspiring address.
   Difficulty: *Challenging* **Objective:** *Interpretation*

7. The past is contrasted with the future of glorious achievement, when the sun will never set on democracy and freedom.
   Difficulty: *Easy* **Objective:** *Reading*

8. He contrasts the racism and oppression of the past policy of apartheid with the freedom and equality of democracy in South Africa's future.
   Difficulty: *Average* **Objective:** *Reading*

9. Mandela's purpose is to inspire South Africans to come together to make a new beginning.
   Difficulty: *Challenging* **Objective:** *Literary Analysis*

10. Students may use adjectives such as the following to describe the speech: inspiring, optimistic, upbeat, confident, triumphant.
    Difficulty: *Easy* **Objective:** *Interpretation*

Essay

11. Students will probably think that Mandela successfully and persuasively conveys hope. He paints a bright picture of the future of South Africa, which will be its glory, by pointing out the struggle to end apartheid.
    Difficulty: *Easy* **Objective:** *Essay*

12. Students may point out that this part of the speech addresses the promise and potential of a new world. Mandela's philosophical assumptions include a basic belief in unity and in the values of justice and peace. The repeated "Let there be . . ." phrases hint at the rewards if the nation becomes unified. Mandela closes his speech with this message because he wants the people to move forward and not to dwell on the past.
    Difficulty: *Average* **Objective:** *Essay*

13. Students should point out that all of Mandela's words are emotionally charged and would have created an emotional response in the audience. The phrases referring to the past evoke bitter memories of mistreatment, oppression, and violence. The phrases describing the future arouse feelings of victory, hope, and satisfaction. Such words as "victory," "justice," and "peace" would appeal to newfound patriotism.
    Difficulty: *Challenging* **Objective:** *Essay*

14. Students should point out that Mandela's emphasis on freedom, equality, justice, and peace reflects his sense that, as a political leader, he has the responsibility of upholding certain values to his people. At the same time, Mandela's stress on unity and cooperation of citizens suggests that, for a democracy to function in a healthy manner, citizens must heal their wounds, come together, and display tolerance and concern for each other.
    Difficulty: *Average* **Objective:** *Essay*

Oral Response

15. Oral responses should be clear, well organized, and well supported by appropriate examples from the selection.
    Difficulty: *Average* **Objective:** *Oral Interpretation*

Selection Test A, p. 162

Critical Reading

1. ANS: B	DIF: Easy	OBJ: Interpretation
2. ANS: C	DIF: Easy	OBJ: Literary Analysis
3. ANS: B	DIF: Easy	OBJ: Comprehension

4. ANS: D   DIF: Easy   OBJ: Literary Analysis

5. ANS: C   DIF: Easy   OBJ: Reading

6. ANS: C   DIF: Easy   OBJ: Comprehension

7. ANS: D   DIF: Easy   OBJ: Interpretation

Vocabulary and Grammar

8. ANS: C   DIF: Easy   OBJ: Vocabulary

9. ANS: B   DIF: Easy   OBJ: Vocabulary

10. ANS: C   DIF: Easy   OBJ: Grammar

Essay

11. Students will probably think that Mandela successfully and persuasively conveys hope. He paints a bright picture of the future of South Africa, which will be its glory, by pointing out the struggle to end apartheid.

    Difficulty: *Easy*   **Objective:** *Essay*

12. Students should point out that Mandela emphasizes the values of freedom, equality, justice, and peace. He pledges freedom from poverty, deprivation, suffering, and discrimination. He also promises a society in which his people will have hope without fear.

    Difficulty: *Average*   **Objective:** *Essay*

Selection Test B, p. 164

Critical Reading

1. ANS: C   DIF: Average   OBJ: Comprehension

2. ANS: A   DIF: Average   OBJ: Interpretation

3. ANS: B   DIF: Average   OBJ: Interpretation

4. ANS: B   DIF: Average   OBJ: Literary Analysis

5. ANS: B   DIF: Average   OBJ: Reading

6. ANS: A   DIF: Average   OBJ: Interpretation

Vocabulary and Grammar

7. ANS: B   DIF: Average   OBJ: Vocabulary

8. ANS: C   DIF: Challenging   OBJ: Vocabulary

9. ANS: D   DIF: Average   OBJ: Grammar

Essay

10. Students may point out that this part of the speech addresses the promise and potential of a new world. Mandela's philosophical assumptions include a basic belief in unity and in the values of justice and peace. The repeated "Let there be . . . " phrases hint at the rewards if the nation becomes unified. Mandela closes his speech with this message because he wants the people to move forward and not to dwell on the past.

    Difficulty: *Average*   **Objective:** *Essay*

11. Students should point out that all of Mandela's words are emotionally charged and would have created an emotional response in the audience. The phrases referring to the past evoke bitter memories of mistreatment, oppression, and violence. The phrases describing the future arouse feelings of victory, hope, and satisfaction. Such words as "liberty," "justice," and "peace" would appeal to newfound patriotism.

    Difficulty: *Challenging*   **Objective:** *Essay*

12. Students should point out that Mandela's emphasis on freedom, equality, justice, and peace reflects his sense that, as a political leader, he has the responsibility of upholding certain values to his people. At the same time, Mandela's stress on unity and cooperation of citizens suggests that, for a democracy to function in a healthy manner, citizens must heal their wounds, come together, and display tolerance and concern for each other.

    Difficulty: *Average*   **Objective:** *Essay*

"Pecos Bill: The Cyclone" by Harold W. Felton
"Perseus" by Edith Hamilton

Vocabulary Warm-up Exercises, p. 167

A. 1. destruction

2. cyclone (whirlwind)

3. whirlwind (cyclone)

4. capable

5. missile

6. heave

7. extreme

8. fatal

B. Sample Answers

1. To *pursue* a runaway dog, I would drive around with my mom or dad until I found it.

2. A plan I *devised* for getting chores done was to make a list and check off each chore as I did it.

3. If someone displayed too much *arrogance*, I would like to say, "Get over yourself."

4. A feeling of love would give me a *radiant* glow.

5. A task that is a *mere* nuisance is taking out the garbage each week.

6. My friend once exhibited *fearless* behavior by going into a dark cave to look for his little brother.

7. I think the most *wretched* weather of all is when it is very hot and humid.

8. When I grow up, I would like to live in an *abode* that is comfortable, spacious, and airy.

Reading Warm-up A, p. 168

Sample Answers

1. (twister, tornado, cyclone); Even from the basement, we could hear the *whirlwind* blow over the roof of our house.

2. cause terrible damage; The aftermath of a *cyclone* might include uprooted trees and ruined buildings.

3. (deadliest); *Fatal* means "resulting in death."

4. weather; An *extreme* weather condition that I once experienced was a storm so violent that it knocked out all the power in my town.

5. (tornado); *Destruction* means "the act of ruining or greatly damaging."

6. moderate damage; One positive thing I am *capable* of is doing complicated algebra problems.

7. (dangerous); When the pitcher threw the ball, it had the force of a *missile*.

8. toss cars through the air and turn whole houses to sticks and stones; A heavy boulder would require a strong *heave* to move it.

Reading Warm-up B, p. 169

Sample Answers

1. happines of creativity; My sister looked *radiant* on the day of her wedding.

2. bad fortune; A wild horse would be difficult to *pursue* because it can run at great speeds.

3. This was no simple game. I intended no harm; it was a *mere* accident.

4. (live with his father in); My own *abode* is a four-bedroom house.

5. Labyrinth; The Labyrinth is a maze from which there is no way out except death; therefore, it is a miserable, *wretched* place.

6. (a way for them to fly); Another word for *devised* is "invented."

7. Icarus decided he could fly much higher; A person who is displaying *arrogance* would be all puffed up with pride, ignoring what others might say or do.

8. (Icarus); I read about the *fearless* actions of the fire fighters on 9/11; they went into the burning Twin Towers to rescue the helpless people inside without fear for their own lives.

Writing About the Big Question, p. 170

A. 1. standard, honesty/responsibility, involvement
  2. character, intentions
  3. justice
  4. serve
  5. wisdom

B. Sample Answers

1. Your honesty might be tested if your parents asked you to tell truthfully how you spent your time after school; your honesty might be tested if a store clerk gave you back too much money in change by mistake.

2. The **choices** a person makes can tell a great deal about his or her **honesty**. For example, if you receive too much change by mistake from a store clerk and you notice the error, you have an **obligation** to return the extra amount, since otherwise the clerk may get in trouble.

C. Sample Answer

In some situations, heroes have a responsibility to risk their own lives. Ocean lifeguards, for example, shoulder this responsibility every day as part of their job. They can never predict the exact ways in which their obligation to serve the public may put them at risk. All they can do is use their training and skills the best they can in order to save swimmers in distress.

Literary Analysis: Tall Tale and Myth, p. 171

Sample Answers

1. Both Pecos Bill and Perseus are courageous and accomplish seemingly impossible tasks. However, Pecos Bill has a playful side that is missing in Perseus. Also, the romantic element in "Perseus" (his rescue of Andromeda and marriage) is not present in "The Cyclone."

2. In "Pecos Bill: The Cyclone," many of the fantastic elements center on the conflict between Pecos Bill and the storm. For example, Pecos Bill jumps on the cyclone's back and refuses to let go no matter how hard the cyclone bucks. Other fantastic or exaggerated elements involve the prairie dogs and the badgers. In "Perseus," the hero encounters a number of fantastic or monstrous beings: the Gray Women, the Gorgons, and the sea serpent. Perseus is aided by gods and acquires supernatural equipment, such as the winged sandals, the sword, the mirror, the silver wallet, and the magic cap.

3. The mood in "Pecos Bill: The Cyclone" might be described as exuberant, and the tone might be described as tongue-in-cheek and lightly ironic. In "Perseus," however, the mood is serious and the tone is suspenseful.

4. Both tales are exciting and suspenseful with a number of twists and turns. Oral storytelling would enhance the humor in "Pecos Bill: The Cyclone" and also the bizarre, unusual aspects of Perseus' adventures, such as his encounters with gods and monsters.

Vocabulary Builder, p. 172

A. Sample Answers

1. After the tyrant usurped the king's throne, most people denounced him as an illegitimate ruler.

2. The professor's arguments were so convincing that even the skeptics accepted her conclusions.

3. When Eugene made such tactless comments to our hosts, we felt mortified.

4. The sounds of revelry from the party next door were raucous and loud.

B. 1. D; 2. C; 3. B; 4. B

Open-Book Test, p. 174

Short Answer

1. Tall Tales: humor; ridiculous situations, traditional story Common Features: exaggerated events, larger-than-life heroes, oral tradition
Myths: heroes with a divine parent, doings of gods, religious origin
"Pecos Bill" and "Perseus" both have larger-than-life heroes.

Difficulty: *Average* **Objective:** *Literary Analysis*

2. "Pecos Bill" is a tall tale because of the larger-than-life central hero and exaggeration, which makes the story humorous.

"Perseus" is a myth because it explains the actions of gods, and Perseus is a mythic hero.

Difficulty: *Easy*   **Objective:** *Literary Analysis*

3. Human figures shape human life in "Pecos Bill," and the gods shape human life in "Perseus."

Difficulty: *Average*   **Objective:** *Literary Analysis*

4. They are both larger-than-life heroes.

Difficulty: *Easy*   **Objective:** *Interpretation*

5. It is hyperbole, because it is an exaggeration and an unbelievable, ridiculous detail.

Difficulty: *Challenging*   **Objective:** *Literary Analysis*

6. Felton's attitude is tongue-in-cheek or amusing.

Difficulty: *Challenging*   **Objective:** *Interpretation*

7. "Pecos Bill: The Cyclone" is humorous. "Perseus" is serious and suspenseful.

Difficulty: *Average*   **Objective:** *Interpretation*

8. The cyclone can watch, it has deliberate action and intent to spoil a celebration. It has the emotions of jealousy and resolve.

Difficulty: *Challenge*   **Objective:** *Interpretation*

9. Danaë does not want Acrisius to know where Perseus is.

Difficulty: *Average*   **Objective:** *Interpretation*

10. The people were enjoying noisy merrymaking of feasting, dancing, playing music, and gift-giving.

Difficulty: *Average*   **Objective:** *Vocabulary*

Essay

11. Students should point out that both Pecos Bill and Perseus are larger-than-life heroes who accomplish superhuman feats that benefit humanity. Perseus is characterized somewhat more seriously and realistically than Pecos Bill.

Difficulty: *Easy*   **Objective:** *Essay*

12. Students who believe that Perseus is not heroic may say that he is merely a lucky young man whom Hermes and Athena help for inexplicable reasons. He could not have succeeded without divine help, for aside from his love for his mother and his desire for Andromeda, he demonstrates no extraordinary qualities. Those who feel Perseus is heroic may say that he is the son of Zeus, has pride and love for his mother, that he meets all challenges (unquestioning faith in gods, travel, monsters, Polydectes), that he thinks quickly in Polydectes' banquet hall, and that he slays the sea serpent out of a desire to rid the world of evil.

Difficulty: *Average*   **Objective:** *Essay*

13. Students should explain that monsters and awesome natural forces represent ultimate foes for human beings. Monsters and natural forces are very unlike humans. They often possess such power that they seem impossible to defeat; they pose the potential of instant and gruesome death; and they threaten not only the

human hero, but all who are human. Thus, defeating such a creature or force is a victory for the hero as well as for all humanity.

Difficulty: *Challenging*   **Objective:** *Essay*

14. Evaluate students' responses on clarity, coherence, and specific support. In general, students should point out that both heroes take on the responsibility of improving the human condition by battling fantastic monsters or destructive natural forces.

Difficulty: *Average*   **Objective:** *Essay*

Oral Response

15. Oral responses should be clear, well organized, and well supported by appropriate examples from the selections.

Difficulty: *Average*   **Objective:** *Oral Interpretation*

Selection Test A, p. 177

Critical Reading

1. ANS: B	DIF: Easy	OBJ: Literary Analysis
2. ANS: D	DIF: Easy	OBJ: Comprehension
3. ANS: C	DIF: Easy	OBJ: Comprehension
4. ANS: C	DIF: Easy	OBJ: Comprehension
5. ANS: A	DIF: Easy	OBJ: Literary Analysis
6. ANS: B	DIF: Easy	OBJ: Interpretation
7. ANS: A	DIF: Easy	OBJ: Literary Analysis
8. ANS: B	DIF: Easy	OBJ: Comprehension
9. ANS: C	DIF: Easy	OBJ: Literary Analysis
10. ANS: D	DIF: Easy	OBJ: Literary Analysis
11. ANS: B	DIF: Easy	OBJ: Interpretation
12. ANS: A	DIF: Easy	OBJ: Interpretation
13. ANS: D	DIF: Easy	OBJ: Interpretation

Vocabulary

14. ANS: A	DIF: Easy	OBJ: Vocabulary
15. ANS: A	DIF: Easy	OBJ: Vocabulary

Essay

16. Students should point out that both Pecos Bill and Perseus are larger-than-life heroes who accomplish superhuman feats that benefit humanity. Perseus is characterized somewhat more seriously and realistically than Pecos Bill is, however.

Difficulty: *Easy*   **Objective:** *Essay*

17. Students should define *conflict* as a struggle between opposing forces; they should define *suspense* as a feeling of uncertainty about what will happen next in a story. In "Pecos Bill," the conflicts are chiefly external, pitting the cyclone against the awesome strength of the hero. Suspense is created as the cyclone struggles mightily to throw Pecos Bill off its back. In "Perseus," the conflicts are also external: Acrisius vs. Danaë and Perseus, Polydectes vs. Perseus, Perseus vs. the

Gorgons, and Perseus vs. the sea monster. Suspense is created by Perseus' lengthy quest to carry out his mission and to overcome difficult obstacles.

Difficulty: *Easy* **Objective:** *Essay*

18. Students should point out that Pecos Bill takes on the responsibility of taming the destructive giant cyclone so it is not quite as harmful to people. Perseus takes on the responsibility of battling fantastic monsters, so the islanders can live in peace and happiness.

Difficulty: *Average* **Objective:** *Essay*

Selection Test B, p. 180

Critical Reading

1. ANS: C	DIF: Average	OBJ: Literary Analysis
2. ANS: A	DIF: Average	OBJ: Comprehension
3. ANS: B	DIF: Challenging	OBJ: Interpretation
4. ANS: D	DIF: Average	OBJ: Interpretation
5. ANS: C	DIF: Average	OBJ: Comprehension
6. ANS: B	DIF: Average	OBJ: Literary Analysis
7. ANS: D	DIF: Average	OBJ: Interpretation
8. ANS: B	DIF: Average	OBJ: Comprehension
9. ANS: C	DIF: Challenging	OBJ: Interpretation
10. ANS: A	DIF: Average	OBJ: Comprehension
11. ANS: C	DIF: Average	OBJ: Literary Analysis
12. ANS: A	DIF: Average	OBJ: Interpretation
13. ANS: A	DIF: Average	OBJ: Literary Analysis
14. ANS: B	DIF: Average	OBJ: Literary Analysis
15. ANS: B	DIF: Average	OBJ: Interpretation
16. ANS: A	DIF: Challenging	OBJ: Interpretation

Vocabulary

17. ANS: C	DIF: Challenging	OBJ: Vocabulary
18. ANS: A	DIF: Average	OBJ: Vocabulary

Essay

19. Students may take the view that Perseus is heroic or that he is not heroic. Those who believe that Perseus is not heroic may cite the fact that he is merely a lucky young man whom Hermes and Athena help for inexplicable reasons. He could not have succeeded without divine help, for aside from his love for his mother and his desire for Andromeda, he demonstrates no extraordinary qualities. Those who feel that Perseus is heroic may say that he is the son of Zeus, that readers identify with his pride and his love for his mother, that he meets all challenges (unquestioning faith in gods, travel, monsters, Polydectes), that he thinks quickly in Polydectes' banquet hall, and that he slays the sea serpent out of a desire to rid the world of evil.

Difficulty: *Average* **Objective:** *Essay*

20. Students should explain that monsters and awesome natural forces represent ultimate foes for human

beings. Monsters and natural forces are very unlike humans. They often possess such power that they seem impossible to defeat, they pose the potential of instant and gruesome death, and they threaten not only the human hero, but all who are human. Thus, defeating such a creature or force is a victory for the hero as well as for all humanity.

Difficulty: *Average* **Objective:** *Essay*

21. Evaluate students' responses on clarity, coherence, and specific support. In general, students should point out that both heroes take on the responsibility of improving the human condition by battling fantastic monsters or destructive natural forces.

Difficulty: *Average* **Objective:** *Essay*

Writing Workshop
Comparison-and-Contrast Essay: Integrating Grammar Skills, p. 184

A. 1. B; 2. B

B. Students' answers will vary.

Vocabulary Workshop 1, p. 185

1. chip off the old block
2. let the chips fall where they may
3. chip on his shoulder
4. something's fishy
5. have a fit
6. fit to be tied
7. start from scratch

A. You are a **chip off the old block**! I cannot believe you lied to me.

B. What do you mean, lied? **Let's start from scratch here**.

C. Well, I knew **something was fishy** from the start.

D. I give up. I do not understand you. **Let the chips fall where they may!**

Vocabulary Workshop 2, p. 186

Sample Answers

Hey Men! Do you go out in the evening sporting a **five o' clock shadow**? Is everything in your wardrobe **a dime a dozen**? Well, it is time to **look out for number one**! Yes, you. You can be **dressed to the nines** every day at a low price. **Put two and two together**. Come to Gregory's Suits today and we will make sure that you walk out **dressed to kill**. So come in today!

Benchmark Test 12, p. 188

MULTIPLE CHOICE

1. ANS: B
2. ANS: C
3. ANS: D
4. ANS: D

5. ANS: A

6. ANS: B

7. ANS: D

8. ANS: D

9. ANS: A

10. ANS: C

11. ANS: B

12. ANS: B

13. ANS: B

14. ANS: C

15. ANS: D

16. ANS: C

17. ANS: B

18. ANS: D

19. ANS: A

20. ANS: A

21. ANS: D

22. ANS: B

23. ANS: A

24. ANS: B

25. ANS: C

26. ANS: B

27. ANS: C

28. ANS: A

29. ANS: C

WRITING

30. Students' essays should indicate strong points of comparison and contrast as well as meet the requirements of the bulleted list.

31. The student should adopt the voice of the person he or she chooses and create journal entries that view events from that person's perspective.

32. Students should use the appropriate formatting and tone for a friendly letter. Each paragraph should support the main purpose.